# NATURAL FICTIONS

# NATURAL FICTIONS

## George Chapman's Major Tragedies

## A. R. Braunmuller

DELAWARE

Newark: University of Delaware Press
London and Toronto: Associated University Presses

Associated University Presses
440 Forsgate Drive
Cranbury, NJ 08512

Associated University Presses
25 Sicilian Avenue
London WC1A 2QH, England

Associated University Presses
P.O. Box 39, Clarkson Pstl. Stn.
Mississauga, Ontario,
Canada L5J 3X9

The paper used in this publication meets the requirements of the American National Standard for Permanence of Paper for Printed Library Materials Z39.48-1984.

**Library of Congress Cataloging-in-Publication Data**

Braunmuller, A. R., 1945–
    Natural fictions : George Chapman's major tragedies / A.R. Braunmuller.
        p.    cm.
    Includes bibliographical references (p.    ) and index.
    ISBN 0-87413-404-8 (alk. paper)
    1. Chapman, George, 1559?–1634—Tragedies.    2. Tragedy.
I. Title.
PR2454.B73   1992
822'.3—dc20                                                         89-40764
                                                                              CIP

PRINTED IN THE UNITED STATES OF AMERICA

To my teachers
Edward Partridge
Ronald Rebholz
Eugene Waith

And for the authentical truth of either person or action, who (worth the respecting) will expect it in a poem, whose subject is not truth, but things like truth? Poor envious souls are they that cavil at truth's want in these natural fictions. . . .

—Epistle Dedicatory, *The Revenge of Bussy D'Ambois*

# Contents

# Note on Texts and References

This book employs a series of abbreviations for frequently cited works:

*Bussy*                George Chapman, *Bussy D'Ambois*, ed. Nicholas Brooke, The Revels Plays (London: Methuen, 1964).

*Comedies*             Chapman, *The Plays of George Chapman: The Comedies*, gen. ed. Alan Holaday (Urbana: University of Illinois Press, 1970).

*Hero and Leander*     Christopher Marlowe, *The Poems*, ed. Millar MacLure (London: Methuen, 1968). This volume includes Chapman's continuation.

*Homer*                Chapman, *Chapman's Homer*, ed. Allardyce Nicoll, Bollingen Series 41, 2 vols. (New York: Pantheon, 1956).

*Letter-Book*          Chapman et al., *A Seventeenth-Century Letter-Book: A Facsimile of Folger MS. V. a. 321* with transcription, annotation, and commentary by A. R. Braunmuller (Newark: University of Delaware Press, 1983). This volume contains copies of letters and other documents by and about Chapman.

*OED*                  *Oxford English Dictionary.*

*Poems*                Chapman, *The Poems of George Chapman*, ed. Phyllis B. Bartlett (New York: Modern Language Association, 1941).

*Tragedies*            Chapman, *The Tragedies of George Chapman*, ed. T. M. Parrott (London: Routledge, 1910). This text is cited for all of Chapman's tragedies other than *Bussy D'Ambois;* it has been collated with and corrected from Chapman, *The Plays of George Chapman: The Tragedies*, gen. ed. Alan Holaday (Cambridge: D. S. Brewer, 1987).

# NATURAL FICTIONS

In quoting from early books, manuscripts, and modern original-spelling editions in English, I have made several typographic changes: i/j, u/v, and long *s* appear as they would in a modern text; scribes' and printers' abbreviations have been silently expanded; where a text is predominantly black letter or italic with Roman for emphasis, I have adjusted the texts to Roman with italic for emphasis. Most of these changes have also been made in French and Latin quotations, but I have not adjusted them to modern standards of spelling and accent. Throughout I have tried to make references and quotations as understandable and unantique as possible and have therefore preferred to emend Parrott's modern-spelling text of the tragedies rather than quote the more recent original-spelling edition. Speech prefixes are given in full, no matter what the practice of the cited edition. The titles of Chapman's nondramatic poems and translations follow the editions cited above and are unmodernized, hence, for example, *Ovids Banquet of Sence, Odysseys, Teares of Peace*. References to plays cite act, scene, and line; arabic numerals mark the conventional sections of classical texts and other works divided into books, parts, chapters, cantos, "sestiads," and the like. Chapman's translations of Homer's epics are cited by volume and page references to the edition listed above and, where appropriate, by book and line numbers.

# Preface

Reviewing a 1944 production of *Love for Love* at the Haymarket Theatre, the precocious Kenneth Tynan admonished his readers:

> Gielgud is an actor who refuses to compromise with his audience: he does not offer a welcoming hand, but binds a spell instead. They must accept him on his own intellectual level or not at all. This aloofness and rigid dignity of his represent his only unique quality: some day he must read the tragedies of Chapman, when he will discover that he is the only actor in Europe today who could play Bussy, Clermont or Byron with anything like the icy poise the parts demand.

Although one may guess Gielgud knew Chapman's plays in 1944, we are, alas, unlikely to experience the performance Tynan wished; but the 1988 Old Vic production of *Bussy D'Ambois* (or half of it) showed that other actors and another director might accomplish some of what Tynan imagined, and more. His assessment of the qualities an actor needs to undertake the role of a Chapman hero vividly describes some of the playwright's qualities—intellectual, icy, poised. These qualities do not immediately recommend themselves to a contemporary sensibility. Chapman's drama also requires actors capable of instant passion, sudden transformations from apparent stoicism to Marlovian excess, moves from icy intellectuality to grandiosely or operatically conceived emotions that reach beyond what ordinary people and typical audiences find possible or credible. These qualities also do not recommend themselves to contemporary sensibilities.

Chapman's drama requires an audience that can encompass, and then applaud, all these seeming contradictions, paradoxes, and oxymora. In part, this book represents an effort to imagine, to re-create, that audience. Chapman quite deliberately and programatically did not make the task easy: he claimed that the reader's or spectator's imaginative torsion echoed and validated the poet's enterprise. Since I believe Chapman's own views—it may not be too grand to say "philosophy"—of art deserve respect, the historical subject George Chapman has a large, but I hope neither monolithic nor unquestioned, place in the pages to come. Numerous writers have provocatively maintained that aesthetic, especially literary, criticism needs to reify the "author" in order to proceed about its self-interested business. For example, Roland Barthes writes in *Image-Music-Text:*

> To give a text an Author is to impose a limit on that text, to furnish it with a final signified, to close the writing. Such a conception suits criticism very well, the latter allotting itself the important task of discovering the Author (or its hypostases: society, history, psyche, liberty) beneath the work: when the Author has been found, the text is "explained"—victory to the critic.

This critical view, endorsed and extended by Michel Foucault and Jacques Derrida, has value and interest, but it elides an early modern development of the medieval concept of aesthetic authority, the idea that allows Chaucer to find in his "Auctour" a blanket certification for what often prove deviant or idiosyncratic moves within literary tradition. In the English Renaissance, the evolving profession of writing and the slowly recognized significance of print technology led some writers—most spectacularly Ben Jonson—to reify themselves.

My argument supposes that George Chapman, Jonson's friend and competitor, similarly tried to reify his authorship, tried, that is, through prefaces, dedications, commentaries, narrative asides, and apodictic digressions to restrict and control the understanding of his work. Or, as Chapman put it in his *Justification of Andromeda Liberata,* "At least, in mine own writing, I might reasonably and conscionably be master of mine own meaning." Chapman's program was less formalistic than Jonson's, but at least as mimetically and diegetically realized. To understand this effort and—I will argue—its failure requires taking both effort and ideas seriously without necessarily endorsing them or treating them solely in contexts Chapman or his contemporaries would have regarded as apposite. Despite its romantic inflection, Milan Kundera's aphorism offers some guidance: "To be a writer does not mean to preach a truth, it means to *discover* a truth." Chapman began and continued as a preacher of truths but became and continued to be a discoverer of countervailing ones. In the Homeric terms he so loved, Chapman's story is both *Iliad* and *Odyssey.* This preface should conclude with a succinct and inviting analysis of "natural fictions," but the early modern and plain modern overtones of the phrase defeat quick statement, escape both eloquence and apothegm. Only time, the reader, and the book will tell.

# Acknowledgments

For the many conversations and kindnesses here recalled, my gratitude; to those people not recalled, I give thanks and of them I beg forgiveness. The dedicatees will variously and acutely estimate the result of their tutelage: while they bear no responsibility, they might perhaps find some recompense. John Loftis and Charles Prouty guided my first studies of Chapman's drama. Over several years, Eugene Waith, David Bevington, and George Hunter read versions of this text; they graciously, conscientiously, and sternly noted the weak and the strong, the likely and the implausible. What survives cannot entirely please them but is better for their care.

Not so easy to define, but just as welcome, were the advice, comments, and obiter dicta of Thomas Berger, Lee Bliss, Robert Dent, Reg Foakes (whose first words to me were to ask why I was writing about Chapman), Gail Kern Paster, and Norman Rabkin (whose generosity even a parent might hesitate to endorse). They will recognize, even as they may kindly fail to record, their influence. This book has been improved by the direct and passing remarks of Michael Allen, Steven Bates, Robert Dent, Charles Gullans, Fritz Levy, David Stuart Rodes, Alan Roper, and the late Richard Sylvester, paleographic master. In New Haven and London and many places else, I have profited from the knowledge and advice of Harris Friedberg, John Hodgson, and William Keach. More recently, Gerald Snare shared his very different Chapman, and those differences shaped my sense of another dramatist of the same name. For any teacher, it will be redundant to say that my students taught me more than I taught them.

Indefinable as these debts may be, there are others more precise. My work was generously and disinterestedly supported by the National Endowment for the Humanities, the Folger Shakespeare Library, and the Academic Senate of the University of California, Los Angeles. Without the Beinecke Library, the British Library, the Bodleian Library, the Folger Library, the Huntington Library, the Public Record Office, and especially their immensely knowledgeable and improbably helpful personnel, this book would have been flatly impossible. I recall the help of Jeffrey Aaron, Victoria Hayne, Peter Merrill, Barbara Mowat, Elizabeth Niemeyer, David Paisey, Sandy

Powers, Lily Stone, Betsy Walsh, and Laetitia Yeandle. Stephen Parks generously gave me a talismanic image of Chapman that has overseen many revisionary nights. Jeanette Gilkison and Edith Lufkin, who battled technological obstacles I could not overcome alone, made this work possible, as did Jay Halio. Finally, and at a very late stage, Rae Jean and Robert Goodman made the computer, hitherto an obstacle, an ally.

# Introduction: "The Most Curious Maker of Them All"

In a verse epistle to Henry Reynolds, "Of Poets and Poesie" (1627), Michael Drayton reviews the great names and great accomplishments of an age virtually past. When he calls George Chapman "the most curious maker of them all," he speaks as one of Chapman's friends to another.[1] Chapman was a "curious maker" in several Elizabethan senses: he was ingenious, and his poetry and drama are highly wrought, complicated, and intricate in reference, allusion, and syntax. The two main modern senses of the adjective, gradually crowding out the older ones in the seventeenth century, also apply. Like his own preferred readers, Chapman had a "searching spirit," a curiosity in exploration. And he certainly was cantankerous, intent upon separating himself from other poets and other men, "curious" by being unlike any other fellow poet or dramatist. Perhaps his long-time friend Ben Jonson comes closest to being like Chapman. Speaking of Jonson, Chapman might sometimes be describing his own work. In a poem commending *Sejanus*, for example, Chapman praises Jonson's ability to collect "Pearles and deare Stones, from richest shores & streames" and then to place "In more then Goulden Verse, those betterd spirits" (*Poems*, pp. 358–59). Years later, when the friendship had evidently died, the case is altered:

> will thy fortune still
> (Spight of all learning) backe the witt thy will,
> Though thy playe genius, hange his broken wings
> Full of sicke feathers, and with forced things
> Imp thy scaenes, Labord and Unnaturall?[2]

Precisely the same praise and the same accusation have been attached to Chapman. The *Sejanus* poem itself borrows heavily from Plutarch; unsurprisingly, therefore, it compliments Jonson's ability to take and improve the best from others. And many people have, alas, turned Chapman's later complaint about Jonson back upon its author. Critics attack his scenes as labored and unnatural, full of forced things and "affected labour."[3] How could it be otherwise if, as Chapman claimed, his soul's "genuine formes struggle for birth, / Under the clawes of this fowle Panther earth" (*Poems*, p. 382)?

With honorable exceptions, the naysayers have generally prevailed, from Chapman's day to this. They complain of his obscurity, of his secretive plundering (even in the great Homeric translations), and of what Swinburne elegantly called Chapman's "taste for extravagance of paradox and shocks of moral surprise."[4] Yet this last phrase also identifies an extraordinary variety. Attempting to subdue that variety, to resolve the paradoxes and soften the shocks of moral surprise, modern interpreters have dissolved Chapman's writing into its sources, transformed him into a Christian moralist, or regarded him as a Neoplatonist suddenly converted to stoicism.[5] Such criticism too often becomes schematizing, and the poet's frequently exciting inconsistencies collapse into moribund but safely coherent system. The tragedies have proved especially susceptible to disintegration. And if they did not serve as rags and bones to be redistributed to their proper owners, they could always, Peer Gynt–like, be melted down and recast with the proper number of button loops to ornament the vest of Renaissance humanism, or Renaissance Neoplatonism, or whatever Renaissance orthodoxy the critic chooses.

As the critics and Chapman exchange salvos of notes and learning, it is easy to forget that he was a highly paid comic dramatist and a vastly more popular tragic dramatist than Ben Jonson. Chapman himself provides a way back into his art and an escape from the treadmill of much modern criticism. Unlike most Renaissance English dramatists, Chapman has a well-developed and frequently articulated theory of art. Those emphatic ideas invite us to consider the relation between the theories and the imaginative realities he created. While the theory has some inconsistencies, Chapman pursues several main topics throughout the epistles, prefaces, and commentaries he attaches to his work. His central tenet remains that poetry offers eternal truth to its subjects and its recipients. Art can penetrate the confusing, the false, and the transitory to manifest and confer clarity, truth, and eternity. The creation of poetry and the reader's or spectator's recreative response demand great effort but promise great rewards. The poet sees as other men do not. Untutored, worldly vision most often looks asquint. With the poet's aid, however, true and false may be separated, and we may come to recognize them as they are.

Chapman regarded this enterprise as Promethean, but the poetic fire bringer gradually concentrates more and more on the earthly dust. Through Chapman's career, that is, theory and practice diverge. Commenting on Book 16 of the *Iliads*, Chapman described the "soule of a Poeme" as "most ingenious imitating the life of things" (*Homer,*

1:346). During his career, Chapman's honest vision of "the life of things"—a world of chance and transience, of politic manipulation and pragmatic immorality—produced dramatic realities that resist his art's power to reshape mundane experience into transcendent meaning. Ingenious imitating remains, but the plays—fine, persuasive, excellent in many ways as they are—work against the theory. His plays testify to the truth of Jonathan Dollimore's generalization: "The received view that Renaissance literary theory has little relevance to Renaissance literary practice is misleading; certainly it has little direct critical application, but it does have considerable relevance."[6]

Like every other Renaissance artist, Chapman sought to understand the value of secular life. More deeply than many, he understood the sway of Fortune, the confusion of daily existence, and the attractions of power. He responded by making our world—our best world—into poetry because this world and the other world meet in art. Correlatively, Chapman's belief in poetry's transcendental and eternal qualities decreed that only poetry could make history intelligible. Only poetry can find experience's true shape; only art can discover the moral of existence. The poet's art penetrates hidden truths, divine and natural, and that same art offers eternity to its subjects.[7] Chapman's presentation of pattern or randomness, of history and revelation, of heroism and pragmatism, depends upon the closest interaction of artistic means, artistic theory, and metaphysical belief.

ꝺ  ꝺ  ꝺ

Just how familiar might Chapman have been with the "life of things" he sought to imitate ingeniously? How familiar was he with Renaissance courts and courtiers, Tudor-Stuart politicians and political events? His audiences, especially at an indoor theater like the Blackfriars, with its clientele of courtiers and inns of court dandies, contained searching spirits who were, or sought to be, daily examples of the figures Chapman dramatized, daily practitioners of the actions he created. Whether or not such spectators expected minute, photographic realism (and we may suppose they did not), Chapman's own didacticism and his culture's pervasive belief that history, feigned and otherwise, instructed by example make the question relevant.

Chapman had a network of friendships, associates, and dependencies that gave him direct experience with the political worlds represented in his major tragedies. Consider, for example, his association with Henry, Prince of Wales, his "most deare and Heroicall Patrone" (Epistle dedicatory to Epicede [Poems, p. 253]). Following E. K. Chambers's lead, many critics have claimed that Chapman was made "sewer-in-ordinary" to Prince Henry virtually from his arrival in

England as a boy of nine.[8] Earlier assertions notwithstanding, this claim rests on an undated and unascribed copy of a petition in a Folger Library manuscript now published as *A Seventeenth-Century Letter-Book*. In the manuscript, this petition (from someone who claims to have been sewer-in-ordinary to Prince Henry for "above Nine yeares," but who has now lost his place following his master's death) is surrounded by copies of authentic Chapman items, but the petition is probably not by him at all.[9] No surviving list of Prince Henry's household from the earliest in the domestic state papers (10 October 1605) to the latest (ca. April 1613) mentions Chapman, although other sewers (who earned twenty pounds annually) and members of the household above and below stairs are amply documented.[10] It seems very likely, however, that the poet is, as Roy Strong says, the " 'Mr. Chapman' who received cloth [livery] for the Prince's funeral in the capacity of one of the 'Gentlemen extraordinarie servauntes to the Prince.' "[11] A gentleman extraordinary received livery but no fixed salary and paid only occasional, "extra-ordinary," attendance upon the Prince.[12] Such a position accords perfectly with Chapman's printed and authentic manuscript references to Henry's request that he complete the Homeric translations, his many years of unpaid work on the project, the Prince's promise of three hundred pounds for the translation, and his deathbed promise of a life pension.[13] While the claim about Henry's last promise may be exaggerated, Chapman provides plausible details about the Prince's court, and Henry's customary attitude toward artists and scholars suggests he might well have said the things the poet reports.

Whatever Chapman's exact status—more probably gentleman extraordinary than sewer-in-ordinary—there can be no doubting the poet's familiarity with Henry's circle of artists, scholars, and courtier-aristocrats. For example, Chapman collaborated with Inigo Jones, surveyor to the prince and later surveyor of James's Office of Works, on *The Memorable Maske*, "performed before the King, at Whitehall" to honor the marriage of Henry's sister Elizabeth (1613), later dedicated his translation of Musaeus (1616) to Jones, and received the posthumous tribute of a funeral monument erected at Jones's expense and still to be seen (although now recarved and not easily deciphered) in St. Giles-in-the-Fields, London. Chapman was a good friend of Michael Drayton, "the Prince's poet," who wrote a commendatory verse for Chapman's Hesiod translation (1618) and praised him in the epistle I have already quoted. They both published grandiose folios with title pages designed, perhaps, by Inigo Jones and engraved by William Hole, another member of Henry's artistic cadre.[14] To Sir Henry Fanshawe (1569–1616), "the favourite of Prince Henry, and had the Prince lived to be king . . . Secretary of State," Chapman inscribed a copy of the first twelve books of the *Odysseys* (1614) "For my right worthie Knighte, my exceeding noble friende, Sir Henry Fanshawe. A pore Homericall new yeare's gift."[15] As even this brief sketch suggests, Chapman had sustained firsthand experience of the group at St. James's, direct experience, that is, of an increasingly popular and politically active heir apparent, as well as the more remote experience of James's court implied by writing the masque for Princess Elizabeth's wedding.

However financially unrewarding Chapman's association with Prince Henry may ultimately have been, it was an association with a brilliant, even avant-garde, artistic group and a court of promising, young aristocrats and a select group of older ones. Chapman also had some experience, we may infer, of grittier political realities. In May 1593, twelve days before his murder, Christopher Marlowe was summoned to appear before the Privy Council; court officers were instructed to seek him at the country house, Scadbury, Chislehurst, Kent, of Mr. Thomas Walsingham (1568–1630), second cousin of Sir Francis Walsingham, the man for whom Marlowe is usually supposed to have served as an intelligence agent. Marlowe had presumably retreated from London's then-virulent plague (as all who could afford to did) and, it seems likely, was engaged in writing *Hero and Leander.* Ingram Frisar, another of Thomas Walsingham's dependents, ended Marlowe's living link with his patron, but the printer of the first known edition of *Hero and Leander* (1598) appropriately dedicated it to the now Sir Thomas Walsingham. Chapman followed suit by dedicating his continuation (also 1598) to Audrey (Shelton), Lady Walsingham, and describes her husband as "my honored best friend, whose continuance of ancient kindness to my still-obscured estate though it cannot increase my love to him" will encourage Chapman to "make my hearty gratitude speak; to which the unhappiness of my life hath hitherto been uncomfortable and painful dumbness" (*Hero and Leander,* p. 44).

So far, the evidence suggests that the two poet-acquaintances (probably poet-friends) were also joint sharers in the Walsinghams' patronage. Those patrons were well placed, with Lady Walsingham as a lady of Queen Elizabeth's bed chamber, Sir Thomas as M.P., J.P., and an important county gentleman with court connections good enough to get him the reversion of the Keepership of Eltham Park. Consequently, when Charles de Gontaut, Marechal de France and Duc de Biron (ca. 1562–1602), arrived as an ambassador from the French king in September 1601, it is unsurprising that the Privy Council directed Sir Thomas Walsingham to meet Biron at Dover, escort him to Gravesend (where he would be met by aristocratic envoys), and then assist his retinue onward to Sittingbourne.[16] Shortly after Biron's return to France, he was convicted (justly) and executed for plotting against his king. Englishmen followed Biron's last days closely, in part because they had recent, similar experience in the Earl of Essex's attempted rebellion, in part because this traitor had only months before been Elizabeth's guest.[17] Biron's was a celebrated career in war and peace, in loyalty and treason, a life ripe for the dramatizing, as Chapman demonstrates in his *Conspiracy and Tragedy of Charles, Duke of Byron* (1608), which includes a scene representing Biron's visit to England.

Chapman's dedication of the printed quarto begins by conventionally depreciating the event, since vernacular plays had in fact only recently achieved sufficient status to merit such dedication:

> Sir, Though I know you ever stood little affected to these unprofitable rites of Dedication (which disposition in you hath made me hitherto dispense with your right in my other impressions),

Chapman decided to go ahead to avoid the charge of ingratitude and because the dedicatee had a special interest in the plays;

> yet, lest the world may repute it a neglect in me of so ancient and worthy a friend, having heard your approbation of these in the presentment, I could not but prescribe them with your name; and that my affection may extend to your posterity, I have entitled to it, herein, your hope and comfort in your generous son. . . . (*Tragedies*, p. 151)

This dedication contains the striking but hitherto unremarked information that Chapman "heard" his patron's "approbation," his applause, his compliments, "in the presentment"; that is, the dedication claims author and patron together watched a performance of the play(s) at the Blackfriars in 1608.[18] That patron, the man who shared the dedication with his son, is none other than Sir Thomas Walsingham, who was by now indeed an "ancient and worthy" friend, since Chapman had gratefully remarked Walsingham's "ancient kindness" a decade earlier. Whatever the vicissitudes of Chapman's career since his gratitude in 1598, Sir Thomas and Lady Walsingham had become increasingly prominent at court, to the point that a few months later (December 1608) Lady Walsingham's "lodging by the Tilt Yard" was the scene of the marriage between Robert Cecil's only son, William, and the Earl of Suffolk's daughter, Katherine Howard.[19]

Sitting in the Blackfriars Theatre and approving Chapman's plays, Thomas Walsingham was watching a dramatic representation of a hero and events he had himself known and experienced less than seven years before. Little wonder, then, that he approbated the plays in the presentment, since he virtually participated in them. But Walsingham and the Blackfriars audience were watching more than the Duc de Biron; they were also invited to see, through him, the Earl of Essex. While the censor has evidently cut a scene representing Byron's interview with Queen Elizabeth, Byron is allowed to mention that Elizabeth discussed the Essex rebellion with him (*Tragedy*, 5.3.139ff) and he explicitly denies that they are "parallel . . . in life and fortune" (4.1.135). Of course everyone else thought the men were parallels, and a French work of 1607 purports to retail Elizabeth's remarks to Byron.[20] Playwright, historical subject, and audience could hardly be more closely linked than this. Besides saying much about the synchronization of political event and political drama, the episode demonstrates Chapman's historical links with and involvement in the material he dramatized. It is, moreover, a tidy demonstration of the poet's claim to clarify and make comprehensible historical event through artistic shaping; just as Sidney and countless others claimed should happen, Chapman instructs his patron and his audience on the meaning of their experience. Representing Byron and, obliquely, Essex, and still more obliquely, Thomas Walsingham, Chapman lifts event into example.

Finally, it is worth asking whether Chapman knew the broad outline of life at the contemporary French court—details ignored or omitted by the historians he consulted. In *Bussy D'Ambois*, the Duke of Guise and King Henry III debate the relative merits of English and French courtly protocol:

> *Guise.* I like not their Court-form, it is too crest-fall'n
> In all observance; making semi-gods
> Of their great nobles; and of their old Queen
> An ever-young, and most immortal Goddess.
>
> . . . . . . . . . . . . . .
>
> *Henry.* The world is not contracted in a man
> With more proportion and expression,
> Than in her Court, her Kingdom: our French Court
> Is a mere confusion to it:
> The King and subject, Lord and every slave
> Dance a continual Hay; our rooms of State,
> Kept like our stables; no place more observ'd
> Than a rude market-place: and though our custom

Keep this assur'd deformity from our sight,
'Tis ne'ertheless essentially unsightly . . .

(1.2.10–13, 24–33)

This imagined distinction between the two national courts would have made perfect sense to contemporary courtiers in each. The Scottish court, as it happens, was modeled on the French, and Bishop Godfrey Goodman (1583–1655) noted that the Scottish James VI stopped at York on his way to London in 1603 to "take state" and "put his court into an English fashion" because "there was no such state observed in Scotland . . . [but] no king, I am sure, in Christendom, did observe such state and carried such a distance from the subjects as the kings and queens of England did. . . ."[21] The modern historian of James's English court has succinctly drawn the distinctions between the Elizabethan court and the Franco-Caledonian: Elizabeth's was formal, private, and distant, restricting "intimacy between monarch and subject"; James's was largely unprivate, with crowds of people in the monarch's intimate chambers, thereby making access to James easier. In sum, "The English court was designed for the preservation and manipulation of distance; the Scots for the management of relatively free and open access. . . . the English etiquette was English, while the Scottish was French."[22] James's English court was a mixture of the two styles and could not help but be a noticeable change from Elizabeth's, a change indirectly but subversively registered in Chapman's historically accurate account of the differences between the French and English practices.

❧ ❧ ❧

The roll call of Chapman's most distinguished patrons—Essex, Prince Henry, Robert Carr—contains a traitor, an heir apparent who died young, and a disgraced accessory to murder. Chapman's personal experience of bounty thwarted begs to be explained through the same theory and the same model he applied to his plays' historical subject matter.[23] As in his experience of patronage, the signal quality of Chapman's tragic worlds is change, but his theory and his finest nondramatic poem, the continuation of Marlowe's *Hero and Leander,* stake his claim for poetry's power not merely to resist transience, but to supersede it altogether. *Hero and Leander* shows how Chapman's desire "to set downe uncommon and most profitable coherents for the time" (*Homer* 1:548) could produce a truly eternal art. Both strengths and weaknesses follow from Marlowe's insistent concern for variety; just as insistently, Chapman's completion looks beyond the immediate toward other principles ("higher," perhaps; certainly uncommon and profitable). Chapman easily, quickly, sees through or past his poem's characters and actions; in their stead he finds Ceremony and Eronusis and Hymen and all the other schemes of thought that, for him, give the story meaning and his readers their chief reward. When Chapman's *Hero and Leander* works best, it reveals his sense of the particular's relation with the universal. He shows time-bound, morally fallible humankind living within an eternal pattern of moral prescription and moral meaning. When Hero chooses to hide her love and continue as a priestess, for example, the narrator promptly decrees that she is "architect / Of all dissimulation" (4.312–13). Later, the poet indicates the layered relations among the gods, his human subjects, and the mythical and fictional characters of the "Tale of Teras": "Examples," we learn, "profit much; ten times in one, / In persons full of note, good deeds are done" (5.11–12). In these passages and many more, we are urged to join various extremes, to see the patterns into which any episode may fit, to discover the soul within the body, the permanent in the temporary.

Narrative poetry allowed Chapman almost unfettered opportunities to exploit his theory's bias toward abstraction and generalization. The drama does not provide similar opportunities, and Chapman developed new methods, for example, the Herculean topoi and various generic conventions of *Bussy D'Ambois*. Another method becomes almost a mandatory scene. The best instance occurs near the end of *Byron's Tragedy* (5.3.189–238), where no fewer than five characters offer, sequentially, comprehensive interpretations of Byron's behavior.[24] Their comments epitomize the intense, constant pressure—throughout Chapman's tragic drama—to discover an ethical and intellectual context, a system of principles, in which events and individuals may find or be given significance. Characters and actions cannot just be; they must mean. In *Bussy*, the *Byron* plays, *Chabot*, even *The Revenge of Bussy*, individuals and groups insistently interpret. Indeed, these heroes make symbols of themselves more readily than any others in English Renaissance drama. They claim kinship with Hercules, with Orpheus, with Apollo, with Alexander, with Cato, with "man in his native noblesse"—all on slender acquaintance and, often, less self-consciousness. Yet, these claims are not merely ironic traps set to spring closed as soon as they are uttered. The asserted similarity or identity always grows from a truthful seed. Likewise, the interpretations other characters make and their deductions concerning the universal frame all contain both some truth and some ironic or pathetic fallacy.

Jacobean dramaturgy included versions of this device almost as a matter of course.[25] Webster's villains, for example, often withdraw into commentator roles that flash new lights over the action, and Shakespeare—in the opening of *Antony and Cleopatra* or the two officers' argument preceding Coriolanus's arrival in the forum—uses a related method to reveal possible interpretations of the stage action. Chapman differs from his contemporaries in two basic ways: he always suggests or shows that each partial speaker has grasped a partial truth, and he rarely limits a speaker's views by implying individual prejudice. His characters often form a very odd chorus: they are never wholly correct nor do they ever adopt plainly idiosyncratic attitudes. Such interpretive episodes have led readers to decide that Chapman is ambivalent or equivocal or incoherent or ethically confused. That may be, but the process is so often dramatized that it must also arise from conscious design. The audience, like the characters, enters the process, for they must understand too, and like the characters, they often get trapped between valuing the process and weighing the product. Many characters, even the heroes themselves, seem to be feeling their way into knowledge. At the same time, the exploration is compelled, not voluntary: neither heroes nor peripheral characters can forbear (self-) defining no matter how contradictory or transient the conclusion.

As a good if somewhat muddled and syncretic Platonist (or Stoic-Platonist; the mixture is evidently not impossible), Chapman sought certainties within mutability. His theory, whether artistic or ethical in any given moment, proposed surety amid confusion. The dramatist's "peculiar tragic theme" has been called "the conflict of the individual with his environment and the inevitable issue of that conflict in the individual's defeat,"[26] but it is more accurate to describe Chapman's interest as humankind and our relation with change. Bussy and Byron, for example, believe themselves the masters of change: their self-images require that they think so. Yet they have frail weapons, flawed even before the conflict begins. More flexible men defeat the heroes, men who either stand and wait, or exploit instantly. As *Hero and Leander* assures us, "The use of time is Fate." Bussy and Byron have partly understood Machiavelli's lesson: temporal events are discrete. Every historical moment is utterly different from every other, and only analysis and flexible policy can meet that variety. These characters have not yet recognized that their self-definitions and, more important, their definitions in others' eyes, are also momentary. They cannot see themselves as part of some other individual's historical moment, and this blindness leads them to risk manipulation, or worse.

Chabot recognizes change—dim, incalculable forces of mutability beyond reason's reach—and he accedes to change, although he maintains his self-hood. The plays repeatedly show that adhering to a fixed system makes defeat inevitable because the rules of the game are themselves unstable. Although Chabot understands this fact, he chooses to remain faithful, bring change what it may. Bussy and Byron are often hyperbolically incredulous that mere events can destroy *them*. The multiple views of these earlier heroes underscore their worlds' inexplicable nature. As with the "perspective," anamorphic art, if there are so many views, can any one be true? Chapman struggles to create a superior realm of pure vision. Bussy escapes to that unchanging world; Byron also escapes, but much less certainly. Chabot has no such goal, no such assurance. His tragedy grants more intrinsic finality or reality to the sublunar world than do the earlier plays. In effect, *Chabot* describes not the way things are *here*, but the way things *are*.

If we accept Chapman's concentration on change, the much-debated division of his plays into Ulyssean and Achillean, or Neoplatonic and Stoic, becomes less important and less helpful.[27] His philosophy is never purely one or the other, as it could hardly hope to be since centuries of Christian syncretic thought also influenced him deeply. These pagan philosophies entered Chapman's creative process at its most intense concern—the discovery of meaning within worldly mutability. Chapman treats his philosophical ideas seriously, but they are fundamentally tools to explore change and permanence. While no one will ever accuse him of a Shakespearean negative capability, Chapman nonetheless practiced his trade successfully in both comedy and tragedy. That success inevitably meant putting ideas and philosophies into conflict. Thus, his various tragic characters and actions partly represent an intellectual experiment focused on the issues of social and political change and man's relation with such changes.

Given his conservative artistic theory, it is not surprising that Chapman first responds to the problem of change with a fairly rigid system. He posits a separation of worlds and attempts to define a hierarchy of values. We may well find his reaction old-fashioned; Ernst Cassirer described Chapman's single most important intellectual creditor, Florentine Neoplatonism, as the apex of a "retrogressive movement, the attempt at restoring Scholastic forms of thought."[28] Later, however, his allegiance to system, to social dogma, and to transcendentally sanctioned ethical codes begins to abate. This evolution may have many sources: Chapman's own artistic dissatisfaction, for example, or a developing conviction that his theories cannot account for the facts his plays so acutely, if painfully, record. Whatever their origins, these changes did take place. The tragedies are the evidence. At the experiment's end, *Chabot* studies a situation in which a man finds he can be true only to himself while living in a world where change and particularity, atomization of responsibility and uncertain standards, prevail.

These increasingly paradoxical plays again reflect Chapman's artistic quandary. He proclaims a theory that promises truth in every poetic reality, and he creates dramatic worlds that never seem quite fully interpreted. His favorite perspective-metaphor becomes more ominous as it approaches his own artistic condition. That metaphor insinuates an element of relativism into Chapman's abstract and absolutist poetic. He seeks dominion over a swirling ambiguity of choice: the heroes decide, command, or select, but their unstable environment often slides away into further complexities. His characters must adopt an unpredictable course, a wild dedication to unpathed waters and undreamed shores. The theory claimed to offer the "right line," the correct view, the profitable coherent, but the characters and action—in each work after *Hero and Leander*—become successively more ambiguous and blended. Universal and particular diverge; neither Chapman's theory nor his poetry can put them together again. The origin of this separation must lie within his own creativity; after all, he chose to portray dramatic worlds that refract as diversely as any Renaissance graphic "perspective." Those worlds resist art's order, and hence, for Chapman, resist meaning.

Chapman selected the chaotic, multifarious world of contemporary history as his dramatic arena. He made that choice, I believe, for two principal reasons. First, tragedies about familiar historical events immediately balance a world of change against art's eternalizing, illuminating power. Second, historical tragedy appeals to the audience's daily experience; it offers, as Chapman claimed, "delineation of human lives" and "memorable Examples for the use of policie and state."[29] The Italian theorist Robortello put it more bluntly: "Si nos verisimilia movent, multo magis vera movebunt."[30] Yet the choice of history makes Chapman's task very difficult. For all its immediate didactic appeal and its vivid depiction of an impermanent world requiring artistic lucidity, "history" was the focus of Renaissance thinkers' most intense and disorienting scrutiny. Scholars claim to find Renaissance philosophy insipid and derivative; the same cannot be said for Renaissance historiography or the philosophy of history. One might even claim that history, drawing legal philosophy and theories of method into its orbit, replaces philosophy at the center of Renaissance thought.[31] The period revolutionized historiography, and many new developments, often lurking within Chapman's very sources, ran precisely contrary to his theoretical convictions. Brief examination of the intellectual, if not demonstrably textual, similarities between

Chapman's tragedies and contemporary historical theory reveals the extent of his dilemma.

Studying the tragedies, especially the *Byron* plays, leaves no doubt that Chapman thought deeply about historical change, about the uses of history (as lesson, or model, or irrelevant evidence, for example), and about socio-political institutions and their permanence or mutability. Chapman's French sources and contemporary Italian and French political theorists show that his dramatizing of the past reflects a major current—perhaps the most influential one—in progressive Renaissance historiography. W. J. Bouwsma has explored the complex interdependence among humanist concepts of reality, Italian (later European) historiography, and specific political structures: particularity, scepticism of hierarchy, suspicion of systematic or programmatic historical patterns, emphasis upon moral and intellectual flexibility to meet the world's potentially infinite variety, and selective appeal to medieval religious schemes joined with a willing use of realpolitik. All these attitudes characterize "advanced" historiography.[32] All may be illustrated—by act and scene—from Chapman's tragedies.

Alongside changing attitudes toward history and historical writing came numerous formal changes in history plays and historical tragedies. Playwrights gradually abandoned morality-derived forms to embody historical material and historical perception. Chronicle histories tended to be unanalytic and usually embraced traditional moral hierarchies and widely accepted cosmologies.[33] So long as such chronicles served as dramatic source material, any playwright less gifted than Shakespeare would continue to employ a form A. P. Rossiter called "moral history."[34] When readers and audiences began to find that "modern" humanist historiography satisfactorily represented political reality, the drama (and literature generally) could not so easily use formal means appropriate to the earlier model. Changes—in history writing or dramatic writing—came neither swiftly nor completely, yet such very different plays as Ford's *Perkin Warbeck* or the Fletcher-Shakespeare *Henry VIII* imply attitudes greatly changed from those that produced *Gorboduc* or *Edward II*.[35]

Machiavelli and Guicciardini, analyzing recent Italian history, proposed principles of flexible political morality—bluntly, *qui nescit dissimulare nescit regnare*. Giving such ideas dramatic form, playwrights also sense a new uncertainty over moral action in the world; eventually, the drama might portray a universe where "flexibility" became license.[36] Many studies of the drama in the period from 1575 to 1642 do indeed depict an increasing scepticism and finally the near-abandonment in some playwrights' work of prescriptive norms altogether.[37]

Such general statements require extensive qualification, but it is fair to say that during this period absolute moral standards—social, political, and personal—in the drama become harder and harder to maintain and open to more frequent and sharper questioning.

The history of history and of historical drama suggests the context for Chapman's own tragedies. He made an unusual and even dangerous choice when he selected contemporary, public themes.[38] Yet that singular choice and his staunch artistic theory cannot conceal some extraordinary changes in the major tragedies. The most important may also be the most obvious: the transcendental world, whether Neoplatonic, Stoic, Christian, or some synthesis, gradually becomes indistinguishable from the mundane. Explicit hierarchy, moral standards, and prescriptive injunction all blend with court intrigue, diurnal passion, and politic motive. Royalty loses its hierophantic power. Chapman's kings grow passionate, and their passion signals their creator's reluctance to assert a supramundane existence. The king becomes a man, powerful enough to ruin the hero but subject to the same analysis of motives and actions. Coincidence (the discovery of Bussy's adultery) or sudden changes of allegiance (La Fin's betrayal of Byron) that were explained through assertions of social-moral-political responsibilities now give way to, or exist alongside, scrupulous analyses of purely power relationships (*Byron's Tragedy*) and private animosities (Francis's envy of Chabot). Chapman moves toward a world in which the survivors are those who can meet each shift of chance or fortune, and the losers are those who perceive and act prescriptively. The failures see not what is but what should be, as Byron does in his disastrously mistaken perception of Henry's court. Simultaneously, the plays lose a vigorous sense of the hero's natural habitation, that transcendent place where a Bussy achieves apotheosis. In brief, Chapman's tragedies gradually devalue the hero's sacrifice.

❦    ❦    ❦

Chapman's four best tragedies reveal, then, that his poetic practice gradually diverges from his theory. He becomes a different poet, but emphatically not a worse one, and not because his most fundamental beliefs changed. Relentlessly pursuing certain human situations, Chapman uncovers much that his art cannot shape as the theory predicted. The works in question span Chapman's career as a tragic dramatist, from *Bussy D'Ambois* (ca. 1604; published 1607) through the ten-act *Conspiracy and Tragedy of Charles, Duke of Byron* (published in 1608 and apparently written just prior to publication) to *Chabot, Admiral of France* (written ca. 1614).[39]

The importance of Chapman's conception of his art and of "Art" in *Hero and Leander* cannot be overemphasized. Many of art's most positive qualities appear in the poem: art as prophecy, art as patterning of raw experience, and art as inseparably connected with a transcendental realm of moral sanctions and perfected acts, perhaps even a realm of Providence's eternal present. Poetry and art share in the very existence of the supernatural, just as in Neoplatonic theory the image shares qualities with the entity imaged.[40] Without a firm conception of this superior world—the place whence the goddess Ceremony comes, for instance—art cannot exist and cannot be espoused by the poet. Art loses its power to discover the eternal within the apparently transient; without the world beyond, art loses the power to prophesy, for it has nowhere to seek or promise certitude; perhaps most important to Chapman, his art—bereft of transcendence—loses its authority, for it has no principles to make "illustrate." The full significance of this possibility—the loss or even the nonexistence of the suprahuman and supraexperiential—becomes clear as Chapman moves from the serene certainties of *Hero and Leander* through the experimentation of *Bussy* and the *Byron* plays to the final pessimistic vision of *Chabot*.

*Bussy* shows the playwright struggling to express his conception of the transcendental, the world beyond the world of court politics and manipulation, the world to which all but his last hero, Chabot, ultimately appeal. *Bussy* also clearly demonstrates Chapman's confusions of technique and genre; such confusions arise directly from his uncertainties about art's value as an evincer of pattern and meaning. Each of the *Byron* plays makes extensive use of art as a measure of morality and as a means of illuminating patterns in the action that might otherwise be overlooked. In these plays, too, the protagonist's major opponent becomes more important, and the relative moral status of hero and opponent becomes increasingly ambiguous. *Chabot* is an excellent concluding study, for it shows the almost complete disappearance of the transcendent world, the utter perversion of art (now used to create false patterns), and the near equilibrium of attention paid to the hero, Chabot, and his chief opponent, Francis I.

Although Chapman has not lacked hardy scholar-knights pursuing erudite grails, even the most stalwart pause before his other two canonical tragedies, *The Revenge of Bussy D'Ambois* and *Caesar and Pompey*. No wonder. The plays are pretty poor stuff: the former suffers by comparison with either *Bussy* or *Chabot*, and the latter clearly out-Catilines Jonson's own Roman failure. Despite special pleading and Chapman's own prefatory complaints, the two plays misfired with the contemporary audience (stage and/or study). The mutation of taste has not so far rescued them. The two plays have

received most attention from those readers who wish to construct a
Neoplatonic/Stoic (or Achillean/Ulyssean) dialectic for Chapman's career. The versified Epictetus of *The Revenge*, for example, does suggest a growing interest in that "good Greek moralist." The play's
dedicatory epistle, however, aligns Chapman with Plato: "Yet (with
the most divine philosopher, if Scripture did not confirm it) I make it
matter of my faith, that we truly retain an intellectual feeling of good
or bad after this life, proportionably answerable to the love or neglect
we bear here to all virtue, and truly humane instruction."[41] The soul's
immortality, personally important to Chapman and thematically important to the play, would surely be a matter of indifference to a Stoic.
Nor does the dialectic fare very well when applied to the sweep of
Chapman's dramatic and nondramatic writing. Neoplatonic his earliest verse and *The Gentleman Usher* (?1602) certainly are, but so are
the (largely translated) "Hymn to Hymen" (1613) and the elaborate
*Andromeda Liberata* (1614) at the other end of his public career.[42]
Many of the images that conclude *Bussy* are Stoic in origin, while
*Chabot* manages to recoup some of Chapman's earlier qualities, largely
through rejecting supposedly Stoic material.[43] I have deliberately
avoided characterizing Chapman's ideas as univocally Christian or
Neoplatonic or Stoic because these labels do not advance interpretation very far. If a pattern is to be found, it must come from within the
oeuvre, from the created response to history and to tradition.

The Stoic cast of *The Revenge* and *Caesar and Pompey*, so far as it
exists, does not produce good drama or literature, but merely muddle.
That muddle derives from Chapman's inability or unwillingness to
give up his concern for the conflict between inward and outward
directed thought and action, for learning versus policy, for the relation
between transcendence and life as it is lived with daily doubt, discon-
tent, difficulty. Chapman could not convert Stoicism into satisfying art
as he could convert Neoplatonic thought; his deepest continuing
interests resisted Stoic formulations. One very general way to examine
Chapman's interests, and one way to draw together an extremely
heterogeneous career, is through the organizing subject of this study—
his attempt to portray an artistically crafted reality. As I hope to show,
Chapman's confidence in his artistry had the deepest possible effect
upon his poetic practice.

# 1

# "Spirit to Dare and Power to Do": The Two Worlds of *Bussy D'Ambois*

Chapman's continuation of Marlowe's *Hero and Leander* has a double conclusion. In one voice, the narrator concludes the poem's plot and sadly proposes the moral judgment the lovers deserve:

> O sweet Leander, thy large worth I hide
> In a short grave; ill-favour'd storms must chide
> Thy sacred favour: I in floods of ink
> Must drown thy graces, which white papers drink,
> Even as thy beauties did the foul black seas.
> I must describe the hell of thy dis-ease,
> That heaven did merit. . . .

>                                                                (6.137–43)

In another voice, he raises them and their story into eternal pattern:

> Neptune for pity in his arms did take them,
> Flung them into the air, and did awake them
> Like two sweet birds, surnam'd th' Acanthides,
> Which we call thistle-warps, that near no seas
> Dare ever come, but still in couples fly,
> And feed on thistle-tops, to testify
> The hardness of their first life in their last. . . .

>                                                                (6.274–80)

The narrator then offers a point-by-point analysis of the goldfinch's plumage to illustrate that its "Colours . . . as we construe colours, paint / Their [Hero and Leander's] states to life" (6.288–89), and concludes the metamorphosis and the poem by recalling Musaeus's status as a "first" poet: "This true honour from their love-deaths sprung, / They were the first that ever poet sung" (6.292–93).

Blending these conclusions required the use of metamorphosis and the invocation of artistic theory and the history of poetry. *Bussy*

*D'Ambois* offers some of the same difficulties Chapman met and overcame in *Hero and Leander*. Like the poem, the play presents us with two lovers who violate their society's proclaimed moral and social codes. Once again, Chapman must judge individuals and actions that a conventional moralist would unhesitatingly condemn, but which the dramatist finds attractive and even noble. Despite such elegant models as John Lyly's *Gallathea*, *Bussy D'Ambois* cannot easily invoke metamorphosis as a dramatic solution to the problems Chapman has created. Instead, Chapman places his characters in a court as violent and seedy as any in Jacobean drama. That court world has little place for heroism or grandeur or delicacy, spiritual or physical. With a very few exceptions, the world in which Bussy and his love, Tamyra, attempt to survive is one that uses its supposed moral codes as hypocritical justifications for self-serving and brutal ambition. Moreover, far from withdrawing into sensual delight on Abydos's shore, Bussy energetically attempts to advance himself in the very political arena that defies his claims to superior spiritual and psychological stature. *Bussy D'Ambois* has a peculiar instability because Chapman has strengthened the contradictions he so carefully resolved, or at least concealed, in *Hero and Leander*. Everywhere one looks, the stakes have been raised: hero and heroine are made morally ambiguous; their enemies are both repellent and successful; their friends are equivocal and even demonic; their world is dangerous, power-mad, and yet supposedly the hero's chief desire.

This extraordinary and often paradoxical variety produces a complicated drama that many audiences, from the seventeenth century onwards, have found confusing and even incoherent. To interpret the play, readers and spectators often fasten on the hero and his seemingly endless contradictions. The prologue for a revival in the 1630s praised "the height and pride / Of D'Ambois' youth and braverie," while a few decades later Dryden attacked Bussy as a "bully hero."[1] Millar MacLure offers a more temperate view: "The hero is not all in the play, but has in the poet's imagination another life the shadow of which falls, often very undramatically, into the business of the action."[2] Debating Bussy's personality, we risk losing an important point: the play itself dramatizes that debate. At the very start, Monsieur, the courtier ambitious to replace his brother, King Henry III, invites Bussy to "live . . . at the well-head" (1.1.83), that is, to come to court and, Monsieur hopes, assist his treachery. Bussy consents after extracting the promise of some money. When Maffé, Monsieur's steward, arrives with the coins, he cannot understand what merit his master finds in the threadbare Bussy. Maffé tries out various identities for the hero: poet, "poor soldier," jester, and finally a morality-play Vice with a "wooden dagger" (1.1.161, 173, 200, 204). Their angry exchanges end when Bussy beats Maffé for his presumption, but each of the steward's sarcastic suggestions has enough truth to make Bussy's nature an issue from the beginning. `

As the other characters attempt to define Bussy, they also define themselves. The many different views of Bussy in fact arise from many different views of the world and from the speaker's sense of his own place, as well as Bussy's, in that world. To some extent, this reciprocity occurs in all drama (and in life), but Bussy arouses such extreme responses and seems himself to be so unusual that Chapman can employ the hero as a scalpel drawn across the court's corrupt body. The court's social formulas have trouble containing Bussy, and so do the court's manipulative politicians, and so, finally, does the court's ordinary, very political, language. A scattered group of speeches—some of them Bussy's own—argue that his qualities are rare, even unprecedented, in the postlapsarian world. These speeches have a disruptive energy completely at odds with the insidious, soothing elegance of the usual court dialect. We hear the first example almost as soon as Bussy arrives at the French court. The newly spruce courtier proceeds at once to a series of bawdy and offensive exchanges with the Duchess of Guise, wife of Monsieur's great rival. Bussy's attack horrifies Monsieur because it threatens open and disastrous conflict with the very man most likely to oppose any attempted usurpation. Yet Monsieur cannot contain his admiration for Bussy's confident bravery:

> His great heart will not down, 'tis like the sea
> That partly by his own internal heat,
> Partly the stars' daily and nightly motion,
> Ardour and light, and partly of the place
> The divers frames, and chiefly by the Moon,
> Bristled with surges, never will be won
> (No, not when th' hearts of all those powers are burst)
> To make retreat into his settled home,
> Till he be crown'd with his own quiet foam.
>
> (1.2.138–46)

The speech dignifies Bussy, lifting him from bawdiness and blackguardism to a level not only of natural force, but especially of *action*.[3] Bussy's actionless valor is a crucial paradox in the play. Monsieur begins to subdue that paradox when he justifies Bussy's violent language, that is, when he explains the sea's motion. Two causes for the ocean's surging have clear human referents: "His [the sea's] own internal heat" (line 139) corresponds to the hot valor, the sense of merit and worth, that Bussy displays; "the place / The divers frames" (lines 141–42) represents "the shape of the land which bounds the sea's movement"[4] and, applied to Bussy, signifies the court itself. Monsieur's other two ventures into oceanography at first seem to have no referential value for the man and the human situation he is describing and hence seem to represent a collapse into nonsense by an overstimulated poet (or speaker).

Examined more carefully, the two remaining causes—"the stars' daily and nightly motion, / Ardour and light" and "the Moon"— reveal important ideas about Bussy's nature, his significance, and his passion's force. Any hint, or anything more than a hint, of astral "influence" seems irrelevant: the play refuses to employ astrology or astrological explanations. These lines loosely associate Bussy with the moon, the stars, and the planets, in the sense that those heavenly bodies spur or excite man's actions. Whether or not the play owes a clear debt to Giordano Bruno's *Lo Spaccio della bestia trionphante* (1584), as Maurice Evans has argued, this speech does further suggest some variety of the Renaissance's endemic assignment of specific virtues to specific heavenly bodies.[5] These assignments derive not only from ancient astrological lore, but from the hermetic tradition, from the manifold mythological and fabulous allegorizations of the stars and constellations, and from other sources as well.[6] Monsieur, for one, is prepared to see the hero in a supramundane frame as well as a courtly one. Bussy's human actions give life to the stars' allegorical meanings. When Monsieur also finds the sea and Bussy moved "chiefly by the Moon," he proposes a more earth-bound explanation for Bussy's fiery language. A later conversation (4.1.1–46) describes first the moon and women as idolon and reflection, one of the other, and then the moon's tertiary influence over men, via women. "Chiefly by the Moon," then, may invoke changeable Luna as Woman raised to astronomical power. Monsieur openly links Tamyra with the Moon: "Your wife, you know, is a mere Cynthia, / And she must fashion horns out of her nature" (4.1.120–21).[7]

I have emphasized the referential value of Monsieur's words. When he invokes the stars and moon to explain Bussy, the hunt for referents becomes more difficult because Monsieur has shifted from one kind of discourse (pragmatic, quasi-physical) to another one, more vague, more mythic, and more mystical. Throughout the play, the characters seek an idiom, an analogy, or a scheme of thought to define Bussy. Monsieur's wavering reflects the play's binocular view of the hero and his language, both "earth-exempt," as Chapman phrased it in *Hero and Leander,* and passionately variable, like moon and tide.

Even Bussy himself cannot always express the vision Chapman hopes to body forth. When Bussy stands accused of murdering his courtly opponents in a duel, the "pardon scene" finds him confident of his difference but slightly unclear as to its precise nature:

> since I am free
> (Offending no just law), let no law make
> By any wrong it does, my life her slave:
> When I am wrong'd and that law fails to right me,
> Let me be King myself (as man was made)
> And do a justice that exceeds the law:
> If my wrong pass the power of single valour
> To right and expiate; then be you my King,
> And do a Right, exceeding Law and Nature:
> Who to himself is law, no law doth need,
> Offends no King, and is a King indeed.
>
> (2.1.194–204)[8]

*Law* undergoes some curious permutations here. In the first half of the speech, one law is clearly the positive law of the kingdom, which may fail (because created for ordinary men) "to right" a man such as Bussy. He claims royal and prelapsarian sovereignty over himself ("as man was made"); hence, he may execute a justice that exceeds mere positive law. Bussy then makes a concession: his strength may not be sufficient to rectify the wrong done him. In such a case, the king must "do a Right, exceeding Law and Nature." Apparently, *Law* refers to human, positive law, a law which may well not avenge Bussy's injury; *Nature* is Bussy's own extraordinary condition. This concession is immediately tempered. Bussy believes it unlikely that his Nature and the law he acknowledges would ever lead him to do anything "past the power of [his own] single valour / To right and expiate."

This glimpse of a man "who to himself is law" flowers in one of the play's most celebrated speeches. Preparing to reconcile Bussy and the Duke of Guise after an especially vulgar exchange, King Henry describes Bussy as

> A man so good, that only would uphold
> Man in his native noblesse, from whose fall
> All our dissensions rise; that in himself
> (Without the outward patches of our frailty,
> Riches and honours) knows he comprehends
> Worth with the greatest: Kings had never borne
> Such boundless eminence over other men,
> Had all maintain'd the spirit and state of D'Ambois;
> Nor had the full impartial hand of Nature
> That all things gave in her original,

Without these definite terms of Mine and Thine,
Been turn'd unjustly to the hand of Fortune—
Had all preserv'd her in her prime, like D'Ambois;
No envy, no disjunction, had dissolv'd
Or pluck'd out one stick of the golden faggot
In which the world of Saturn was compris'd,
Had all been held together with the nerves,
The genius and th' ingenuous soul of D'Ambois.

(3.2.90–107)

As Jonathan Goldberg has pointed out, Henry is also praising himself here, identifying the "founding myth for the imperium in" Bussy.[9] Difficulties with this speech come not so much from Henry's (self-)praise as from the definition of *fall* and the general interpretation of "the world of Saturn." The overall effect is not in doubt: Henry speaks with great moral as well as secular and quasi-religious authority. Bussy differs from other courtiers because he belongs to an existence that they long ago forfeited. Although Edwin Muir helpfully distinguishes Henry's use of *fall* from the word's Christian connotation, most readers have made the mistake, certified by numerous Renaissance allegorizations, of assimilating "the world of Saturn" to Eden and its loss to the orthodox Christian Fall of Man.[10]

Louis Bredvold traces two interpretations of the Golden Age in the Renaissance.[11] One group of authors looked back to the Golden Age as a time when society restrained no human activity, a time when love was free, ownership unknown, honor not invented, and life easier than it ever after was to be. This libertine conception of natural law (in effect, doing what comes naturally) receives delicate embodiment in the famous chorus of Tasso's *Aminta*.[12] Many Stoic writers, wishing to use the topos for other purposes, attacked this conception as ethically empty. Untested innocence is neither a virtue nor truly understood "innocence." This second important use of the topos progressed via Cicero's and Seneca's philosophical writings to medieval and Renaissance political theorists.[13] These writers emphasized the innate virtue of people living close to the divine principles implicit in Nature; since the Golden Age, such natural law has needed civil, or positive, human law to eke out the defects of human nature.[14] The whole subject recurs in Thomas Starkey's famous *Dialogue between Reginald Pole and Thomas Lupset* (ca. 1533), which also serves as a handy compendium of arguments for and against the active and contemplative lives.[15] Chapman seems to lean toward the Stoic interpretation of the Golden Age, but the alternative arguments, so freshly and recently treated in Tasso's influential pastoral romance, were also available. The familiar topos emphasizes Bussy's ambiguous nature and the complexity of his choices and actions. The Golden Age speech encourages us to see Bussy as a man close to the original laws of nature, now distorted in most modern men, but also as a man who may share that primitive and excessive individualism that society's laws have been invented to control.

Henry's speech cannot be pressed too far toward specific referents; as Harry Levin notes, the Golden Age topos becomes "a source of precept and allusion" in Seneca's drama and the English playwrights (including Chapman) who imitated him.[16] Functioning largely as grandiose elevation, the portrait of Bussy as a Golden Age survivor echoes in literary and elegiac terms his displacement from the transcendental to the political world. Henry's praises are as ominous as they are complimentary. R. B. Waddington observes, "D'Ambois is a threat to the equilibrium of the state that has evolved. . . . What is natural in another context becomes monstrous. . . ."[17] The political, fallen world requires kings; a world where Nature's hand has been turned to the hand of Fortune cannot comprehend Bussy, a man so far from his time and place that they have themselves become myths.

Most courtiers do not share Henry's admiration, but even they cannot always conceal their wonder and their fear at the spectacle of Bussy's career. The ironic comments upon the hero's bravado express awe as well as scepticism. While Monsieur only once rises to the eloquent height of "His great heart will not down," at other times and in different circumstances he admits his admiration: Bussy possesses an "advanced valour" (3.2.299); he is a "spirit" (4.1.91); he has "strange gifts in nature" (3.2.349) and "organs and faculties" to equal the greatness of "Augustus Caesar" (4.1.99–100). "Violent Guise," perhaps recognizing in Bussy a nobler exemplar of his own chivalric code, cannot believe that Nature would

> give a whole man valour, virtue, learning,
> Without an end more excellent than those
> On whom she no such worthy part bestows.
>
> (5.3.34–36)

The play's courtly speakers lack a language to describe Bussy, or at least to describe one aspect of the hero. They struggle to find terms—demon or prelapsarian man or blustering bully—for what they have never experienced. This difficulty extends to Bussy himself. He, too, flounders when he tries to define himself as the outsider he feels he is. Linguistic difficulties echo the social and psychological ones. If a definition could be found, Bussy could be "placed" in the court world,

and, of course, the politicians could then control and manipulate him
as they control and manipulate more orthodox individuals. Even as
Chapman establishes this extreme vision of the hero as demigod, he
promotes a very different version. Bussy also appears as an archaic
soldier-swordsman-brawler, a man whose valor preys upon his reason.
This Bussy is ripe for the blandishments of power and susceptible to
the finely tuned system of rewards and punishments that Monsieur
and the other politicians operate so well. This Bussy is not only more
recognizable to the courtiers, he is also more familiar to Chapman's
audience. Behind him stretches a long line of blood-and-thunder
tragic heroes from plays by Marlowe and Peele and other popular
dramatists.[18] Two crucial episodes define this vision of Bussy: his
original decision to go to court, and his adulterous love affair with
Tamyra. Given Chapman's paradoxical bent throughout the play, we
cannot be surprised when neither episode offers a clear-cut evaluation
of the hero.

There is no reason to suspect hypocrisy when Bussy decides to "rise
in Court with virtue" (1.1.126), although several ominous words and
events suggest that it may not be so easy as he thinks. What are his
announced motives? His valor and general merit demand recognition
in "Honour" and "Reward" (1.1.2). The only place they may be
gained, he thinks, is the active world, the court. One may object that
Bussy errs in seeking a community he has bitterly attacked (1.1.84–
104), but Henry III himself represents at least a partial answer. He is
at once the supreme courtier, a moral and honorable man, and eventually Bussy's chief friend in court. When Tamyra threatens to tell the
king of Monsieur's attempted seduction (2.2.100, 106–7), she proclaims Henry a moral man and the court (potentially) a moral place.
Moreover, Bussy's decision suggests that virtue must act if she is truly
to be herself.[19]

There are qualifications. Bussy's "spirit" and his desire for honor
may produce passionate excess (as in the striking of Maffé) and his
questionable decision to use Monsieur's designs ("killing of the
King") for his own very different ends. Indeed, Bussy's excessive
concern for honor and praise make possible his passionate involvement with Tamyra and hence lead to political manipulation and death.
The hint that Bussy may already be flanking policy with policy (cf.
4.2.155ff.) first appears when he recognizes Monsieur's schemes and
decides to accept preferment nonetheless:

> What will he send? some crowns? It is to sow them
> Upon my spirit, and make them spring a Crown
> Worth millions of the seed crowns he will send:

But he's no husband here; a smooth plain ground
Will never nourish any politic seed;
I am for honest actions, not for great:
If I may bring up a new fashion,
And rise in Court with virtue, speed his plough. . . .

(1.1.119–26)

By countermining, Bussy hopes to blow up Monsieur's project and substitute his own.

"Merit" alone does not suffice; it requires a "raiser" (1.1.134–35). Bussy abandons a locale where virtue is evidently its own (but only) reward for the court, where merit needs political help, and where, presumably, vice is not automatically punished. When Bussy first meets the King, their exchange hints that Bussy has ventured more than he has gained:

*Henry.*    I like your alteration, and must tell you,
          I have expected th' offer of your service;
          For we (in fear to make mild Virtue proud)
          Use not to seek her out in any man.
*Bussy.*    Nor doth she use to seek out any man:
          He that will win, must woo her; she's not shameless.
*Monsieur.* I urg'd her modesty in him, my Lord,
          And gave her those rites, that he says she merits.

(1.2.61–68)

The King's implicit reproach—that "mild Virtue" has been made proud—stings Bussy to a defensive retort.

Just as Bussy's career and language often recall Hercules',[20] so too the hero's decision echoes the "Choice of Hercules," often represented pictorially as taking place in a "green retreat" (1.1.45). In many graphic works, Hercules reclines or rests on his club in positions that recall Bussy's own (for example, *He lies down,*" the stage direction at 1.1.33).[21] Fulgentius (*Mythologia,* 2.1), drawing on Plutarch, who in turn borrowed from Plato, had allegorized the "Judgment of Paris" as the choice among the active, the contemplative, and the sensual lives.[22] Ficino later compared the judgment of Paris with the choice of Hercules and defined the second as the choice between the active life and the sensual life.[23]

One traditional distinction between the contemplative and active lives—pastoral virtue and urban vice—does not solve the ambiguity of Chapman's allusions. Civic humanists, sometimes recalling Aristotle's jibe that the philosopher exists to make men good,[24] encouraged the argument that the educated, virtuous man should enter society rather than withdraw from it. *Nennio, or A Treatise of Nobility* (translated 1595) appeared with a commendatory poem by Chapman and made no judgment between the relative merits of the active and contemplative lives, although the sensual life received short shrift and the dangers inherent in social activism were discussed.[25] Literature could reconcile the heroic with the pastoral code, as Spenser's Sir Calidore demonstrates, and a paradigm for Bussy's hopes appears in *Faerie Queene* 1.10, when Red Crosse first ascends the mount of contemplation and then returns to the life of chivalric and moral action. Finally, the dramatic tradition in Peele's *Arraignment of Paris* defined the triadic choice as contemplation, heroic action, and sensuality.[26] Chapman varies the topos: Bussy chooses to leave a withdrawn life (but perhaps not a purely contemplative one) for an active life that includes the danger of sensual temptation.

These plain references to a common literary debate have ambiguous applications. The structural device is common in Chapman's plays: shifting patterns for the stage action underscore the complex choices the characters themselves must make. Rather than inhering in the hero's response to events, ambiguity and indeterminacy instead control the very presentation of those events and seem to be part of dramatized life itself. *Bussy D'Ambois* applies the "world-turned-upside-down" topos to topoi themselves and to many other conventional patterns. This tactic, which became a peculiarly Jacobean one, gives the play some of its unsettling quality, but it also has potentially unsettling consequences for Chapman's art. Excess pattern and multiple formal alternatives within the art work foster doubt that any single or unified set of patterns and forms exists. If the power of art to shape its subject matter, to make it "illustrate" as Chapman wrote, gets out of control, it may die of its own too much. The artist, discovering many different and contradictory patterns for his action, may begin to doubt the eternally endorsed truth of any single pattern and consequently the truth of his art itself. Chapman's slippery treatment of Bussy in the first scene raises these questions, and the remainder of the play does not entirely answer them.

Bussy's choice takes him to court, the passionate locus where Nature, "stark blind herself" (5.3.4), subserves Fortune. Psychologically, Bussy's choice rests upon his valor or spirit and his desire for noble action, honor, and fame. Only by playing upon these traits can Monsieur secure Bussy's consent:

> . . . as the light
> Not only serves to shew, but render us
> Mutually profitable: so our lives

In acts exemplary, not only win
Ourselves good Names, but doth to others give
Matter for virtuous Deeds, by which we live.

(1.1.76–81)

Although Bussy and the audience recognize that the appeal merely
cloaks Monsieur's design upon the throne, Bussy succumbs: "What
would you wish me to do?" Thus, while Chapman gives the scene
certain features of a classical topos and Monsieur ornaments his discourse with allusions to Neoplatonic ideas of the soul's impotence[27]
and to the medieval morality tradition,[28] the true emphasis falls upon
spirit and its expression. To Bussy, the court seems the only place
where he may properly be himself, and suggestions that he has compromised his principles only underscore his desire's power.

Bussy, "a man of spirit beyond the reach of fear" (1.1.46), reveals
his nature as soon as he arrives at court. Fleering courtiers quickly
surround Bussy and treat him as a jester, incongruously costumed for
their amusement. Bussy disdains the courtiers' "ridiculous jollity" (a
nice pun), and two of them respond with telling jibes:

> *Pyrrhot.*  O strange credulity! Do you think yourself
> such a singular subject for laughter, that none
> can fall into our merriment but you?
> *Barrisor.* This jealousy of yours sir, confesses some close
> defect in yourself, that we never dreamed of.

(1.2.182–86)

Barrisor's insult superficially refers to the "perfumed Ass . . . dis-
guised with a Lion's case" (lines 187–88), but it also points up Bussy's
overquick sensitivity. Bussy challenges his tormentors to a duel, kills
them, and when he next appears, stands accused of "wilful murders"
(2.1.149).

Although Monsieur manages to win a pardon for Bussy, his protégé
refuses to accept a conditional liberty and soon becomes the King's
new favorite. Monsieur now realizes that he cannot employ Bussy's
"mettle" in his campaign to reach the throne. He identifies the cause:

> . . . I fear him strangely,
> And may resemble his advanced valour
> Unto a spirit rais'd without a circle,
> Endangering him that ignorantly rais'd him,
> And for whose fury he hath learn'd no limit.

(3.2.298–302)

Bussy interrupts his musing "master," just as Monsieur had once found Bussy in his "green retreat."[29] Bussy insinuates that Monsieur has again been plotting against the King, and this accusation becomes a leitmotif of the flyting scene that follows. MacLure has described these exchanges as a "savagely attractive . . . *contentio veritatis.*"[30] The reiterated phrase—"killing of the King" (3.2.347, 356, 371, 411)—demonstrates Bussy's devotion to Henry. His valor serves the monarch, as does his satire; he is the King's "eagle." Monsieur's faults, as Bussy lists them, do not add significantly to the previous hyperbolic ledger of immoralities: treason, perjury, duplicity, vindictiveness, tyranny, atheism, lust, and satanism. In contrast, Monsieur chooses as Bussy's central fault the very quality that made him attractive as an agent of treason:

> . . . I think thee then a man,
> That dares as much as a wild horse or tiger;
> As headstrong and as bloody; and to feed
> The ravenous wolf of thy most Cannibal valour
> (Rather than not employ it), thou would'st turn
> Hackster to any whore, slave to a Jew
> . . . . . . . . . .
> That in thy valour th' art like other naturals,
> That have strange gifts in nature, but no soul
> Diffus'd quite through to make them of a piece,
> But stop at those humours that are more absurd,
> . . . . . . . . . .
> That in that valour (which is still my dunghill,
> To which I carry all filth in thy house)
> Th' art more ridiculous and vainglorious
> Than any mountebank; and impudent
> Than any painted bawd. . . .
>
> (3.2.336–41, 348–51, 357–61)

These are strong lines, and exaggerated, but the duel forces us to admit they have a certain painful truth.

Horror at his failure to control Bussy—in fact, fear of any uncontrollable human quality (the politician's nightmare)—drives Monsieur's rage and feeds his sick language. This fear of what may not be manipulated, of passion beyond pragmatic restraint, forces Monsieur to seek some means of destroying his erstwhile favorite. Conferring with Montsurry and the Guise, Monsieur decides to "set snares for his gadding greatness . . . amongst our greatest women." "For," he says smuttily,

there is no such trap to catch an upstart
As a loose downfall; and indeed their falls
Are th' ends of all men's rising: if great men
And wise make 'scapes to please advantage
'Tis with a woman: women that worst may
Still hold men's candles. . . .

(3.2.143–48)

Sexual passion and vulnerability to political control are here explicitly associated, as they often are in Jacobean drama. To feel desire or to respond to another's desire necessarily means subjecting one's fate to another's power. Bussy's enemies soon discover his affair, and Tamyra's adultery astonishes Monsieur as much as his inability to direct Bussy's "advanced valour." A politician's success depends upon knowing all human qualities—good, but more often ill—and a precise calculus of human relations.

Monsieur's very life requires that he know what evil lurks in the hearts of men and women. The speech that ends with the simile of Bussy as "a spirit rais'd without a circle" begins with Monsieur's amazed meditation upon Tamyra's guilt:

O the unsounded Sea of women's bloods,
. . . . . . . . . . . . .
Where never day shines, nothing ever grows,
But weeds and poisons, that no statesman knows. . . .

(3.2.286, 291–92)

What Monsieur does not know can hurt him. Pragmatic, reductionist knowledge is courtly power. While he can control neither Bussy's valor nor Tamyra's lust, Monsieur can employ—through Montsurry—his knowledge to destroy them.

Sexual passion and valor correspond to one another in the play's action and in its metaphysics: they are complementary, and they contradict the most deeply held patriarchal convictions of early modern England.[31] The play's view of sexuality (limited almost solely to Tamyra) thus illuminates much in Bussy himself. Tamyra's "licentious fancy / Riots within" (2.2.42–43). Violent words and images crowd her first passionate speech: *rageth, tosseth, insolent fury, riots* (2.2.38, 40, 41, 43). When she compares her passion to an earthquake, she describes the violent upwelling of unconscious desire, a lightning tendril from that shadowy abyss as well-known (if not so suavely or frequently invoked) by Elizabethans as by post-Freudians.[32] Many features of the play support this interpretation not only of sexual passion but of all passion. Some of Montsurry's ravings, for instance, vividly prefigure the explosion of suppressed and perverted fantasy when Ferdinand discovers his sister's marriage to Antonio (*The Duchess of Malfi*, 2.5). Tamyra helplessly invokes name, house, and religion. Remembering Hero's self-torment by "strange thoughts . . . that spake straight, and wish'd their mother slain" (*Hero and Leander* 3.225, 228), we recognize such lines as these:

> They come, alas they come, fear, fear and hope
> Of one thing, at one instant fight in me:
> I love what most I loathe, and cannot live
> Unless I compass that that holds my death:
> For love is hateful without love again,
> And he I love, will loathe me, when he sees
> I fly my sex, my virtue, my renown,
> To run so madly on a man unknown.
> See, see the gulf is opening, that will swallow
> Me and my fame for ever; I will in,
> And cast myself off, as I ne'er had been.
>
> (2.2.168–78)

The last line rings true to the experience of losing a known, accepted personality in the sudden internal onslaught and triumph of another darker and more passionate self.

As Brooke says, the adulterers "are placed . . . outside the shelter of the moral order,"[33] yet Montsurry, the "injured party," has himself compromised that order. When Tamyra reports Monsieur's attempted seduction, her husband consoles her: "That Prince doth high in virtue's reckoning stand / That will entreat a vice, and not command: / So far bear with him . . ." (2.2.124–26). As in *Hero and Leander*, Chapman attempts simultaneously to condemn immorality and to gain our sympathy for the lovers' "set and cunning world of Love" (2.2.195). In this second aim, he succeeds brilliantly. The understanding and sympathy expressed in Tamyra's invocation to night cannot be denied:

> Now all ye peaceful regents of the night,
> Silently-gliding exhalations,
> Languishing winds, and murmuring falls of waters,
> Sadness of heart, and ominous secureness,
> Enchantments, dead sleeps, all the friends of rest,
> That ever wrought upon the life of man,
> Extend your utmost strengths; and this charm'd hour
> Fix like the Centre; make the violent wheels

Of Time and Fortune stand; and great Existence
(The Maker's treasury) now not seem to be,
To all but my approaching friends and me.

(2.2.157–67)[34]

Outside the moral order, prey to political necessity, Tamyra begs for a new world beyond Time, motion, and Fortune.

Bussy is the guarantor—the only begetter—of the lovers' security. His valor must conceal, defend, even create, the very world they inhabit. Bussy's valor and Tamyra's desire now appear as the reciprocal passions they truly are. Tamyra's confessor, Friar Comolet, recognizes this reciprocity in his strange instructions to Bussy:

> Come worthiest son, I am past measure glad,
> That you (whose worth I have approv'd so long)
> Should be the object of her fearful love;
> Since both your wit and spirit can adapt
> Their full force to supply her utmost weakness. . . .

(2.2.179–83)

Despite the sexual innuendo here, subsequent scenes also support the idea that Tamyra's passion matches Bussy's "full force." Indeed, his valor may be what most attracts her. Awaiting the King's verdict on the duel, she claims, "Though his great spirit something overflow / All faults are still-born, that from greatness grow" (2.2.2–3). These are her first words in the play.

Immediately after their first (and only) assignation, Tamyra fearfully confesses that she has "set open all the doors of danger" (3.1.2) and laments Sin's "dangerous siege . . . and the tyranny / He exercises when he hath expung'd" (3.1.9, 10–11). Bussy responds to these military metaphors with his own view of morality as chivalrous contest: "Sin is a coward Madam, and insults / But on our weakness, in his truest valour: / And so our ignorance tames us . . ." (3.1.18–20).[35] He then commits his valor, as Comolet had asked, to protecting Tamyra:

> Sooner shall Torture be the sire to Pleasure,
> And health be grievous to men long time sick,
> Then the dear jewel of your fame in me
> Be made an outcast to your infamy. . . .

(3.1.34–37)

Bussy's grand avowals satisfy Tamyra: "It rests as all Kings' seals were set in thee"; in fact, valorous speech is Bussy's only response to her affection. Later, when the trap of revenge and manipulation has nearly closed around the lovers, Tamyra cries for help and Bussy loudly threatens (4.2.8–10). The Friar is much more practical; he summons hellish spirits for assistance, and his pragmatism endangers Bussy's rhetoric for it may seem mere rodomontade without substantial force. Valor actively joins with sexual passion when Bussy decides to go to Tamyra, no matter what the cost:

> I must fare well, how ever: though I die,
> My death consenting with his augury;
> Should not my powers obey when she commands,
> My motion must be rebel to my will:
> My will, to life. . . .
>
> (5.2.68–72)

Reading the bloody characters of the letter Montsurry has tortured his wife to write, Bussy merges all the meanings of *blood* and *spirit:*

> So much elixir of her blood as this
> Dropp'd in the lightest dame, would make her firm
> As heat to fire: and like to all the signs,
> Commands the life confin'd in all my veins;
> O how it multiplies my blood with spirit,
> And makes me apt t'encounter death and hell:
> But, come kind Father; you fetch me to heaven,
> And to that end your holy weed was given.
>
> (5.2.91–98)

The irony is strong, but it does not overpower Bussy's heroic love. While Tamyra may be infirm in chastity, her endurance of Montsurry's torture demonstrates her firm fidelity to Bussy. He has long claimed that her "blood . . . commands the life confin'd in all my veins"; that command now issues in action.

In the extended parallel between valor and sexuality, Bussy's commitment to valor and to Tamyra has often appeared merely verbal, without any significant action (until the very last moment) to ballast his rhetorical protestations. At the same time, Tamyra's love has caused her great suffering. Similar contrasts occur throughout the play and form its most difficult challenge. Yet, properly understood, the paradox of massively rhetorical valor joined with near inaction points to the essential structure of the play, its metaphysics, and the true estimate of its hero.

The playwright portrays Bussy as a man at once subject to passion (both valor and sexual desire) and keenly aware of and participating in a world far removed from sublunar passions and concerns. Chapman's design includes the simultaneous moral condemnation and poetic elevation apparent in *Hero and Leander*, but also develops along several particularly dramatic lines. Employing the familiar plan of dividing between two individuals emotions shared by both, Chapman gives Tamyra the aggressive role in the love affair. Later, when the lovers must conceal their secret, Tamyra and Comolet take the leading "politic" parts—Bussy glowers and threatens. Moreover, Bussy's emotional response to Tamyra's advances is usually portrayed in terms of his heroic frenzy, his valor. His reciprocal affection becomes evident only late in the play when rejection and transcendence of such concerns are near. Thus Chapman shifts the brunt of moral outrage and condemnation from Bussy to Tamyra. The hero appears as a passive sexual object (an extremely unhistorical position), needing Comolet's instruction in the *ars amatoria* and responding to most of Tamyra's advances in the no less passionate but more heroic idiom of valor. Chapman's treatment of the love affair led him to create the only female character in Elizabethan and early Jacobean drama worthy of comparison with the greatest of Shakespeare's or Webster's or Middleton's tragic heroines.

Two passions—physical desire and valor—mingle in the love affair to form a special case of the play's most striking feature: the discrepancy between the hero's words and his actions.[36] A much more straightforward but less explicable example never occurs on stage. Relegating Bussy's duel against the sneering courtiers to a report speech (albeit a very grand one) epitomizes Chapman's curious design. Any contemporary playwright would have assured Chapman that his audience would love such a spectacle.[37] Why not stage the duel? A partial explanation would diagnose Chapman's common malady: his blood cried out for Seneca's. As it is, *Bussy D'Ambois* contains a brilliant Nuntius speech, and Chapman certainly made a good deal of it. Epic techniques and references to Hector, Paris, and the "Spartan King" (Menelaus) dignify a trivial and envious court contention; allusions to great deeds of war against Henry of Navarre, "the sole soldier of the world" (2.1.104), link the contest with the most recent of the great European land wars. Such phrases as "an oak . . . in Arden," "travels through Armenia," and wounds that "might as they open'd, shut, and never kill" (2.1.94, 118, 80) all contribute a reflected glory of romance. Bussy finally becomes that most exotic and mysterious of beasts, "an angry Unicorn" (2.1.119). Still, these allusions, marvelous and strange, and the perhaps understandable urge to imitate Seneca cannot fully account for Chapman's decision. A better answer requires a further paradox. In characterizing his hero, Chapman follows a curious principle: Bussy should be bold, but not too bold. As with the love affair, to display rather than report Bussy's physical heroism would anchor him in the passionate world and, by inference, subjugate him to that world's chief determinants, Fortune and politics.

By holding Bussy slightly aloof from passion, Chapman risks making his hero seem a hollow man. Various characters do hint that Bussy's claims and his true merit may not be quite so "firm as heat to fire." When Monsieur reminds Bussy that the Guise is "nobler born," for example, the hero responds stridently: "He is not, I am noble. / And noblesse in his [its] blood hath no gradation, / But in his merit" (3.2.76–78). Monsieur has clearly won the argument over mere facts of birth, and Bussy retreats to quibble on innate as opposed to inherited nobility. Yet the fact remains that Bussy repeatedly proclaims his own nobility and assumes a privilege and sovereignty that would have shocked any orthodox sixteenth-century royalist as much as Napoleon's self-coronation threatened the aristocracy of his time. Although Henry obviously regards Bussy as more than a braggart, his portrait of man in his "native noblesse" includes a double-edged compliment. Such a man, says the King, "knows he comprehends / Worth with the greatest" (3.2.94–95). Henry's emphasis upon internalized honor—"native noblesse" requires no court trappings or patches of frailty—stresses Bussy himself guarantees his own claims to "manly freedom."

Chapman's design forces him to walk a line between miring Bussy in a passionate, heroic world and allowing him to seem a deluded, boastful near maniac. In the first four acts, Chapman relies upon a few isolated awestruck speakers, upon the energy of Tamyra's love, and upon Bussy's own self-description. Yet the mostly satiric and/or threatening speeches that demonstrate the hero's virtuous valor have a concrete and precise reference that distinguishes them from Montsurry's insanely disjointed rant during the fourth and fifth acts. Thus, while Bussy's valor and deeds exist *only* in language, it is the play's most vigorous and exciting idiom. To compare Bussy's speeches with Tamburlaine's and call both "symbolic action," however, obscures Chapman's design.[38] Marlowe successfully distributed Tamburlaine's activity between dramatized events and "high astounding terms": deeds and claims interact and support one another. In contrast, Chapman has excised or elided every possible opportunity to show Bussy's actions prior to the fifth act. The structure and language of Bussy's speeches, his affair with Tamyra and its assertion of valor as the reciprocal of sexual desire, the avoidance of dramatized action, and the various doubting remarks made by Bussy's associates all produce a delicate and artful balance between passionate, worldly involvement and heroic, transcendental aspiration.

Chapman refuses to allow the audience any grip on Bussy's nature. Just as the court has trouble defining the hero, so, too, the audience cannot fit him into the tidy categories their theatrical experience or their knowledge of humankind has prepared for them. However degraded or offensive, the court world appears much more plausible than the cloudy, transcendental world painted in the extraordinary speeches describing Bussy as superhuman. I am not suggesting that the audience shares the court's values, only that it has precisely the same difficulties and for precisely the same reasons. If Bussy truly is what he claims to be and if he is what Chapman sometimes leads us to believe he is, our language and our schemes of perception must inevitably fail to comprehend the hero. We can, if we wish, follow Monsieur in emphasizing and exploiting the hero's valorous, bawdy, passionate qualities. We can make him a ruffian, an adulterer, and in many ways a blustering jester, complete with dagger of lath. This simplified version of Bussy will not really work. Not only does it fail to explain his transcendent and "Golden-age" claims, it also ignores the complexity of the most significant piece of evidence for a view of Bussy-as-passionate-ruffian—his love affair with Tamyra.

At the play's conclusion, the central characters make a final, almost convulsive, effort to interpret the hero. His political opponents, Monsieur and the Guise, deliver their judgments while they oversee, as "Fate's ministers" (5.2.61), the hero's murder. Even in this arch-political moment, Monsieur cannot control his admiration. He begins in a low key, continuing the sceptical dissociation of word and thing he displayed in "wooing" Tamyra. "Nature," he claims,

> Gives that which we call merit to a man
> (And believe should arrive him on huge riches,
> Honour, and happiness), that effects his ruin. . . .
>
> (5.3.18–20)

Monsieur doubts any definition of worth ("that which we call merit") unless it produces tangible reward—"huge riches, / Honour, and happiness." These rewards might be abstract, but we have learned Monsieur's meaning: for riches, the thousand blood-stained crowns he offers Bussy; for honor, his superficial courtship and covert propositioning; for happiness, usurpation. When Guise disagrees, Monsieur freely grants Bussy's innate qualities: he is one

> . . . on whom Nature spent so rich a hand,
> That, with an ominous eye, she wept to see
> So much consum'd her virtuous treasury. . . .
>
> (5.3.39–41)

Monsieur's philosophy requires that Bussy be great, so long as he is also destroyed. The Guise, who does not observe "like a worldly man" (5.3.26), does not need to support his personal philosophy by praising a man whose death he has just arranged. Even without Monsieur's self-protective compulsion, the Guise overgoes his companion's praise:

> But with as much decorum she [Nature] may make
> A thing that from the feet up to the throat
> Hath all the wondrous fabric man should have,
> And leave it headless for an absolute man,
> As give a whole man valour, virtue, learning,
> Without an end more excellent than those
> On whom she no such worthy part bestows.
>
> (5.3.30–36)

The Guise's principle of decorum simply contradicts Monsieur's position. In fact, both characters are right. From a worldly standpoint that "by th' events / Values the worth of things," Bussy's rare qualities lead but to the grave. At the same time, the hero's "wondrous fabric" does gain him "an end more excellent" than any dreamed of in Monsieur's philosophy.

The Friar, politic even as a ghost, enters immediately after this argument and urges Tamyra to "devise / How to prevent" Bussy's murder. She and the Ghost then duplicate the exchange between Monsieur and the Guise by proposing an interpretation of Bussy's approaching death:

> *Tamyra.*  Man is a tree, that hath no top in cares;
>             No root in comforts; all his power to live
>             Is given to no end, but t' have power to grieve.
> *Ghost.*   'Tis the just curse of our abus'd creation,
>             Which we must suffer here, and 'scape hereafter:
>             He hath the great mind that submits to all
>             He sees inevitable; he the small
>             That carps at earth, and her foundation-shaker,
>             And rather than himself, will mend his maker.
>
> (5.3.66–74)

Tamyra's speech aptly summarizes her role: all her passion has been spent to grieve. Comolet echoes Bussy's repeated recognition that some principle called Fate—"Fate is more strong than arms, and sly than treason, / And I at all points buckled in my Fate" (5.3.87–88)—organizes human lives. The Friar also recalls the definition of a great, virtuous man that Bussy and the King jointly espouse in the pardon scene. Bussy enters, followed by his murderers, whom he drives off the stage. At last, the vaunted strength matching Tamyra's love bursts into action, and he challenges Montsurry to appear. Montsurry mocks his hirelings' fears that Comolet (or Bussy?) is more than human:

> Cowards, a fiend or spirit beat ye off?
> They are your own faint spirits that have forg'd
> The fearful shadows that your eyes deluded:
> The fiend was in you. . . .
>
> (5.3.114–17)

Just as he overcomes Montsurry and grants Tamyra's plea for her husband's life, Bussy is shot from behind. At once, he applies his own individual standards of honor and nobility to the Fates, as he had earlier to Sin: "O then the coward Fates / Have maim'd themselves, and ever lost their honour" (5.3.120–21).

The hero himself now tries to define the meaning of his life and death. At first, he accepts the worldly significance Monsieur's politic philosophy would give such a death:

> . . . is my body then
> But penetrable flesh? And must my mind
> Follow my blood? Can my divine part add
> No aid to th' earthly in extremity?
> Then these divines are but for form, not fact:
> Man is of two sweet courtly friends compact;
> A mistress and a servant: let my death
> Define life nothing but a Courtier's breath.
>
> (5.3.125–32)

"Two sweet courtly friends" are no true friends at all. Thoughts of manhood and Roman valor bring Bussy back from this empty belief to a renewed confidence in the immortality fame confers. Both the reference to "look upwards even in death . . . like a Roman statue" (5.3.136, 144) and the concern with honor are typical of Chapman's tragic heroes.[39] While Bussy still seeks the meaning of his death in human terms—as an example to men who may requite his fall with "all their sighs together (for their frailties / Beheld in me)"—he has now rejected Monsieur's pragmatic interpretation. Comolet's ghost and Tamyra intercede for pardon, and Bussy realizes (for the first time, apparently) the torture Tamyra has suffered. Bitterly contemptuous, he reads the ultimate meaning of his death in her wounds:

> O, my heart is broken,
> Fate, nor these murderers, Monsieur, nor the Guise,
> Have any glory in my death, but this:
> This killing spectacle: this prodigy. . . .
>
> (5.3.178–81)

In his last moments, Bussy reviews the possible interpretations of his life: from Monsieur's scepticism, to his own original estimate of honor and fame, and now to the gory characters of illicit but true passion graven in Tamyra's body. His last conception of his life's meaning is a moral emblem:

> O frail condition of strength, valour, virtue,
> In me like warning fire upon the top
> Of some steep beacon, on a steeper hill;
> Made to express it like a falling star
> Silently glanc'd—that like a thunderbolt
> Look'd to have stuck, and shook the firmament.
>
> (5.3.188–93)

As he dies, Bussy claims the "condition of strength, valour, virtue" already given him by Monsieur and the Guise, but fears he will prove only a warning beacon, not a fixed star.[40] The Friar's ghost allays this fear in his final eulogy:

> Farewell brave relicts of a complete man:
> Look up and see thy spirit made a star,
> Join flames with Hercules: and when thou set'st
> Thy radiant forehead in the firmament,
> Make the vast continent, crack'd with thy receipt,
> Spread to a world of fire: and th' aged sky,
> Cheer with new sparks of old humanity.
>
> (5.3.268–74)

Psychologically and metaphysically, this splendid speech recalls Monsieur's "His great heart will not down, 'tis like the sea." Comolet has transcended his limited role as agent of Tamyra's blood. He offers a grand vision of the hero's significance.

As with Bussy's heroic claims and Tamyra's active sexuality, Chapman shrouds the Friar in ethical ambiguity. He panders, of course, and teaches Bussy the art of love. Such a characterization would hardly disturb the audience, accustomed to good friars (like Lawrence in *Romeo and Juliet* or Francis in *Much Ado About Nothing* or Bonaventura in Ford's *'Tis Pity She's a Whore*), bad and bawdy friars (like those in Marlowe's *The Jew of Malta*), and comic friars (like Bungay in Greene's *Friar Bacon and Friar Bungay*). The problem arises neither from the Friar's unseemly conduct, nor his sympathy for the lovers, but from this powerful and evocative eulogy. If the speech's verbal energy, felicity, and feeling alone represent endorsement, we could not doubt Chapman's design. Yet he seems determined to make his task as difficult as possible: after all, a less ambiguous character might easily have delivered the eulogy. Montsurry himself might have been an effective choice, chastened but human and stubborn as he eventually appears. Alternatively, other playwrights might have chosen to separate the religious spirit from the bawdy.

We cannot dismiss the eulogy's rhetorical power, nor deny its splendid finish to a major dramatic interest. Choosing the Friar as pander, Chapman underscores Tamyra's moral dilemma and her love's power: this "bar" is indeed made "engine" to amorous "fury." Moreover, the Friar's status as an intermediary between this world and the next (albeit a Christian, not a heroic or pagan one) suits Tamyra's and Bussy's love affair. His spiritual associations, again, give him access to the demonic, but paradoxically benign, kingdom of Behemoth, Cartophylax, et al. Finally, he delivers the eulogy as an umbra, a spirit haunting life and vainly attempting to rescue Bussy. Making the priest/pander a ghost intensifies Chapman's ambiguous presentation, since contemporary attitudes toward spirits are notoriously complex, but this development pushes the Friar further into that other world where he situates the dead hero. Despite Chapman's idiosyncratic emphasis of one friarly trait and complete suppression of others, the choice makes sense. A clerical ghost and spiritual pander fit Chapman's transcendental design and his persistent flouting of mundane interpretations—the court's or the audience's.

Throughout the play, Bussy has existed in two worlds. His satiric speeches, Monsieur's political manipulation, and Tamyra's passionate excess define one world. The other world appears intermittently in the court's awe, in Henry's words, and finally in the play's last scene when the hero assumes his true place among the stars. This dichotomy profoundly affects the play. When Bussy apostrophizes his fame and its human preservers, for example, he puns on "worthless" ("without value or significance" and "not corresponding to my worth"):

> . . . that a thunder
> Of all their sighs together (for their frailties

Beheld in me) may quit my worthless fall
With a fit volley for my funeral.

(5.3.155–58)[41]

The hero's characterization is riven along the divide between high thoughts of his true place and the necessity for action in a world he never made and for which he is quite unfit.[42]

Bussy's frail humanity—his passion for honor, for fame, for a secular grandeur to match his claim of transcendental stature—betrays him through Tamyra's love into the politicians' hands. He "cannot help . . . Against these base foes that insult on weakness, / And still fight hous'd behind the shield of Nature" (4.1.38, 35–36). The middle section of the play concentrates on Bussy's gradual domination by Luna/Tamyra, a goddess he attempts to meet with strength and chivalric language. Through her guidance and his willing service, he sinks to meeting policy with policy. Each subsequent scene shows Bussy slowly accepting his limited earthly powers, revealing "the great mind that submits to all / He sees inevitable" and recognizing his fate in this world.

Montsurry's role in achieving the revenge action is obvious. In the drama of Bussy's divided consciousness, however, Montsurry has a more subtle and important part. His insane jealousy contrasts brilliantly with Bussy's valorous response to Tamyra's love, just as his random and perverse language measures Bussy's grandiloquent but tightly logical and self-confident professions. Oddly, Montsurry's hysteria makes Bussy's own exaggeration more comprehensible and more appropriate. The parallel between the two lovers of Tamyra goes further. In the delicately modulated reconciliation and separation of Tamyra and Montsurry that intervenes between Bussy's death and the Ghost's eulogy, we see the mundane response to passion, to Luna, finely executed. Only parting—"to the open deserts" for Tamyra, to a life embittered by the irreconcilability of love with honor for Montsurry (5.3.243, 248–49)—can subjugate passion. Bussy entirely transcends Luna's empire. He breaks through the very sphere of the moon and starts anew, in conflagration and purification, the cycle of human history.[43] Henceforth he will remain—not form, but fact—in the stars' immutable sphere, a moralized constellation to serve as a beacon of hope for the old humanity he has left behind.

Readers have tried to solve the play's paradoxes by associating Bussy's characterization with Renaissance allegories of Prometheus and Hercules or with the extreme method of Giordano Bruno in *Lo Spaccio della bestia trionphante*. Clearly, they respond to a quality manifest in the play. Bussy claims and has ascribed to him values that are evidently not of this world, either the court world specifically or the world of man in the iron age generally. The principal effect of the love affair is to show that Bussy is sometimes contiguous with the world of ordinary mortals but also has qualities that world cannot explain. Indeed, Bussy himself cannot explain his meaning any better than Monsieur, or the Guise, or Tamyra, or Montsurry. The effort to interpret the hero and to show him seeking his own interpretation makes challenging drama and, often enough, emotionally moving dramatic action. Yet the play—like *Hero and Leander*—finally moves the problem into a transcendent arena. The hero's apotheosis may seem implausible or a desperate shift because it follows hard upon so much "personal and exact life" (*Tragedies*, p. 341), but it is the play's version of the metamorphosis that concludes *Hero and Leander*. Chapman moves his hero into a space and time to which only poetry has access. It is difficult to ignore the corollary that the play has put a sharply observed world, quite hostile to metamorphosis and any other poetic transvaluation, into conflict with a hero and a theory proclaiming just those values. Despite Bussy's sardonic jest that he "can poetise" (1.1.184), I do not mean to suggest that he is a poet or poet-surrogate. He is, sometimes and with brilliantly caught lapses, a human who represents a world of value that is poetic and can only be expressed in poetry. As Chapman's subsequent tragedies were to show more and more clearly, however, Maffé's contempt—"By your no better outside, I would judge you / To be a poet" (1.1.160–61)—may finally win the day.

# 2

# War and Peace in *The Conspiracy of Charles, Duke of Byron*

Like many other works in Chapman's canon, his two plays on the Duke of Byron have received rigidly dichotomized interpretations. The critical either/or first compares Byron's character with King Henry's and then moves outward to the political and vaguely philosophical issues the play contains. An idealized Henry and a treacherous Byron fall neatly into the larger pattern of Achillean versus Stoic heroism that underlies most studies of the plays. When these two plays do not conform to the mold, as often they manifestly do not, Chapman's bad, old Marlovianism, his unregenerate affection for Achilles, bears the blame and mars the grand design.[1] Chapman presents a world of high politics much more subtly modulated than such exclusive interpretations allow. In this world, no motive is pure, no decision ideal, no action perfect. Henry is a good king, concerned with the business of running a modern state threatened by anarchic feudal demands and religious schism; Byron is a traitor, intent upon self-glorification, though it bring chaos again. Yet, the king's own words and his courtiers' political manipulations substantiate Byron's criticism however selfishly it may be motivated, and Byron's conception of himself, debased and betrayed though it may be, deserves our consideration and respect. His final apotheosis transcends the ambiguous world in which the play has taken place and in which Henry must remain.

Less obviously than *Bussy D'Ambois*, the *Byron* plays offer almost too many interpretive structures: a pattern of ascent and descent; the competition of Virtue and Fortune; humor psychology; magic and astrology (hence determinism and free will); and political morality.[2] Such structures, however, satisfy only in part, ignore or slight important scenes, speeches, or motives, and eventually seem an imposition, a fraudulent claim to a particular kind of shape. A more comprehensive explanation, one that allows Byron and Henry their full scope while also respecting the *Conspiracy*'s political dimension, depends upon another dynamic conflict: war and peace. War and peace, the clash of their representatives, and the dialectic of memory and forget-fulness in which that clash occurs are elements around which a complex, sometimes paradoxical interpretation may develop.

🌰   🌰   🌰

Chapman distributes common experience among several characters, almost doubles characters, and thus clarifies this dialectic and incorporates it into the play's dramatic architecture. Nearly a reflexive device for Chapman, the technique is rarely so developed in other Renaissance drama. As he did in *Hero and Leander* and *Bussy D'Ambois*, the poet divides events and responses common to two characters and attributes some to one, some to the other. The technique offers economical exposition, a consequent plenitude of realized experience, and a sense of mutual sensation and shared fate. Although the goddess Ceremony, for example, appears only to Leander and her significance is made clear only to him, the reader realizes, through allusions and parallel situations, that Ceremony's presence and meaning function throughout Hero's experience too. In *Bussy*, Tamyra's presence implicitly elaborates upon Bussy's character. The tension, the danger, and the deep affection of their adultery are all expressed by Tamyra, while Bussy's few responses are gruff or hyperbolical. Still, the fact of their love and the vigor of their early scenes together convey information about Bussy without distracting the audience's close attention from other features of Chapman's heroic characterization and his analysis of the political and private problems of Bussy's presence at court.

*Byron's Conspiracy* employs this tactic very fully, and the device points to a fundamental issue. Given the facts that Byron is a great soldier and a great traitor, Chapman develops La Fin and the Duc D'Aumale as, respectively, a soldier and a traitor. This much the playwright had from history.[3] He enriches these doubling characters through Byron's responses to them, or more exactly, to the facts of their careers. In La Fin, Byron's heroic anger is reduced to petty resentment; in Aumale, Byron's future appears, although he mistakes its significance.

Aumale is the simpler, more poignant example. He first appears, an exile at the Archduke Albert's court, listening to a painful but sympathetic recounting of his treachery. Bellièvre, one of Henry's ambassadors, expresses his sorrow that Aumale's "obstinacy . . . [in] . . . mortal enmity against the King"

> Should force his wrath to use the rites of treason
> Upon the members of your senseless statue,

Your name and house, when he had lost your person,
Your love and duty.

                                                    (1.2.57–60)


Aumale's dignified response, "I use not much impatience nor complaint" (line 63)[4] seems to end the matter, and one is left with the
impression—accurate enough—that rebellion in France is common,
the punishment swift and condign. The traitor's presence shadows the
scene, and Byron chooses Aumale to illustrate his aphorism, "The
bounds of loyalty are made of glass, / Soon broke, but can in no date
be repair'd" (lines 145–46). Chapman rarely manages to unite exposition with reflection so neatly, but in character doubling he finds a
method that yields binocular vision of an event. The hero's puzzlement at one of the "rites of treason" used against Aumale—"And (for
a strange reproach of his foul treason) / His trees about it [Aumale's
razed house] cut off by their waists" (lines 152–53)—illustrates his
spiritual insensitivity. Generally, Byron is blind to any sort of external
symbolism. We need not know the customary sanctions of felling a
noble family's trees to see Henry's gesture as a symbol of Aumale's
dishonor, his plunge from a tradition of fidelity, his separation and
exile from his native soil, and the extirpation of any vestige of his
family's long life in France. It is, after all, not a very difficult symbol,
and hardly a "strange reproach." Byron's blindness to such signifi-
cances misguides him throughout his life. Imagery of natural, organic
growth, of fruition and nurture, represented allusively by the trees in
this passage, is crucial in Byron's struggle with Henry. Each in his own
way seeks to be a creator, although their creations differ markedly.
These created worlds, and their metaphoric representations, also directly reflect the two opponents' ability to manipulate symbols. For
the moment, though, pairing Aumale with Byron serves several purposes: the dialogue with the man himself and Byron's reference to past
events give the play temporal depth; we learn that traitors exist in
France and that they are punished; Byron, it appears, does not entirely understand the significance of treason or its punishment.
    La Fin, too, partly echoes Byron's situation: both are old soldiers,
now unneeded. Berowne's remark, "'Tis some policy / To have one
show worse than the king's and his company" (*Love's Labour's Lost*
5.2), provides a model for La Fin's function. Discussing double plots,
William Empson describes what he calls "pseudo-parody to disarm
criticism": two similar characters or characters sharing similar ideals
are distributed between an heroic and a pastoral plot.[5] One character
draws the audience's criticism, or disbelief, or laughter, while leaving
the other unscathed. It is *pseudo*-parody because the heroic half of the

pair is not in fact meant to be qualified by the pastoral alter ego. That alter ego satisfies certain psychological needs in the audience and makes the naturalistic concession, for example, that cowards exist as well as heroes.

As a method of deflecting incredulous or hostile reactions, pseudo-parody suits a tragedy whose hero strains common definitions of human behavior. Paradoxically, the danger here is that pseudo-parody will tip over into parody proper: of Byron's two doubles, La Fin most threatens an unequivocal response to Byron's merit and an unprejudiced attention to his transformation. Still, instead of flattening Byron's high aspirations to the trivia of his own goals and personality, La Fin accentuates Byron's unique qualities and makes us more sympathetic to the grand traitor. In part, Chapman distinguishes them through dramatizing La Fin's fear of Byron. The two men have radically different aims, and that difference, we assume, corresponds to an equal difference in their respective characters and virtues. We see, too, the antipodal difference in Henry's treatment of the two men.

La Fin's role also recalls a traditional use of the foil: his character presents aspects of Byron's character—anger, quick resentment at injury, a sense of discarded or ignored merit—in debased form. Consequently, we transfer our horror at Byron's decay from the traitor to the agent of treason, a character very similar to Byron in some skewed fashion. Unlike other Renaissance playwrights, Chapman does not pile up parallel, simultaneous examples of the hero's situation. When they are first introduced, neither La Fin nor Aumale mirrors Byron's situation in the way that Laertes or Fortinbras does Hamlet's, or Gloucester, Lear's, or Bajazeth, Tamburlaine's. The essential difference is that La Fin and Aumale are not what Byron is, but what he may be.

Initially, Byron and La Fin appear similar because both are veteran warriors; their doubling implies that they may become similar in other ways as well. In particular, Byron fears that what has happened to La Fin—exclusion from court despite a good war record—may also happen to him.[6] La Fin says of Byron:

> since he came from Flanders
> He heard how much I was threaten'd with the King,
> And hath been much inquisitive to know
> The truth of all, and seeks to speak with me. . . .
>
> (2.1.27–30)

The doubling device (La Fin, Aumale) chiefly provides proleptic versions of some future Byron. The play's opening thrusts us into the swirl of plot and counterplot; Byron's interest in Aumale and La Fin and his ignorance of their full significance have been made clear. The transtemporality of Byron's doubles—we have in effect a sequence of time-lapse photographs of days in the life of Byron—distinguishes Chapman's technique from the foil characters of Shakespearean or Marlovian drama.

Right from the start, then, with Aumale and Byron at the Archduke's court and the conspirators' first moves against the hero, the device of character doubling accentuates the most important subjects in the play: Byron's past in war, his present in peace, and their dual link in time and memory, as embodied in Henry's favor. This technique achieves complex meaning through its transtemporality, through its powerful presentation of possible events and futures, and more simply, through explicit reference to past traitors and former men of war.

ॐ  ॐ  ॐ

While Chapman does use several subsidiary characters as Byron's chronological parallels, the play also develops a special aspect of prediction—magic and demonic power. Just as La Fin's present may contain hints of Byron's future, so, too, the exile's putative ability as a sorcerer serves a proleptic purpose. What La Fin claims may happen through magic does come to pass; the forebodings of La Fin and La Brosse do prove well-founded. For example, La Fin tells Byron (accurately enough, as events prove):

> I care not how I tempt your conquering fury,
> I am predestin'd to too base an end
> To have the honour of your wrath destroy me,
> And be a worthy object for your sword.
>
> (2.1.75–78)

Henry warns Byron against "that ill-aboding vermin," La Fin, and then attributes to La Fin's "ominous" haunts all the appurtenances of witchcraft and demonism: "Throats of ravens," "infected houses," "howls of dogs . . . at midnight," "apparitions," "spirits clad in black men's shapes, / Or ugly women's, the adverse decrees / Of constellations. . . ." By throwing this catalogue into metaphoric descriptions of La Fin, the audience has its thaumaturgic thrills, and Chapman maintains his intellectual superiority too.

The play hardly grants magic and witchcraft respectability. Byron's judges doubt that sorcery had any irresistible influence upon his actions. Even were the black arts to be an admitted possibility, Henry's chancellor cleaves to a modern, Christian point of view in saying, "Witchcraft can never taint an honest mind" (*Tragedy* 5.2.174) and, in his summation,

> For witchcraft, I esteem it a mere strength
> Of rage in him, conceiv'd gainst his accuser,
> . . . . . . . . . . . . . . .
> Suppose it true, it made him false; but wills
> And worthy minds witchcraft can never force.
>
> (5.2.282–83, 285–86)

Thus, in the two *Byron* plays more clearly than in many contemporary plays, the necromantic props have a metaphoric or symbolic basis. Chapman will employ the paraphernalia for intrinsic dramatic purposes but eventually conceives all witchcraft as a metaphor of weakness. Byron leant toward treason; witchcraft only rationalizes, through irrationality, his fall.

Astrology is treated more circumspectly, as befits a profession patronized by many Elizabethan nobles, but in the end it, too, seems a method of transferring responsibility. Shakespeare's sceptical Cassius—"the fault . . . is not in our stars, / But in ourselves"—appears here as the English counsellor who advises Byron that a "wise distrust" in stellar influence or counsel is best. Several theatrical and dramatic purposes are served, however, through allusions to the influence and portents of stars. La Brosse's dejected sense of helplessness despite astrological forewarning is a good example: "we know all their [the stars'] working / And nought can do, or nothing can prevent! / Rude ignorance is beastly [bestial], knowledge wretched!" (*Conspiracy* 3.3.7–9). "Our knowledges do light us but to err" (*Tragedy* 5.3.195) recalls these musing comments. It is a succinct, Websterian statement of the human position, uniting as it does all experience and prediction with surprise and sudden loss. Distant, mysterious, and quasi-magical, the stars are also convenient targets for Byron's boastful sallies. Occasionally, they show up his aspiration for the degenerate egocentrism it so often is:

> . . . one poor cup of wine
> More than I use, than my weak brain will bear,
> Shall make them drunk and reel out of their spheres
> For any certain act they can enforce.
>
> (*Conspiracy* 3.3.123–26)

It is Byron's head that first reels and then falls. Although he does not recognize the fact, his own case sadly disproves his maxim, "Virtue in great men must be small and slight, / For poor stars rule where she is exquisite" (*Tragedy* 5.2.186–87).

❦ ❦ ❦

Act 2, scene 2 of *The Conspiracy* encapsulates the problem of what might be called the erosion of heroic military virtues in peacetime. To further Byron's estrangement from the King, Savoy praises and then overpraises the hero in the King's presence. The device, which should tell us as much about Henry as it does about Savoy, works very well. Piqued that his own accomplishments should be slighted, Henry responds by denigrating Byron's martial successes. Savoy, aware that Byron is "past measure glorious; and that humour / Is fit to feed his spirits . . . with praise of his perfections; / The taste whereof in him so soothes his palate" (1.1.70ff.), immediately reports Henry's most damning remarks to Byron (3.2.45ff.).

These politic moves and successes are not the scene's main substance, as several critics have claimed.[7] More important, the scene serves as a near "set speech of report"[8] and analyzes the war-peace-memory dynamic. Had Chapman chosen to dramatize a greater length of time in Byron's career, Savoy's speeches (in quite different psychological circumstances, of course) would be given to an anonymous messenger, or to a minor lord making a postbattle situation report.[9] Here the scene recalls and substantiates Byron's claims about his past glory and importance. Henry's response reminds us of every old soldier's deepest anxiety: forgetfulness. Henry's willed amnesia is of two kinds: he attempts to forget by denigrating Byron's past military contributions, and he tries to forget war as an entity. We know, from the play and from history, that Henry was an excellent soldier, "the sole soldier of the world" (*Bussy*, 2.1.104), but he never appears in that role (rarely even in metaphoric or hypothetical speech); he alludes to it only in pejorative or neutral comparisons with a more glorious present peace. That is, Henry's early reluctance to meet Savoy's taunts—"No question he [Byron] sets valour in his height, / And hath done service to an equal pitch" (2.2.89–90)—indicates not merely gracious assent to a vassal's praise, but also an eagerness to forget—a desire to talk of matters other than war and to direct the conversation away from war and warriors as quickly as possible.

Like *Troilus and Cressida*, Chapman's two plays are about time and the meaning of the past and of men from the past in a changed present. Henry gives clear and early warning that he has made the transition from war to an uneasy but ever more stable peace (1.1.112ff.). Byron blindly relies upon his martial valor; the men who trap him and condemn him do everything they can to forget it.

Grimeston occasionally suggests that Byron's intrigues had no other (and no deeper) motive than a desire to create a situation—war—in which his talents might once again be burnished.[10] Grimeston's analysis echoes in the plays when Byron claims he must "ruin" France "to re-advance it" (*Tragedy*, 1.2.35) and when he castigates the "base fruits of a settled peace" (*Tragedy*, 4.1.1ff.).

Byron's past deeds are truly "alms for oblivion" in Time's wallet; his arms profit him nothing in a war-weary world that is sceptical of soldiers and of war. If no arms, then no man. While Byron attempts to find peace in nothing but war, Henry extinguishes both Byron and war. Hence, for Byron, time past determines the virtues that are to contend with Fortune in time present. Henry, possessing virtues of both war and peace, manages utterly to avoid the wheel of Fortune that Byron attempts to shackle.

Henry's reasons for exiling La Fin immediately link the King's program for peace with the action he takes in banishing a man of war:

> I will not have my train
> Made a retreat for bankrouts, nor my Court
> A hive for drones: proud beggars and true thieves.
> . . . . . . . . . . . . . . .
> Though I am grown, by right of birth and arms,
> Into a greater kingdom, I will spread
> With no more shade than may admit that kingdom
> Her proper, natural, and wonted fruits;
> . . . . . . . . . . . . . . .
> Thou art in law, in quarrels, and in debt
> . . . . . . . . . . . . . . .
> thou seek'st by me,
> In my supportance, now our old wars cease,
> To wage worse battles with the arms of peace.
> (1.1.112–14, 118–21, 125, 127–29)

This excellent speech captures very well Henry's mixed motives and mixed emotions: reminiscence and anticipation, apprehensiveness and self-esteem. Imagery of growth and fruitful husbandry defines the metaphoric arena Henry and Byron contest. Although the King grants that he owes his new kingdom to his "arms" as well as his "birth," he announces the important difference between destructive war and fruitful peace: what might once have been permitted or even encouraged has become intolerable. La Fin's reaction, "Peace must not make men cowards . . ." (1.1.130), foreshadows Byron's similar response. In Henry's statesmanlike moves to pacify the kingdom and to encourage men to return to normal lives after a generation of war and religious schism, soldiers like La Fin and, more nobly, Byron, can see only the abandonment of life as they know it. Thus, they stigmatize peace with the only word they have for life not in battle: *cowardice*. On another occasion, Byron—the man who cannot change from war to peace—misunderstands the man who has changed: the King's "heroic fashions," he says, have been transformed into "an antic vizard" (5.2.18, 19). Here again, the perceiver influences his perceptions as surely as the drunken head makes the stars reel.

Henry's characterization of La Fin—"so vile thyself, / That thou suspect'st perfection in others" (1.1.157–58)—makes an important distinction between La Fin and Byron. Actual warfare means little to La Fin, who merely exercises his satanic arts (the overtones of many scenes justify that adjective) wherever he finds himself. Byron, on the other hand, portrays himself as a creator of order; for him, peaceful order is chaos, and he wishes to return to the battlefield's certitude and the precision of military life. Byron claims he has "put off from this dull shore of ease" (i.e., peace: 2.1.149) and believes that peace breeds only immorality and corruption.

What then of this other existence—peace—so often described in metaphors of natural growth and health? Having exiled La Fin, Henry asserts his interest in procreation: "I have trust in heaven / I am not yet so old, but I may spring" (1.1.201–02).[11] Henry's reasons for sending Byron abroad are part of the king's careful nurture of his kingdom: "I therefore mean to make him change the air . . . To breathe a while in temperate English air" (2.2.46, 49). When La Fin describes himself as a "poor and expuate humour of the court" (2.1.101) and Henry bids Savoy good riddance as a "great wit . . . That . . . infecteth [and] conspires" (5.2.261–66), the imagery links the traitors' banishment with a healthy body's self-purification. Organic metaphors portray Henry as his kingdom's creator and chief husbandman.

Byron, too, views himself as a creator, but a creator who must "ruin" France "to re-advance it" (*Tragedy* 1.2.35). Earlier, he makes the image explicit: "on our Chaos [i.e., the present peace] / Will I sit brooding up another world." Byron's procreation is starkly, violently, different from Henry's "royal issue" (*Conspiracy* 4.1.150):

> . . . I alone
> Took Amiens in these arms, and held her fast
>
> . . . . . . . . . . . . . . .
> Only myself (married to victory)
> Did people Artois, Douai, Picardy,
> Bethune and Saint-Paul, Bapaume and Courcelles,
> With her triumphant issue. . . .
>
> (5.1.147–48, 152–55)

Byron fathers a host of ruined towns; in peacetime, he must divorce his wife, Victory. Earlier in the same scene, Byron juxtaposes "blood of faith" (spilt in battle) with "All my rain is fall'n / Into the horse-fair, springing pools, and mire"; the hero would manure the earth with his own blood.

In this conflict of the warrior with the king, who is both a soldier and a man of peace, we hear Byron's outraged and bewildered questions about the meaning of his past service: "detraction so with spite embru'd . . . drown such good in such ingratitude?" (3.2.77, 78); "Who will he grant, if he deny it me?" (5.1.31); "jest and slight / A man that you should curiously reward . . . you quit my deserts with your grey beard" (5.1.99–100, 113). Byron fears, more than any physical foe, the impalpable shape of forgetfulness. Memory—the King's, the court's—lets slip not only Byron's merit, but also his deeds. In this matter, Queen Elizabeth has some staunch and pointed words, as is her wont in appearances or report upon the stage of her time. It is not only in *Bussy D'Ambois* that Elizabeth's is a "Court indeed; / Not mix'd with rudeness . . . / But as Courts should be, th' abstracts of their kingdoms" (*Bussy*, 1.2.19–21). Here she rebukes Byron, the King's emissary, and complains that Henry "Should check at eight hours' sail . . . [and] stick at the kind rites of peace" (4.1.27, 33). Of Henry's memory and its expression, she says:

> We thank him that he keeps the memory
> Of us and all our kindness; but must say
> That it is only kept, and not laid out
> To such affectionate profit as we wish.
>
> (4.1.18–21)

Precisely Byron's point. Elizabeth's criticism, tempered from Grimeston's yet more astringent lines, chimes so closely with Byron's that we must accept the axis of past and present, memory and oblivion, as central to the play.[12]

Queen Elizabeth evidently endorses Byron's complaints, the very complaints that urge him towards treason, and that agreement confuses the play's ethical and political values. Unless we accuse Chapman of radically misunderstanding his play, we must recognize that this seeming confusion arises from two sources: a modern bias toward critical theory drawn from naturalistic drama and the Jamesian novel; and a dramatic program especially clear in Chapman and in his devoted admirer, John Webster.[13] The modern prejudice for certain kinds of consistency and plausibility distorts Renaissance drama and has received excellent, if not wholly effective, rebuke in Chapman's case particularly.[14] Elizabeth's disconcerting words also emphasize a cardinal quality in the playwright's design: Chapman often employs contradictory causal and explanatory schemes. Speech, character, and event must be referred to the proper universe of discourse, or ambiguity and contradiction will destroy the work. Multiplied perspectives— the hero's development through reflecting secondary characters, for example, or Elizabeth's unexpected hostility toward a fellow monarch—produce a shifting dramatic world peopled by anamorphic characters who are themselves fairly simple but various as they are viewed.

❦   ❦   ❦

The scene between Henry and Savoy, as well as Chapman's skillful handling of natural imagery, show that an analysis of Byron and his acts must begin with his misunderstanding—not so much of himself ("Who cannot friend himself is foe to any . . ." [2.1.131])—as of present conditions in France. Byron's mistaken analysis of peace means that he will also be blind to the nature of his opposition to Henry and, more generally, to the court.

In several important arguments with the King, Byron reveals both his theoretic understanding of "The Court" (as, for example, a standard satiric target in the drama) and his utter ignorance of this specific court. In act 3 Henry warns Byron against trusting La Fin; Byron responds by proclaiming himself one of those "men in themselves entire" who does not "build . . . outward, nor depend on props" (3.2.227, 229). This definition of personal self-sufficiency is one Chapman almost uniformly espouses and one Byron has constantly claimed for himself; it is also a characterization Byron has been shedding throughout the play. Byron moves from self-praise to a defence of La Fin that turns upon Henry's very rejection of him:

> So rare are true deservers lov'd or known,
> That men lov'd vulgarly are ever none,
> Nor men grac'd servilely for being spots
> In princes' trains . . .
> The stallion, Power, hath such a besom tail
> That it sweeps all from justice, and such filth
> He bears out in it that men mere exempt
> Are merely clearest. . . .

(3.2.232–39)[15]

With characteristic hyperbole, Byron then describes a day when courts will attract all the corrupt individuals in the nation, and one will go to "prison or the pillory" for honorable friends. Elsewhere, too, this description of the court sounds a sympathetic vibration among those myriad Elizabethan and especially Jacobean passages criticizing the court and its morality. Policy is a "botcher-up of king-doms" without "one patch . . . that can mend / The brack" between Henry and Byron (5.1.34–36).

All that Byron has to say about policy and courts, kings and corruption, is true: Savoy and his fellows demonstrate it with their "hidden drifts" and their very perversion of Byron's loyalty. No viewer, however monarchist, can ignore the evidence that Henry him-self more than once practices the duplicity of state that Byron so decries and in which he becomes so enmeshed. Throughout the two plays, Henry's concern for Byron seems ultimately self-interested. The King shows little sympathy for or understanding of Byron the man; for Henry, France's stability and her future Bourbon rulers alone matter. His actions towards Byron, in fact, amply support Byron's sense that La Fin's treatment portends the same for men to whom the King and France owe much more than to that poor "sweeping" of the court. Perhaps Henry's gravest insensitivity to Byron's nature comes at the very end of *Conspiracy*. Aware that Byron is one of those men who use compliments "as their state potatoes [aphrodisiacs]" (3.2.16), Henry nonetheless laughs at Byron's exaggerated claims to greatness and merit. This laughter finally shocks Byron into recognizing the changes that have occurred in the shift from war to peace. Only personal humiliation so threatens him that he must commit active treason rather than drift with treason's current. His treason must be motivated by his private experience, by personal sensation rather than abstract conceptualization:

> Slight my services?
> Drown the dead noises of my sword in laughter?
> (My blows as but the passages of shadows,
> Over the highest and most barren hills)
> And use me like no man . . . ?
>
> (5.2.21–25)[16]

Henry exploits this intensely egocentric and introverted nature when he employs Byron's trusted friend, La Fin, as a spy. The new politics easily destroy a naive and outdated warrior ethic that treats all experi-ence as a series of personal relations. Byron yet retains a pathetic dignity despite his obvious redundancy—a heroic ruin amid modern rubble.

Although Peter Ure's remark seems generally true, that Chapman often has a character express a sentiment consistent on the ethical level but incongruous on the political level of a play's discourse, we need not invoke that explanation here. Like Shakespeare's Brutus, Byron maintains two sets of mental constructs—generalized political or social analysis alongside personal or private speculations and concerns— with little interchange between the two. Hence, having decided to meet Savoy and La Fin on a personal plane, partly because of La Fin's war service and their military bond, Byron does not recognize that his analysis of the court applies *a fortiori* to the men he defends. Just as Byron meets personal appeal with personal response, no matter how irrational or unfounded, he also counters abstraction with abstraction, no matter how ill-applied or ironically ill-considered. As the conspiracy develops, Henry gradually forgets the personally valorous (and personally loyal) Byron and instead substitutes a fearsome impersonal presence that threatens political chaos. Byron counters that dehumanization with his own version, a satiric (and ironically accurate) analysis of courtly politics. Both Byron's misplaced trust and his principled—but effectively impersonal—political suspicion have a single source: his bewilderment and confusion in a world newly celebrating the rites of peace.

Thus, the rift in Byron's character between the personal and the public worlds, each with its appropriate set of acts, responsibilities, principles, and even vocabularies, grows directly out of his life-long military service. The world of battle requires constant personal vigilance. Byron's instant responses, his high sense of personal importance, his impatience with any disorder or disarray in the links between cause and effect, make him an admirable soldier, an excellent leader, and an obedient follower.[17] Once away from the battlefield, once severed from its demand for personal ties among men, Byron's language no longer serves to exhort and to encourage, but becomes merely ludicrous. His quick decisions and immediate reactions become threats. His rough and formulaic analyses—perfectly suited to the frightening simplicities of war and death—no longer serve as guides to action in a peaceful world made complex by conflicts violence can not resolve.

Interpretations of the play that argue for the conspirators' corruption of Byron, whether or not that corruption is "Machiavellian," imply but rarely state that Byron falls from some psychological or moral or political eminence. That height, simply, is heroic self-sufficiency, a quality Byron more and more strenuously claims even as it is stripped from him. He states his ideals (and, we believe, his nature) at the opening of the play:

> O, 'tis a dangerous and a dreadful thing
> . . . . . . . . . . . . .
> To trust our blood in others' veins, and hang

'Twixt heaven and earth in vapours of their breaths;
. . . . . . . . . . . . . . .
So, when men fly the natural clime of truth,
And turn themselves loose out of all the bounds
Of justice and the straight way to their ends,
Forsaking all the sure force in themselves
To seek without them that which is not theirs,
The forms of all their comforts are distracted,
The riches of their freedoms forfeited,
Their human noblesse sham'd. . . .

(1.2.137, 140–41, 154–61)

Earlier in the same scene, Byron tells Picoté (the plotters' emissary), "I will become . . . their servant . . . In any office but disloyalty. . . ." The allusion to *service* suggests that Byron's self-esteem is as great a dissuasion from treachery as his allegiance to Henry.

These lines, and others in which Byron expresses a growing sense that he may indeed have betrayed what he believes, cannot be dismissed as Chapman's uncontrolled desire to express *his* beliefs or "good sentences," regardless of the speaker. Byron's philosophy of the self is wholly introverted. It is a philosophy of character and human nature that severs the individual from his fellows and thrusts him solely upon his private mental and moral resources. It is, in fact, a philosophy admirably suited to a world of aggression, of uncertainty, of war. Unlike Bussy, Byron "is not voluptuous, / Nor much inclined to women" (1.1.66–67); he lacks a Tamyra to offer us insight and to relieve the constant tension of masculine independence and uncommunication. Byron's confidant is La Fin and, by extension, the other plotters. A lifetime of warfare has taught Byron that he may find support and confidence only among men committed to war. Once the mantle of military service descends, it hides, at least from Byron, self-serving sycophancy and even the fraud of the very claim to comradeship.

Byron never fathoms the deeps of policy and peace that surround him. Like his final impetus to treachery in the fifth act, both his self-awareness and his repentance require direct personal experience rather than conceptions of such imponderables (for him) as peace, statesmanship, and politics.[18] In purely personal terms, Byron does recognize—gradually and only fitfully—that he has abandoned "the freeborn powers of royal man." One of the most striking moments of self-awareness comes as Byron prepares to visit the Astrologer, La Brosse:

The forts that favourites hold in princes' hearts,
In common subjects' loves, and their own strengths,

Are not so sure and unexpugnable
But that the more they are presum'd upon
The more they fail: daily and hourly proof
Tells us prosperity is at highest degree
The fount and handle of calamity:
Like dust before a whirlwind those men fly
That prostrate on the grounds of Fortune lie;
And being great, like trees that broadest sprout,
Their own top-heavy state grubs up their root.
These apprehensions startle all my powers,
And arm them with suspicion gainst themselves.
In my late projects I have cast myself
Into the arms of others, and will see
If they will let me fall. . . .

                                        (3.3.20–35)


For once, Byron sees the connections between his faulty perception of Henry's court and his equally and oppositely faulty perception of Savoy and La Fin. Momentarily he seems to understand that his accurate theory of politicians and court-favor should be applied not to Henry (or not only to Henry) but to those into whose arms he has lately cast himself. Chapman uses a favorite metaphor of self-doubt and inward battle: that of a mind armed against itself. Here, as they do in *Hero and Leander* (see, e.g., 3.200–230), great personal strengths may become the enemies of the self and a strong individual's doubt can equal his self-confidence. Rhymed aphorisms that might have been uttered by a commentator in an earlier *de casibus* tragedy or by the narrator in *Hero and Leander* are now skillfully given to the hero. He stumbles toward truth, striving to bring together gnomic wisdom and personal experience. When Byron continues, we hear resonances of his earlier axiom on the bounds of loyalty: "and will see / If they will let me fall, or toss me up / Into th'affected compass of a throne." The forts in princes' hearts and the compass of a throne are two quite different "bounds" and between them stretches the area of excess, of limitless aspiration or defeat, into which a man "sure in himself" does not venture.

This moment of irresolution, so dangerous and so unfamiliar to a man used to sudden action, gives way to a response more typical of the angry warrior: the great aria that ends the act and includes the lines Shelley used as the epigraph for *The Revolt of Islam:*

Give me a spirit that on this life's rough sea
Loves t'have his sails fill'd with a lusty wind
. . . . . . . . . . . . . . . . . .

He goes before them, and commands them all,
That to himself is a law rational.

(3.3.135–36; 144–45)

These lines, and many speeches like them throughout the two plays, are Chapman's version of the "high astounding terms" Marlowe taught his peers and successors. They are also, of course, the speeches Henry laughs to shame and which, *mutatis mutandis*, another Henry respects when they are spoken by Bussy D'Ambois.

Often enough, such speeches express Byron's fascination with himself, an almost mystic sense of self-destruction in the midst of self-fulfillment and transcendence:

What place is this, what air, what region,
In which a man may hear the harmony
Of all things moving? Hymen marries here
Their ends and uses, and makes me his temple.
Hath any man been blessed, and yet liv'd?
. . . I stand on change,
And shall dissolve in changing; 'tis so full
Of pleasure not to be contain'd in flesh:
To fear a violent good abuseth goodness,
'Tis immortality to die aspiring,
As if a man were taken quick to heaven;

. . . . . . . . . . . . .
. . . like the shaft
Shot at the sun by angry Hercules,
And into shivers by the thunder broken,
Will I be if I burst; and in my heart
This shall be written: 'Yet 'twas high and right.'

(1.2.22–32, 40–44)

Byron begins by associating the music—played by the traitors in order to swell his self-conceit—with the music of the spheres, Apollonian symbols and makers of harmony.[19] Music, with its order and the ever-present metaphor of harmony and sweetness, often represents the well-ordered society, the proper functioning of hierarchy, degree, and loyalty. The traitors' perversion of what is at once a metaphor and a mainstay of Renaissance cosmology calls forth Byron's own misunderstanding of the metaphor and of his position. As he speaks, *changing* (1.28) carries associations of *changes* in music—variations that cannot help, in this incitement to treason, but foreshadow the impending social discord. *Changing* also summons the image of Byron's submission to, or rather embrace of, Fortuna, the goddess against whom, we suspect, his "virtue" will hold little sway. The irony of the events

taking place in this small room of the Archduke's palace finally sur-
faces with enough force to have awakened any man less egotistical, less
married to his own false ideas of transcendence: "They hide the earth
from me with coverings rich, / To make me think that I am here in
heaven" (1.2.50–51). Each word, the suggestion of deceit, the inap-
propriateness of *heaven*, the very "history of Catiline" upon which he
treads, warn and threaten Byron, in the voice of the music and the
figure in the carpet.

While this speech and many others underline Byron's flaws, they
also place him in a much more positive context—a deeply entrenched
Renaissance conception of heroic anger. Byron does not suffer, as
Bussy may, from an unsubstantiated heroism. His sentiments and
transcendental longings might be ludicrous or pitiful, signs of mental
imbalance or ridiculously misplaced self-esteem, if his actions did not
support them.[20] Yet his violence—physical, verbal, imaginative—
cannot be doubted; only destructive nature—the sea that swallows
rivers, the rivers that consume their banks—serves as a proper comparison.[21] This violence and the verbal excess it requires place Byron
alongside other "angry" heroes, like the Hercules whose Senecan fury
he explicitly echoes in this very self-portrait.[22]

As theorists and poets developed an ethic of anger, they faced a
variety of problems, especially justifying anger (a deadly sin) and
distinguishing it from madness. These difficulties explain both the
modern and the contemporary Renaissance ambivalence toward such
characters as Byron. Edgar Wind has traced the humanistic and
Neoplatonic discussions; E. M. Waith has shown how arguments
lauding Paul's angry zeal against the heathen benefited Hercules and
his fellows; and Gordon Braden has examined the particularly Senecan
origins of what he calls "combative selfhood."[23] Translating Homer,
Chapman naturally accepts heroic anger, but carefully separates it
from madness. Pallas Athena explains to Diomed:

> Tis true, Mars hath just rule in warre,
> But just warre; otherwise he raves, not fights. He's alterd
>     farre;
> . . . . .
> He is inconstant, impious, mad.
> <div align="right">(<i>Iliads</i> 5.828–29, 833; <i>Homer</i>, 1:133)</div>

Ordinarily, Chapman applies the word *raves* to Agamemnon rather
than to Achilles, who knows his "soule must conquer th' angrie part"
(*Iliads* 1.216; Homer, 1:30).

Epic and Christian treatments of anger combine in Tasso's

*Gerusalemme Liberata.* Speaking Fairfax's English, Tasso interprets Rinaldo and his experiences in "The Allegorie of the Poem":

> . . . but what this power of the mind, holding the second degree [after Godfrey, "the figure of *Understanding*"] of dignitie is, shall be nowe manifested. The *Irefull* vertue is that, which amongst all the powers of the minde, is lesse estranged from the nobility of the soule, insomuch that *Plato* (doubting) seeketh whether it differeth from reason or no. And such is it in the minde, as the chiefetaine in an assemblie of souldiours: for as of these the office is to obey their princes, which do give directions and commandements to fight against their enimies: so is it the dutie of the irefull, warlike, and soveraigne part of the minde, to be armed with reason against concupiscence, and with that vehemencie and fiercenes (which is proper unto it) to resist and drive awaie whatsoever impediment to felicitie. But when it doth not obey Reason, but suffers it selfe to be carried of her owne violence . . . it fighteth not against concupiscence, but by concupiscence. . . . This violent, fierce, and unbridled furie . . . is . . . principally signified by *Rinaldo*. . . . His returne and reconciliation to *Godfrey*, noteth *Obedience*, causing the *Irefull* power to yeelde to the *Reasonable*. . . . Reason commandeth Anger, not imperiously, but curteouslie and civillie. . . . Secondly, . . . the reasonable part ought not (for heerein the Stoiks were very much deceived) to exclude the *Irefull* from actions, nor *usurpe* the offices thereof, for this usurpation shoulde bee against nature and justice, but it ought to make her her companion and handmaid. . . .[24]

Much that Tasso says about Rinaldo could be said of Byron and attests a conception of the heroic character that valued the "*Irefull* vertue." At the opening of *Byron's Tragedy*, Henry almost uses Tasso's words to report Byron's response to an earlier temptation:

> And plain he told them that although his blood
> (Being mov'd by nature) were a very fire
> And boil'd in apprehension of a wrong,
> Yet should his mind hold such a sceptre there
> As would contain it from all act and thought
> Of treachery or ingratitude to his prince.
>
> (*Tragedy* 1.1.81–86)

Like Rinaldo's anger, Byron's "suffers it selfe to be carried of her owne violence." Byron's concupiscence, unlike Rinaldo's for Armida, is directed toward praise; he lusts for compliment and flattery. Like Rinaldo, Byron obeys (in battle) his prince according to the "dutie of the irefull, warlike and soveraigne part of the minde." In the *Conspiracy*, Byron's anger, like Rinaldo's, climbs to the pitch of madness—

"the short madness of my anger" (5.2.102)—before absolution.[25] Ultimately, Byron is no Rinaldo to seek forgiveness, nor Henry a Godfrey to grant it.

These Renaissance ideas also seriously undermine interpretations of the play that regard Chapman's haphazard allusions to melancholy and choler as an essential system of dramatic structure and characterization. Peter Ure's point, based upon internal evidence rather than ideas of anger and of the angry hero, is also germane: "It is nowhere in the play suggested that this accident of his temperament [Byron as a "choleric man"] controls his *choice*. . . ."[26] The violent or hysterical speeches or actions that some critics have sought to explain by psychology[27] often respond to the actions of others or to the oppressive or confusing situations in which Byron finds himself. The idea of the angry hero is a literary conception of a hero's humanity far older than abnormal psychology or the rudimentary propositions of Elizabethan medicine men.

Byron's social and political situation and Chapman's literary and traditional portrait coincide curiously. The political context prevents Byron from exercising the heroism that speech, act, and tradition assure us he represents. A major source of Byron's verbal excess and threatened physical excess lies in his belief that France's present state deprives him of his past, indeed, of his self-definition. The same may be said of his dramatic presentation, which belongs to a heroic conception that survived in literature far longer than in actuality. Shakespeare's Henry IV and Henry V exploit feudal ethics and institutions even as they destroy them; Hal may consequently ridicule Hotspur's outmoded language and ideals. Similarly, Byron's heroic anger sounds false or petulant or ludicrous when surrounded by Savoy's conspiracy and Henry's nationalism.[28] The hero's dramatic tradition dies with the hero himself. Like some wounded animal, Byron seeks a conflict, or an opponent, a mission upon which to expend his enormous energy. So long as he remains blind to his true enemies and to the true nature of peace and of the court, he continues to be the butt of Henry's laughter and the tool of Savoy's plots. Byron's blindness does at last depart, and his vigor finds its consummation in a magnificently "entire" or "circular" death. One great subtlety of Chapman's plays lies here: he shifts our sympathies, or our perspectives, between past and present, war and peace, Byron the hero and Byron the self-destructive egoist.

ৼ    ৼ    ৼ

The literary tradition Tasso's allegories illustrate can help us interpret Byron's situation, but artistic theory and questions of art's truth enter the *Byron* plays even more directly than through such conventions or traditions. In act 3, Byron himself contemplates the relation between art and truth; his speech illuminates his nature and epitomizes Chapman's use of art and artistic allusion in the play. Pretending a sense of injured merit and sensitivity to Henry's proud condescension, La Fin attempts to force Byron into patent treason. Byron soon unwittingly finds himself tempting his tempter. He asserts his accustomed philosophy of self-reliance; La Fin, he says, should

> profit in experience of the slaveries
> Impos'd on us in these mere politic terms
> Of love, fame, loyalty. . . .
>
> (3.1.26–28)

Byron honestly believes in love, fame, and loyalty, as they may truly and reciprocally exist between sovereign and vassal. To Byron's rather insensitive and unpolitic eyes, La Fin's expulsion proves that the expedient appearance of love and loyalty has replaced those abstractions' essential natures. Unfortunately, Byron's position sounds very much like Picoté's; a skillful sophist might easily guide him from one to the other. Above all, this speech rather alarmingly recalls Byron's befuddlement when trying to understand Aumale's punishment for treason.

Chapman underscores Byron's ethical and imaginative defects in his next speech, where the use of art should warn Byron but instead merely serves his own much more limited and confused purposes:

> There is no truth of any good
> To be discern'd on earth: and, by conversion,
> Nought therefore simply bad; but as the stuff
> Prepar'd for arras pictures is no picture
> Till it be form'd, and man hath cast the beams
> Of his imaginous fancy through it,
> In forming ancient kings and conquerors,
> As he conceives they look'd and were attir'd,
> Though they were nothing so: so all things here
> Have all their price set down from men's conceits,
> Which make all terms and actions good or bad,
> And are but pliant and well-colour'd threads
> Put into feigned images of truth;
> To which to yield and kneel as truth-pure kings,
> That pull'd us down with clear truth of their gospel,
> Were superstition to be hiss'd to hell.
>
> (3.1.47–62)

While Byron's little homily may sound uncharacteristically astute, the speaker misses more than he grasps. The opening elliptical phrases aim to convey Byron's confusion between difficult perception ("no truth . . . To be discern'd on earth") and existence or nonexistence. The first phrase asserts that "good" cannot be accurately judged on earth; "Nought therefore simply bad" apparently jumps to the conclusion that bad doesn't exist since good cannot be certainly distinguished.[29] After all, Byron's persistent limitation has been his "imaginous fancy"; presented with "the stuff . . . for arras pictures," his mind has construed images we know are "nothing so." Chapman even manages to incorporate a temporal element into the simile: Byron contrasts modern, imaginary representations of "ancient kings and conquerors" with their supposed (but equally imagined) historical reality. Similarly, he himself fails to distinguish present "feigned images of truth" (e.g., La Fin's "feigned passion" [3.1.1] in this very scene) from past facts. The hero's tempters are evil artists, creating a false reality.

Byron's speech rebounds in another way. As we know, the simile's chronological element brings the speech closer to Byron's own situation; the basic point lies in "feigned images" versus "truth of any good." For such purposes, the contrast might easily be drawn between the present Henry IV and an image of Henry IV. Byron completes this rhetorical move by mocking the vain or superstitious respect paid royal images as if they were themselves "truth-pure kings." While clinching Byron's point, this conclusion overturns the speech's premise, since Byron originally denied the mind any more than a capricious or selfish ability to distinguish good from bad, truth from falsehood, "feigned images of truth" from "truth-pure kings."

Finally, Byron's instinctive choice of subject—"ancient kings and conquerors"—points the irony. He fails to consider that the subject might be ancient conspirators and traitors, as it was in the "history of Catiline" spread before him in act 1, scene 2. Just as that carpet's prophetic significance along with its associated music and even the simplest symbolic meaning of Aumale's punishment fell on deaf ears and blind eyes, so too, Byron's *own* experience cannot overcome his consistent insensibility to art and its meanings. Although the dramatic speech is necessarily more compressed, the combination of prophecy, interpretation, and irony vividly recalls Hero's "conceited scarf" (*Hero and Leander* 4.37–121).

In the next scene, Savoy and the other plotters again dupe Byron "artistically"; in fact, Savoy even reminds the audience of the earlier scene: "Such tricks the Archduke us'd t'extol his greatness" (3.2.13). The plan is childishly simple:

> *Savoy.*     But is my painter warn'd to take his picture,
>              When he shall see me and present La Fin?

*Rochette.* He is, my lord, and, as your Highness will'd,
        All we will press about him, and admire
        The royal promise of his rare aspect,
        As if he heard not.

                                        (3.2.7–12)

The ruse works perfectly, exceeding, one suspects, even the plotters'
dreams. Byron promises Savoy no mere picture nor even a statue, but
a mountain carved in his likeness, so that Savoy may look from his
Duchy towards "the famous mountain Oros . . . [which] . . . shall
. . . clearly bear my counterfeit" (3.2.155, 164). With the "history of
Catiline," Chapman emphasized Byron's blindness to the practices
made of art; in this scene, Byron ignores (almost fails to hear) among
so many compliments, Roncas's ominous reminiscence:

        I have heard the famous and right learned Earl
        And Archbishop of Lyons, Pierre Pinac
        (Who was reported to have wondrous judgment
        In men's events and natures by their looks),
        Upon his death-bed visited by this Duke,
        He told his sister, when his Grace was gone,
        That he had never yet observed a face
        Of worse presage than this. . . .

                                        (3.2.122–29)

Art, variously shaped, serves as a moral and perceptional touch-
stone in other scenes. One of the most famous speeches in all of
Chapman's drama is the "doctrinal and witty hieroglyphic" of Byron
astride "his brave beast Pastrana."[30] The hieroglyphic, says Savoy,
serves "to express and teach / Kings to command as they could serve,
and subjects / To serve as if they had power to command" (2.2.79–81).
The hieroglyphic thus elicits ideas and principles very close to the goal
of Savoy's plot. Henry's answer, for its pungency and implicit rebuke
to overingenuity, should be as famous as the hieroglyphic itself:

        You are a good old horseman, I perceive,
        And still [i.e., distill] out all the use of that good part;
        Your wit is of the true Pierian spring,
        That can make anything, of anything.

                                        (2.2.82–85)

The couplet summarizes Savoy's actions in the play.
    Another such moral emblem (also called a "hieroglyphic") Byron
ignores completely:

As you may see a mighty promontory
More digg'd and under-eaten than may warrant
A safe supportance to his hanging brows;
All passengers avoid him, shun all ground
That lies within his shadow, and bear still
A flying eye upon him: so great men,
Corrupted in their grounds, and building out
Too swelling fronts for their foundations,
When most they should be propp'd are most forsaken;
And men will rather thrust into the storms
Of better-grounded states than take a shelter
Beneath their ruinous and fearful weight;
Yet they so oversee their faulty bases,
That they remain securer in conceit:
And that security doth worse presage
Their near destructions than their eaten grounds;
And therefore heaven itself is made to us
A perfect hieroglyphic to express
The idleness of such security,
And the grave labour of a wise distrust,
In both sorts of the all-inclining stars,
Where all men note this difference in their shining,
As plain as they distinguish either hand,
The fixed stars waver, and the erring stand.

(4.1.190–213)[31]

The doctrine, sadly apropos, is neatly set off as a verbal picture, an inset scene that Byron fails to understand; of course, he also fails to undertake the "grave labour of a wise distrust" in the stars.

This episode joins several others where Byron does not understand—through pride or obtuseness—the significance of all he sees, hears, or does. Several such significant errors involve art. At his first entrance, Byron strides upon a rug illustrating the "history of Catiline," but ignores reality in favor of vaunting fantasies: "They follow all my steps with music / As if my feet were numerous . . . with Apollo's virtue" (1.2.45–47).[32] Later, he ignores both his own examples drawn from art and the prophetic words of a bystander who looks upon the portrait that incites Byron to one of his most extravagant orgies of self-praise and folly. When Henry still later admonishes Byron against flattery, he specifically criticizes the hero's "credulous eye." Recalling those early Apollonian sounds, Henry mocks the puffery common in prefatory poems: "his tun'd feet / Are of the great last, the perpetual motion" (3.2.257–58). The King's entire speech parodies the words to be found on any Elizabethan poet's lips when puffing a fellow poet's work: "his plumes only imp the Muses' wings. / He sleeps with them, his head is napp'd with bays."

This last series of recondite allusions makes the point that *Byron's Conspiracy* is a literary play, written by a man very much in the world of letters and requiring for greatest enjoyment an audience aware of the vocabulary and special interests of drama and literature. More generally, one concludes that Chapman employs art—genres, vocabularies, overt allusions—as a standard for measuring Byron. Construed naturalistically, it is folly to spread a rug displaying Catiline's conspiracy before a man one hopes to suborn; the conspirators' brashness (and Chapman's), however, disappears alongside Byron's failure to recognize the prophecy for what it is. Chapman employs significant form and a character's response to it for definition of the tragic subject and amplification of the tragic dilemma.

❦   ❦   ❦

Repentance and temporary reprieve come for Byron when Henry abandons his role as monarch of a modern state and assumes a much older, hierophantic role as God's lieutenant. In the reconciliation scene, Chapman resolves several distinct conceptual interests in the play. Byron can now recognize his king as he could not before: "heroic fashions" rather than "an antic vizard" once more hold sway. Henry first analyzes Byron's political and mental situation and offers advice. He finds that Byron's "judgment is not competent" because inwardly troubled. The analogy is with tinnitus:

> For as the air contain'd within our ears,
> If it be not in quiet, nor refrains
> Troubling our hearing with offensive sounds
> (But our affected instrument of hearing,
> Replete with noise and singings in itself)
> It faithfully receives no other voices;
> So of all judgments, if within themselves
> They suffer spleen and are tumultuous,
> They cannot equal differences without them;
> And this wind, that doth sing so in your ears,
> I know is no disease bred in yourself,
> But whisper'd in by others. . . .

(5.2.58–69)

The image diagnoses Byron's illness: a faulty perception that transforms, or deforms, reality.[33] Henry then alludes to one of the play's finest conceits, that of a river overflowing its banks or contending with the sea or finally wasting itself in shallow floods. The conspirators are "streams"

> That make themselves so many heavens to sight,

Since you may see in them the moon and stars,
The blue space of the air, as far from us,
To our weak senses, in those shallow streams,
As if they were as deep as heaven is high;
Yet with your middle finger only, sound them,
And you shall pierce them to the very earth;
And therefore leave them and be true to me.
Or you'll be left by all. . . .

(5.2.72–80)

Byron must learn to distinguish the stream's reflection from the true heaven of fidelity and royal order. The metaphor will be finally resolved only when and if Byron achieves self-awareness, that is, once he can understand figurative language hitherto used unthinkingly. That ability appears only at the end of the ten-act drama: "we should imitate streams, / That run below the valleys and do yield . . ." (*Tragedy* 5.4.152–53). The King achieves a temporary resolution through a prayer addressed to "Innocence" (5.2.85–100): in Byron's earlier phrase, Henry pulls down the hero "with clear truth of . . . gospel" (3.1.61). Successful for a time, the King invokes his power as divine vice-regent and threatens a second Flood: "your fire will be inward, / Which not another deluge can put out" (5.2.83–84).

In a sense, Byron is a tragic hero who must first be awakened to the possibility of tragedy, a man who understands best only those events or persons confronting him directly. His initial solipsism, lost completely only in death, tells him that warfare is life and peace, chaos or cowardice. Confusing these realms, indeed, only gradually understanding that "realms" are at stake, Byron struggles to reestablish life as he knows it. He seeks absolution only under the powerful stimulus of prayer, of Henry's religious and political and "literary" eloquence. Byron's conspiracy is against himself. The play has shown him to be a battledore of war and peace, of pride and ignorance.

# 3

# Rare Virtues and Their Impair in
## *The Tragedy of Charles, Duke of Byron*

*Byron's Conspiracy* ends with a curious comic scene, displaying Savoy's discomfiture when he fails in sophisticated badinage with three court ladies. King Henry, the newly-reconciled Byron, and other courtiers observe the scene, commenting upon it as if it were a dramatic episode played for their benefit:

> *Epernon.* Sir, if it please you to be taught any courtship take you to your stand; Savoy is at it with three mistresses at once; he loves each of them best, yet all differently.
> *Henry.* For the time he hath been here, he hath talked a volume greater than the Turk's Alcoran; stand up close; his lips go still.
>
> (5.2.111–16)

Eventually, Savoy takes an embarrassed though not inelegant leave and flees to his native land. After some jests concerning Savoy's imitation of D'Auvergne's manners, Henry soberly reminds his court that Savoy's "great wit / Can turn him into any form he lists, / More fit to be avoided than deluded" (5.2.261–63).

Superficially an awkward coda to the moving and effective scene in which the King forgives Byron, this comic episode serves as a ceremonious marking of Byron's return: the villainous Savoy becomes a buffoonish victim. Just as Byron's threat has been turned aside, the traitor made socially and politically acceptable, so too his tempter's authority has been diminished, mocked, and then dismissed. Savoy has shifted from politics to drama. His machinations cannot encompass court compliment, much less treason; his actions are not realistic threats, but only the subject of a playlet celebrating Byron's regained fidelity. The released tension moves us smoothly from *The Conspiracy*'s resolution to *The Tragedy*'s quiet and serious opening; Chapman cannot exaggerate the first play's conclusion without simultaneously making Byron's new treason implausible. At the same time, *The Conspiracy* does end comically. The scene emphasizes the traitors' sterility, opposed to Henry's confident blessing of his new son in *The Tragedy*'s opening scene. Finally, this little playlet crowns *The Conspiracy*'s movement in much the same way *The Tragedy*'s parallel entertainment, the masque, reveals some fundamental truths about Henry's reign.

Whether this final scene satisfied all the expectations *The Conspiracy* encouraged is arguable; the episode does, however, give the play a technical conclusion well suited to its transitional location. As a whole, the construction of *Byron's Tragedy* is less noticed, but no less shrewd. Since the historical Byron unobligingly (and unaesthetically) revolted twice, Chapman faced the two-part play problem in an exceptionally acute form. Rather than explain Byron's relapse, Chapman begins the play by juxtaposing new treason with new dynastic hope. The king and his party remain as puzzled as the audience over the *source* of Byron's second fall. Henry and the courtiers quickly, but with natural self-interrogation, sketch Byron's career and indicate that La Fin, "who hath his heart in keeping" (1.1.88), will soon betray his master. Henry then prays over his infant son, asking for future peace, but promising swift royal action in war. A series of short scenes establishes Byron's unsuspecting trust of La Fin as well as Henry's astonished conviction that La Fin's betrayed friend is indeed a traitor. The king decides to recall Byron: whether Byron comes willingly or not, he will have effectively surrendered either himself or his pretended loyalty.

After a curious but revealing glimpse of court life—the "Masque of Virtues"—the play's most finely orchestrated scenes record Byron's response to his summons and his eventual capitulation. Two challenging speeches, one opening act 3 and the other, act 4, frame Byron's decisive actions. These long speeches attack the king and court on moral, philosophical, and political grounds that the play generally—and unexpectedly—substantiates. The two attacks, mingled with Byron's self-serving and increasingly flimsy alibis, prevent any unequivocal arbitration between monarch and noble. On the eve of his arrest, Byron's confident, even flamboyant, self-possession ironically underlines his friends' urgent warnings. At last Henry overcomes his honest scruples and orders Byron's arrest and trial.

When Byron's sentence has been passed and he awaits execution, an observer remarks the hero's extraordinary emotional changes: "he doubts, storms, threatens, rues, complains, implores. . . . And sorrow errs through all forms in his face" (5.3.218, 223). Byron's psychological variety is both cause and consequence of the play's elusive treatment of human and political rights and wrongs. Like *Coriolanus*, which it often resembles at even the verbal level, *Byron's Tragedy* puts several flawed rights into conflict and poses difficult political questions without shirking the practical human realities that contaminate political theory. Chapman repeatedly employs Byron's blunt military acumen against policy and Machiavellianism, even as we recognize that the hero ignores his own entrapment by those very forces. Byron's speeches analyzing and condemning Machiavellianism simultaneously make his self-deception more painful and partly exculpate him from the charge of moral ignorance. Inevitably, the attacks on Henry's religious dereliction and his personal and social ingratitude blur the line between complete admiration and complete condemnation. Such categories have become murkier and murkier because the plays contain an implicit triangular structure in which Byron points to Henry and Henry to Savoy, each uttering the identical curse: "machiavel." The half-truth in Byron's accusation and his disregard of the whole truth in Henry's justify A. P. Rossiter's view that *The Conspiracy* and *Tragedy* are "the most intellectual of Elizabethan plays."[1]

❦   ❦   ❦

*The Tragedy*'s intellectual complexity, and the further complexities of its world, appear plainly in Byron's two most reasoned outbursts against his monarch. In the first, Byron repeats his contention that a king forfeits his subjects' loyalty if he does not keep faith with them: "Dear friend [D'Auvergne], we must not be more true to kings / Than kings are to their subjects" (*Tragedy* 3.1.1–2). Legally, Byron's point has its roots in the feudal vassal-lord relation, which depended upon reciprocal honor.[2] In mid and late sixteenth-century France, the grounds of loyalty and disloyalty were both religious and sociopolitical. Various great nobles, anxious to retain ancient privilege and independence, exacerbated Catholic-Protestant hostilities and thereby hoped to avert the unification and centralization Henry IV sought. The linked religious and political problems became a *casus belli* in France, as they had threatened to do in England after Henry VIII decided Rome wasn't worth a marriage. Such issues turned attention from the issue of a ruler's power to the more modern question, "What is the state and how is it constructed?"[3]

Even as his countrymen grew increasingly dependent upon opaque and general agreements among citizen classes, Byron unceasingly advocates a system of personal rights and duties. The hero sees Machiavelli as a theoretician of "new" principles "That for a day preserve a prince, and ever / Destroy him after" (3.1.6–7). To this political system (or "art," 3.1.10), Byron opposes "simple virtue" and the "right of Nature" (a phrase recalling similar remarks in *Bussy* and common in contemporary political discussion). Byron's elegant fable of the tree of Religion and "that laurel spray / That from the heavenly eagle's golden seres / Fell in the lap of great Augustus' wife" (3.1.15–17) specifically concerns Henry's "playing both ways with religion." Machiavelli would have approved a royal conscience flexible enough to exchange Protestantism for Paris.

Byron's objection is not just the quarrel of Huguenot with Catholic or reactionary noble with "modern" executive. If Byron's case were thus limited, Henry and his court might be justified in countering with the charge of hypocrisy, as they do:

> No question, sir, he was of no religion;
> But, upon false grounds by some courtiers laid,
> Hath oft been heard to mock and jest at all.
>
> (1.3.4–6)

Byron makes much more comprehensive accusations. As a result of Henry's wavering attitude toward religion, "The lamp of all authority goes out, / And all the blaze of princes is extinct" (3.1.41–42), and

> since squint-eyed Envy
> And pale Suspicion dash'd the heads of kingdoms
> One gainst another, two abhorred twins,
> With two foul tails, stern War and Liberty,
> Enter'd the world.
>
> (3.1.30–34)

The medieval flavor of the personifications images the social collapse and moral apocalypse Byron anticipates; his implied medievalism also suggests his social and political values. The specific charge is religion; the much graver charges are a breakdown of social responsibility, the adoption of Machiavellian relativism, and the approach of a new chaos. An effective concluding image underscores the ordinary man's helplessness as he watches portents of political catastrophe:

> Thus, as the poet sends a messenger
> Out to the stage to show the sum of all
> That follows after, so are kings' revolts
> And playing both ways with religion
> Fore-runners of afflictions imminent,
> Which (like a Chorus) subjects must lament.
>
> (3.1.43–48)[4]

Byron, of course, implies that only he can emerge from the chorus and take arms, as protagonist in a metaphoric tragedy, against the tyrant's might. This easy invocation of dramatic terminology links Byron's remarks here with *The Conspiracy*'s use of art as morality. In the second play, Byron becomes more sensitive to artistic fables but often employs them, as in his elaborate man-beast comparisons, to create and support an egocentric dreamworld cut off from court politics.

Byron's second great aggressive speech, at the opening of act 4, joins his earlier obsession, war and peace, with his present concerns, the morality of courts and kings. Almost an aria, it opens, "O the most base fruits of a settled peace! / In men I mean, worse than their dirty fields, / Which they manure much better than themselves . . ." (4.1.1–3). In wartime, men look to "their spirits and freedoms," now "smother'd in their ease." The public's moral and physical dereliction merely reflects "their tyrants and their ministers . . . [who] Grow wild in prosecution of their lusts." Having lost martial self-confidence (and weapons), the cowardly men of peace do not dare oppose authority "though they see their bloods / In their most dear associates and allies, / Pour'd into kennels by it." Although Byron repeats his earlier complaints, the imagery of organic nature and bestial death aptly supports his claim that tyrants destroy humanity. The speech integrates Byron's actions in the two plays by emphasizing his role as sufferer and the king's role as moral cynosure.

Perhaps as further mollification, or to make easy judgments impossible, Chapman has Byron deliver these speeches to the "good" conspirator, D'Auvergne. The Comte is no less culpable than any other traitor, but his motives, though little explored, appear noble and free of the political manipulation that characterizes the foreign agents and their native henchmen. Indeed, Chapman often tempers his pro-Henrician sources, which attack or ridicule D'Auvergne, a prince of the blood royal, as much as they dare. When Byron makes the charges, the stage is momentarily free of the tainted presence of La Fin or Picoté or Savoy. Byron's actions, especially his growing lust for praise, quickly undercut these speeches, but his words do confirm the criticism more objectively displayed in act 2's masque.

Like most masques within plays,[5] Chapman's is not so highly developed as the masque designed for independent performance, nor is it so complex as Chapman's fullest masque-within-a-play in *The Widow's Tears*. The "Masque of Virtues," as it might be called, deserves more attention than readers usually pay it, however, simply because it renders Byron's criticism more than vain denunciation or sullen hypocrisy. While the masque is wholly original, Chapman's putative source, Edward Grimeston, and Grimeston's own source, Pierre Matthieu, mention that in the winter of 1602 the Court was full of Jolity and Sports, the Queene having made a very Rich and Sumptuous Maske, calling fifteene Princesses and Ladies of the Court unto her, which represented sixteene Vertues, whereof the Queene made the first. The Duke of *Vendosme*, beeing attired like *Cupid*, marched before the Queene: but within fewe dayes after he changed that Habite. . . .[6]

Compressing Matthieu's account, Grimeston makes Cupid part of the masque, but the original French source adds that detail only after what seems a conclusive comment on the masque itself:

Ceste nuit [of the masque] valut a la Royne une journee, car en tous les lieus ou le Balet fut veu & admire, tous les coeurs & toutes les voix s'accordoient à ses louages. Le Duc de Vendosme estoit vestu en Cupidon, & marchoit devant la Royne. Il ne demeura gueres en cest habit. . . .[7]

Since Matthieu's marginal note refers to three different locations in which the masque was performed, Cupid may not have been part of the original "sport." Jean Bertaut's "Récit, Pour le Ballet de seize Dames representans les Vertues, dont la Royne estoit l'une" survives, but does not further identify the original participants, nor does its text resemble Chapman's.[8] In any case, Chapman specifies that the queen, Marie de' Medici, should play "Sophrosyne, or Chastity" and that Henriette D'Entragues, the king's current mistress, should play "Dapsile, or Liberality."[9] If Chapman also intended Cupid to be played by the Duc de Vendôme (Henry's bastard son by Gabrielle D'Estrees, an earlier mistress), the "family" group would be complete.

The domestic theatricals are simple but pointed: Cupid introduces the virtues, newly arrived from "shady Arden" to ratify and adorn the "sweet Peace" that Henry's "valour lifted from her grave" (2.1.5–7). Cupid's most recent task has been reconciling a "kind and worthy emulation / 'Twixt these two Virtues, leaders of the train" (2.1.14–15). This "effeminate war," a celebrated scene now censored, showed the Queen striking Henriette; presumably, its loss accounts for the text's abrupt transition to the masque itself.[10] Chapman himself apparently fled to escape arrest when the French ambassador, not surprisingly, complained at his king's wife and mistress scuffling on Albion's perfidious stage.[11] These broils have passed, and the masque's first part ends with a "Court compliment" (2.1.66), a dance by the ladies. Cupid had entered *with a table written, hung about his neck;* this plaque evidently displays a riddle, "another parcel" of the virtues' "courtship" (2.1.68–69), which he poses for the court. Epernon accepts the challenge and thus provides a traditional link between the masquers and their courtly spectators. A dance concludes the entertainment.

On the historical masque's first performance, Matthieu reports, Henry turned to the Papal Nuncio

> & lui demanda ce qu'il luy en sembloit, & si un tel esquadron n'estoit pas beau? Bellissime, respond le Nunce, & bien perilleux.[12]

Matthieu, or the Archbishop, then applies this equivocal remark to the inevitable conflict between "tant de beautez" and "tant de vertus." That potential conflict arises naturally from a masque in which wife and mistress impersonate contending virtues. Chapman's brief entertainment neatly represents the possible ambiguities. While Englishmen might have once accepted the existence of royal mistresses as "inevitable,"[13] that generalization can hardly apply adequately either to an English audience until recently ruled by a virgin queen ever stricter in regulating court morals or to an audience now ruled by a king more eager for minions than mistresses. The English, moreover, certainly feared the proliferation of bastard pretenders to the throne. Francophobia, too, might join a popular interest in theatrical licentiousness with a morally or politically motivated condemnation.

Cupid's conclusion to the masque,

> We'll now turn to our dance, and then attend
> Your Highness' will, as touching our resort,
> If Virtue may be entertain'd at Court . . .
>
> (2.1.125–27)

reminds the audience that the "virtues" have been in Arden and only now seek "entertainment" (i.e., acceptance, permission to remain) at the court. Henry's answer, "This show hath pleased me well for that it figures / The reconcilement of my Queen and mistress," reveals a very natural relief at finding his sacred and profane loves peacefully disposed but in no way suggests that his wife will become sole inheritor of his grace. The harmony symbolized and identified by the masque is political, not moral.[14] Even the political reconciliations quickly collapsed, for Henriette and her half brother D'Auvergne (Charles IX's bastard and last of the Valois) conspired against Henry once more in 1604.[15]

If we imagine that Chapman conveyed the players' historical identities (and the French ambassador's angry protest in 1608 proves he, or the actors, managed the feat), the performance must have been very amusing, balanced as it is between luxuriously decorated piety and courtly sexuality. Similarly, the audience presumably enjoyed the indecent double entendre of Cupid's riddle; like the masque, it pairs crudity and courtship:

> What's that a fair lady most of all likes,
> Yet ever makes show she least of all seeks:
> That's ever embrac'd and affected by her,
> Yet never is seen to please or come nigh her:
> Most serv'd in her night-weeds, does her good in a corner:
> But a poor man's thing, yet doth richly adorn her:
> Most cheap and most dear, above all worldly pelf,
> That is hard to get in, but comes out of itself?
>
> (italic in original; 2.1.88–94)

However amusing, the masque and the riddle (answer: "good fame") must be seen as Chapman's serious attempt to portray Henry as a fallible human being rather than a high-minded Lycurgus or Numa with his gaze fixed firmly on the future. Byron's sometimes petulant charges are neither entirely baseless nor selfishly hypocritical. Chapman's careful structuring of the masque and, more bluntly, the riddle's repetition of the same ambivalence, ensure that Byron's later talk of a vicious peace—implicitly opposed to "virtuous" war in which there is no time for vice or courtship—will recall Henry's less-than-perfect morals. If the King, moral exemplar to his realm, commits adultery and connives at the public acknowledgment of that fact, then the audience may justifiably doubt his sincerity in taking a high moral line. The politically adept monarch, spreading his maker's image broadcast, deserved his two contemporary epithets—"le Grand" and "le vert gallant."

Chapman carefully precedes Byron's charges with the masque and court banter that give them substance and conviction. The court scenes of Henry at play and among his counsellors amplify and define his character, filling in the general outline gleaned from *Byron's Conspiracy*. If that play may be considered an examination of Byron's troubled thoughts of war and memory in peace, then the first four acts of *The Tragedy* may be said to concentrate on defining Henry's responses to nearly overt treason and to his daily life as a great courtier. Until *The Tragedy*'s opening, even Henry's friends, a group including all the critics, would be hard put to characterize him. His only significant acts so far have been to banish La Fin and to forgive Byron. Increased attention and further development produce greater ambiguity and less certain judgment because Chapman now chooses to develop Henry's characterization through two contradictory, or at least divergent, actions. One is his acceptance and encouragement of La Fin, that "centre to impiety," when he decides to abandon Byron; the other is his obvious and moving reluctance to punish the hero.

The problems posed by Henry's use of La Fin are not easily resolved. Even the king's ardent supporters and his equally ardent historians balked at La Fin.[16] Henry himself had earlier banished the man, and his betrayal of Byron (as Chapman only hints) was historically very much a self-protective and self-advancing measure. When a group of Byron's friends publicly murdered La Fin in 1606, they were neither pursued nor punished, and his name came to be a by-word for treachery.[17] Nonetheless, most modern critics agree with Ennis Rees and Peter Ure in seeing Henry as a perfect monarch fighting the good and moral fight against the Machiavellian Savoy and his tool, Byron. Given Henry's patent dynastic concerns and his nearly megalomaniacal concentration on national unity, we must agree "that [in this play] even the politically virtuous must at times use politic means and that no political motive is untainted by egotism."[18] Grimeston and Matthieu offer several maxims commending the King's interest in preventing and discouraging treason by whatever means.[19] While such evidence in a play's source does not carry any weight unless it has demonstrably affected the drama itself, the historians' consensus corroborates Machiavelli's anonymous and ubiquitous influence in the period. Those principles, so long as they appeared shorn of Machiavelli's name and his vigorous rhetoric, were more or less acceptable: much of Bodin's work and even some of James I's contain "Machiavellian" ideas.[20]

A good example of the sly insinuation of politics into contemporary commonplaces about kingship comes in Henry's holier-than-thy-master speech to the Spanish ambassador:

>                      If, because
> We sit above the danger of the laws,
> We likewise lift our arms above their justice,
> And that our heavenly Sovereign bounds not us
> In those religious confines out of which
> Our justice and our true laws are inform'd,
> In vain have we expectance that our subjects
> Should not as well presume to offend their earthly,
> As we our heavenly Sovereign. . . .
>
>                                  (5.1.49–57)

Part of the theory behind this speech might come directly from Bodin or James: citizens are subject to positive, man-made and man-enforced law, which in turn depends upon natural and divine law, to which a sovereign is alone responsible.[21] If a sovereign errs, says Bodin, it lies between him and God; if a subject errs, it lies between the individual and his sovereign, whose power and justice derive from and depend upon God's. So much is traditional. These principles are not, as Robert Ornstein claims, "[free] from the traditional limitations which medieval theorists placed upon royal authority," but he correctly points to a prominent implication of Henry's speech: "According to Henry a king should be just . . . because it would be imprudent to be otherwise."[22]

Political self-interest is matched by a more personal, if less tangible, kind. Henry's response to La Fin's apostasy makes a chilling literary link between two ideas that might be supposed opposites: "you have with excellent desert / Of loyalty and policy express'd / Your name in action" (1.3.12–14). "La Fin" equals "the end" or "the goal." In urging Byron to confess, Henry makes the case for La Fin's betrayal and for the traitor's immediate repentance:

> . . . you disdain submission, not rememb'ring,
> That (in intents urg'd for the common good)
> He that shall hold his peace, being charg'd to speak,
> Doth all the peace and nerves of empire break. . . .
>
> (4.2.221–24)

The issue is blurred, however, when Henry tries to convince D'Auvergne that his honor is more engaged to reveal treason than to keep faith with Byron:

> Think you it not as strong a point of faith
> To rectify your loyalties to me,
> As to be trusty in each other's wrong?
> Trust that deceives ourselves is treachery,
> And truth, that truth conceals, an open lie.
>
> (4.2.180–84)

Henry implicitly recognizes that rebellion against his rule may have an honorable basis, but argues, as Bodin generally does, that there are degrees of honor and that one serves a higher personal honor in serving the nation's honor (and the king's). Issues pitting honor against honor, truth against truth, complicate our responses. If Chapman has shown that Byron betrays his king upon grounds that are hardly idealistic, he also shows that Henry's own devotion to truth and to his realm has a personal and, judged by Henry's professed ideals, a contaminated basis.

In his reluctance to punish Byron, Henry's attitude is much less equivocal. Upon Byron's tardy arrival at court, Henry's first appeal for repentance ("If you conceal my enemies, you are one") receives this sophistical answer:

> Being friend and worthy fautor of myself,
> I am no foe of yours, nor no impairer,
> Since he can no way worthily maintain
> His prince's honour that neglects his own;
> And if your will have been, to my true reason,
> (Maintaining still the truth of loyalty)
> A check to my free nature and mine honour,
> And that on your free justice I presum'd
> To cross your will a little, I conceive
> You will not think this forfeit worth my head.
>
> (3.2.76–85)

Being a friend to oneself is, in Chapman's ethics, a precondition of honor, but no guarantee; moreover, Byron's indecision when faced with Henry's summons undercuts even that first claim. The appeal to a conflict of honors is answered to some extent by Henry's speech to D'Auvergne and further enfeebled by Byron's unwillingness to face his sovereign when explicitly summoned. Finally, in the terms of will and reason invoked here, Byron's own "true reason," not Henry's "will," should have checked his "free nature." Although he has indisputable proof of Byron's treason, Henry ends the interview with the promise that he will discuss the matter further, "Always reserving clemency and pardon / Upon confession, be you ne'er so foul" (3.2.121–22).

Against the direct counsel of a political writer like Bodin, Henry repeats his willingness to grant mercy: "Would he of one thing but reveal the truth . . . He should not taste my justice" (4.2.2, 4).[23] Both Henry and his Chancellor urge Byron's claims upon the royal favor, echoing Byron's own words:

> I never lov'd man like him; would have trusted
> My son in his protection, and my realm:
> He hath deserv'd my love with worthy service . . .
>
> (4.2.7–9)[24]

and

> Your Majesty hath us'd your utmost means
> Both by your own persuasions and his friends
> To bring him to submission, and confess
> With some sign of repentance his foul fault;

. . . . . . . . . . . . . .
You have, in love and care of his recovery,
Been half in labour to produce a course
And resolution, what were fit for him. . . .

(4.2.18–21, 23–25)

These sentiments and Henry's repeated efforts to put them into action leave no doubt that he honestly hopes to save Byron from his merited punishment.

Caught between old loyalties and present dangers, Henry prays for guidance to his Sovereign: "O Thou that govern'st the keen swords of kings, / Direct my arm in this important stroke . . ." (4.2.63–64). His speech recalls the similar musings of Shakespeare's English Henry, who similarly concludes that could "a fool comprise" the "huge counterpoise [to the popular idea of royal freedom] / In cares and dangers . . . He would not be a king, but would be wise" (*Tragedy* 4.2.83–85). Although the prayer's dignity and reverence are a little tempered by Henry's pompous Neoplatonism ("Now I am settled in my sun of height, / The circular splendour and full sphere of state . . ." [5.1.138–39]), he has amply demonstrated his eagerness to grant mercy and his true conception of the responsibilities of a king and a secular judge.

Byron's sophistry and eventually his downright deceit in meeting Henry's offer of forgiveness indicate well the character Chapman builds for him throughout the first four acts. The decline from virtue and the growing disparity between Byron's allusions to Alexander and Camillus and his own corruption achieve grand proportions, unequalled in the earlier play.

Between Byron's first attack on Henry ("we must not be more true to kings / Than kings are to their subjects") and his sophistic response to the proffered royal bounty lie two scenes whose brisk action show Byron to be far more sinful than sinned against. Hard upon the speech denouncing obedience to Henry comes the first of a series of royal messengers, commanding Byron's return to court. The hero's excuse for not coming—"does he think / It is an action worthy of my valour / To turn my back to an approaching foe?" (3.1.83–85)—is at once specious and feeble. Its principal claim (the immediacy of foreign threat), D'Escures quickly denies. The larger issue—Byron's overparticular sense of honor has replaced his duty to Henry—explains the messenger's growing insistence and Byron's ever more captious alibis. Placed in such a personal and self-serving context, his earlier complaint, Henry's ingratitude, begins to sound both petulant and false: "He takes on him my executions; / And on the demolitions, that this arm / Hath shaken out of forts and citadels, / Hath he advanc'd the trophies of his valour" (3.1.136–39). As a champion of all good men against a rapacious and ungrateful king, Byron was admirable and partly convincing; as an individual refusing to accept the consequences of his stand, all the while reiterating his worth in grandiose similes—"I have Alcides-like gone under th'earth . . ." (line 151)—he appears a moral coward with a stock of grand allusion.

Janin succinctly identifies this moral cowardice and the puerility of Byron's excuses:

> . . . these aloof abodes . . . bewray,
> That there is rather firmness in your breath
> Than in your heart. Truth is not made of glass,
> That with a small touch it should fear to break,
> And therefore should not shun it. . . .
>
> (3.1.177–81)

Janin's metaphor recalls, for a reader at least, Byron's striking epigram on the "bounds of loyalty": one may easily lose one's self in treason, but an honorable man is not so easily tainted by the "light breath of report" (line 175). Byron then contradicts himself, first arguing that Henry's ingratitude has "crack'd" his merit, then denying any grudge ("nor am [I] oppos'd / Against my Sovereign" [lines 212–13]) and proffering his old excuse of dishonor in retreat before the enemy.

At court, various nobles speculate upon Byron's recalcitrance and discuss its meaning. Prâlin summarizes the dilemma Byron has created for himself through indecision and feeble pretense: "Come, or be fetch'd, he quite hath lost his honour / In giving these suspicions of revolt / From his allegiance" (3.2.3–5). At the crucial moment, Byron has hesitated between two equally "headless" resolutions: to gild his treason with brass at court or to hammer out a separate course of open revolt. Behind it all, says Prâlin, is Byron's "enchanted glory"—the drowning in self that forfeits all. Byron is, in fact, his own magician, bewitching himself from himself. Epernon's simile of food and amorous satiety (lines 18ff.) demeans the "wonder" at Byron's greatness to a purely sensual aspiration and mundane amazement. This reduction is an important stage in the moral decline extending from Byron's first appearance in *The Tragedy* to his final nadir as a wild beast in act 4. At that first appearance, we quickly recognize Byron's capitulation to moral delinquency and solipsism: La Fin dares to say, "How great a spirit he breathes! How learn'd, how wise! / . . . your unmatch'd and more than human wind";[25] "you do too much ravish and my soul / Offer to music in your numerous breath" (1.2.43, 45, 57–58). Even the early Byron, his humor "past measure glorious," could not have allowed such sycophancy to pass unchecked. This later, more self-engrossed Byron finally slips from evasion to lies:

> . . . to all the censures of the world
> My faith and innocence had been foully foil'd;
> Which, I protest by heaven's bright witnesses
> That shine far, far, from mixture with our fears,
> Retain as perfect roundness as their spheres.
>
> $(3.2.112-16)^{26}$

The second great attack on Henry (4.1.1–24) is again adulterated by Byron's petty indignation (lines 25–26). Soissons attempts to encourage confession by explaining Henry's proffered clemency:

> . . . he is most loth (for his ancient love
> To your rare virtues, and in their impair,
> The full discouragement of all that live
> To trust or favour any gifts in nature)
> T' expose them to the light. . . .
>
> $(4.1.46-49)^{27}$

But Byron can only circle within the prison of his own egotism: "the malignant envies of my foes, / Who pour me out . . . To drown me in myself" (lines 61–63).

Just as the business of act 3 comprised a series of messengers requesting Byron's presence at court, the first two scenes of act 4 show various friends urging him to leave. The first friendly plea comes from a "Captain." His anonymity makes his task more poignant because he expresses a general admiration for Byron; at the same time, court intrigue and political treachery horrify a man hardened to Byron's military service. The Captain brings a letter telling Byron to "retire." When asked his opinion, the veteran cannot restrain his incredulity at Byron's continued stupidity:

> Yet doth that senseless apoplexy dull you?
> The devil or your wicked angel blinds you,
> Bereaving all your reason of a man,
> And leaves you but the spirit of a horse
> In your brute nostrils, only power to dare.
>
> (4.1.106–10)

This powerful speech gives voice to all those silent spectators of Byron's former glory who "wonder of his wisdom and his valour"

(3.2.7). "Power to dare," "the spirit of a horse," now become the dominant motifs: the Captain adduces a series of "strange ostents"— animal deaths and brute madnesses—associated with Byron. The hero finally confirms the equation between man and beast. He becomes a kind of super-brute:

> When men show most their spirits
> In valour, and their utmost dares to do
> They are compar'd to lions, wolves, and boars;
> But, by conversion, none will say a lion
> Fights as he had the spirit of a man.
> Let me then in my danger now give cause
> For all men to begin that simile.
> For all my huge engagement I provide me
> This short sword only, which, if I have time
> To show my apprehender, he shall use
> Power of ten lions if I get not loose.
>
> (4.1.143–53)

Such comparisons logically end in the traitor's final rejection of mercy; irremediably committed to treason, Byron can think only of active physical retort: "I beseech you yield my innocence justice, / But with my single valour, gainst them all / That thus have poisoned your opinion" (4.2.214–16).

In the scene preceding the arrest, various messengers continue to whisper counsels of defeat and withdrawal. Byron responds to all as to D'Auvergne:

> *D'Auvergne.* [*aside to* Byron] We are undone!
> [*Exit* D'Auvergne]
> *Queen.*                                       What's that?
> *Byron.*          I heard him not.
> *Henry.*          Madame, y'are honour'd much that Duke Byron
>                        Is so observant: Some to cards with him. . . .
>
> (4.2.91–93)

Henry's irony ("so observant") begins a series of fine exchanges in which Byron, playing cards, is clumsily symbolic in his blunt military manner, while various court figures twist his words to omens of arrest and death. When these omens are fulfilled, Byron reacts like a trapped animal, sure that he will be immediately dispatched:

> For manhood sake
> Lend something to this poor forsaken hand;

For all my service let me have the honour
To die defending of my innocent self. . . .

(4.2.245–48)[28]

The dehumanization implicit here and alluded to throughout the act culminates in this painful analogy: "And take away my sword; / A proper point of force; ye had as good / Have robb'd me of my soul . . ." (4.2.280–82). *In extremis*, Byron begins to approach the truth of his long parabola. Just as he was the army's "soul" (*Conspiracy* 3.2.100–103), its best and quintessential part, so now Byron sees how much he has allowed his soul to depend upon props of physical and brute strength. This discovery, or concession, must precede the torment and resolution of the final act.

After nine acts of Byron's career, certain unresolved issues now appear plainly. Chapman has been playing a difficult game: in *The Conspiracy*, he engaged our sympathy for Byron through the hero's claims of injured merit, his misguided but valid criticism of politics, and (occasionally) his grand aspiration. In the opening of *The Tragedy*, we find Byron speaking and acting a similar double role: he makes valid satirical, even moral, points, while at the same time he betrays his king. Now, however, Chapman also gradually withdraws our sympathy from Byron by displaying the hero's petulance, his verbal excesses, his complaisant assent to flattery, and his animality.

While our interest in Byron and knowledge of him have been consistently great, it is only in the second play that Henry develops much beyond a rather stereotypical figure performing the expected hieratic ceremonies. The opening scene of *The Tragedy*, however, with its symmetrical echo of the first scene of *The Conspiracy* (a royal son desired and predicted; the infant Dauphin "baptized" by his father's sword) initiates Henry's move toward the center of dramatic, or at least political, interest. Henry always prays well (see *Tragedy* 4.2.63ff. or *Conspiracy* 5.2.85ff.), and his invocation of transcendental powers, the flowering of his role as God's representative (as in *Conspiracy* 5.2.20–84), mark how completely the balance of interest between the King and the hero will be redressed. With the greater attention to the King comes a severer criticism of his actions, his morals, and his claims to absolute ethical superiority. The masque, the use of La Fin, and Byron's two long speeches are the chief vehicles of this criticism.

At the beginning of the fifth act, then, Chapman must both maintain Henry's character (human, but kingly and resolute) and revivify our admiration for Byron. His solution is transfiguration and death. A changed Byron, one whose psychological and verbal links with the old are carefully noted, appears. He is no longer a great noble and a notable traitor, but first a human being attempting to comprehend death and then a great and reconciled hero confidently thrusting upward to heaven. This complex ebb and flow of sympathy and the frequent shifts of focus arise from Chapman's desire to anatomize kings and overproud subjects, to examine the effect of war and peace upon nations and individuals, and, finally, to create a tragic conflict of strength with strength in an ambiguous political world.

The first three scenes of this astonishing close show Byron "amaz'd at death" (5.3.186), responding now violently and brutally, now calmly and sanctimoniously, to his trial and condemnation. Vitry's long speech—almost a Websterian "character"—describes how Byron "disdains / To grace the prison with the slend'rest show / Of any patience" (5.1.109–11) and "as a bird, / Enter'd a closet,"

> wrathful beats his breast from wall to wall,
> Assaults the light, strikes down himself . . .
>
> . . . . . . . . . . .
>            . . . and with a savage will
> Frets, pines, and dies for former liberty:
> So fares the wrathful Duke. . . .
>            (5.1.118–19, 121–22, 127–29)[29]

Thus the Captain's reported "ostents" and Byron's promise to assume the lion's spirit produce "dumb rage," the sick fluttering of a man trapped, body and spirit.

At the trial, allusion to *blood* as both "anger" and "violence"[30] introduces the central tragic perception of the play:

> *Byron.* I grew so desperate that I found my spirit
>     Enrag'd to any act, and wish'd myself
>     Cover'd with blood.
> *Chancellor.*     With whose blood?
> *Byron.*             With mine own.
>            (5.2.105–7)

Before Byron unwittingly sums up that tragic perception, he discovers in aspiration his undoing:

>                What man is he
> That is so high but he would higher be?
> So roundly sighted, but he may be found
> To have a blind side, which by craft pursu'd,
> Confederacy, and simply trusted treason,

May wrest him past his Angel and his reason?

(5.2.168–73)

and

Sometimes the very gloss in any thing
Will seem a stain; the fault, not in the light,
Nor in the guilty object, but our sight.

(5.2.178–80)

A moment later, Byron concludes, "I did deserve too much; a pleurisy / Of that blood in me is the cause I die." His point is well and ironically taken: his aspiration—part of metaphoric "blood"—not his virtue has brought him to trial; the qualities that made a "mighty merit" have also perpetuated a "monstrous crime." Although he falls back momentarily from this enlightenment and still justifies himself as the victim of policy, Byron begins to see that "We have not any strength but weakens us" (5.3.193); or, as Aufidius says, "Rights by rights falter, strengths by strengths do fail."[31]

The trial scene is, appropriately, altogether one of the best in the play. As his death approaches, Byron penetrates closer and closer to recognizing his weakness and its inextricable union with his strengths; at the same time, he tries vainly to justify himself and to convict his accusers and his judges (5.3.15–52 and 179–84). Hard upon this defense and Byron's subsequent condemnation comes a comic vignette displaying Chapman's excellent dramatic sense, in sharp contrast to the relative failure of *The Conspiracy*'s final comic interlude. The hero's rash confidence in his suasive powers leads him to a mimic performance of the court-room scene. Epernon, who knows Byron's true danger, protests in horror, "For heaven's sake, good my lord!" (5.3.24). When the mockery is done, Epernon says, as the audience might, "He said not this, my lord, that I have heard." For the moment, confidence carries Byron beyond truth into a dreamworld where lawyers are not death dealing and he is not a traitor but an innocent safe enough to ridicule legal pedantry. Again, knowing Chapman's very Elizabethan distrust of lawyers (for example, *All Fools*, 4.1.227ff. in *Comedies*, p. 282), we see that curious doubleness in Byron's character and speech: what he says (about kings, courts, politics, lawyers) is generally true but tragically wrong in this specific situation. No mere disparity of knowledge ("dramatic irony") produces this split, which also controls minor character creation. Rather, Byron's character depends upon this tension, or this equivocation, and the entire world of policy is suffused with it.

After the lawyers have entered and delivered their judgment, Byron is "transport[ed]" by bitterness "beyond all colour and . . . proper judgment" (5.3.117–18) and alternately predicts a pardon and sophistically defends his refusal to ask mercy when it is offered. Five nobles remain on stage and comment on the spectacle they have witnessed. Epernon contributes a series of paradoxes on the contraries of human nature, including "We have not any strength but weakens us" and "Our knowledges do light us but to err," gnomic formulas that echo and re-echo Byron's dilemmas and discoveries in the play.[32] Soissons castigates Virtue and the Vidame defends "real Goodness"; their words recall the antithetical interpretations Monsieur and the Guise offer in *Bussy D'Ambois* 5.3. The Vidame's speech predicts certain features of the course that Byron's resolution will take:

> O real Goodness, if thou be a power,
> And not a word alone, in human uses,
> Appear out of this angry conflagration,
> Where this great captain, thy late temple, burns,
> And turn his vicious fury to thy flame
> From all earth's hopes mere gilded with thy fame:
> Let Piety enter with her willing cross,
> And take him on it; ope his breast and arms,
> To all the storms Necessity can breathe
> And burst them all with his embraced death.
>
> (5.3.205–14)

The two remaining speakers emphasize the moral degradation and the psychological disintegration they have seen in the hero.

In sentiment and dramatic purpose, these speeches are important to Chapman's design. No single opinion may unequivocally be called "the author's," nor do the speeches perform the usual function of the classical chorus—commonsensical analysis or exposition, expression of the community's religious or social assumptions, bewailing or praising on behalf of the folk. Each individual offers a partial view; none completely grasps or completely misses the issues and the nature of Byron's life. As fragments of a total vision that does not, perhaps cannot, exist in the drama, each comment reinforces Chapman's presentation of a world of fluid morality, of unlikely or unpredictable chains of cause and effect, a world, in fact, that may best be described (at least as it is shown through Byron's life) by paradoxes: strength and weakness, knowledge and error, fortune and virtue.

In the final scene, a new Byron—fitfully visible in his discoveries at the trial—gradually replaces the old. First intimations of this change appear as rage; Byron, still appalled at death and the manner of his death, shakes off the Bishop's unctuous "resign / Your sensual powers entirely to your soul" with

> Horror of death! Let me alone in peace.
> And leave my soul to me, whom it concerns;
> You have no charge of it; I feel her free:
> How she doth rouse and like a falcon stretch
> Her silver wings, as threatening Death with death;
> At whom I joyfully will cast her off.
>
> (5.4.26–31)

Here speaks an utterly changed man: still aristocratic—his soul a falcon—yet without the physical pride that led him to challenge combat against his detractors. He knows, but surpasses, priestly consolation:

> I know this body but a sink of folly,
> The ground-work and rais'd frame of woe and frailty,
> The bond and bundle of corruption,
> A quick corpse, only sensible of grief,
> A walking sepulchre, or household thief,
> A glass of air, broken with less than breath,
> A slave bound face to face to Death till death:
> And what say all you more?
>
> (lines 32–39)[33]

The earthly life of glory, battle, intrigue, and treason passes away as if a bad dream:

> I know, besides,
> That life is but a dark and stormy night
> Of senseless dreams, terrors, and broken sleeps;
> A tyranny, devising pains to plague
> And make man long in dying, racks his death;
> And Death is nothing; what can you say more?
>
> (lines 39–44)

Secure in his faith of salvation and triumph over death,

> I being a large globe, and a little earth,
> Am seated like earth, betwixt both the heavens,
> That if I rise, to heaven I rise; if fall,
> I likewise fall to heaven; what stronger faith
> Hath any of your souls? What say you more?
>
> (lines 45–49)

he remains vigorous and unyielding:

> Why lose I time in these things? Talk of knowledge!
> It serves for inward use. I will not die
> Like to a clergyman; but like the captain
> That pray'd on horseback, and with sword in hand,
> Threaten'd the sun, commanding it to stand;
> These are but ropes of sand.
>
> (lines 50–55)

Byron, often a hero of words, the hyperbolic equal of Alexander, cuts off his speech and the words of others: knowledge and fortitude are not to be expressed, but known and lived in isolation.

Finding his friends gone, Byron develops the *contemptus mundi* theme of his earlier speech and ends with a sentiment utterly foreign to his former self:

> Oh all the world forsakes me! Wretched world,
> Consisting most of parts that fly each other,
> A firmness breeding all inconstancy,
> A bond of all disjunction; like a man
> Long buried, is a man that long hath liv'd;
> Touch him, he falls to ashes: for one fault,
> I forfeit all the fashion of a man.
> Why should I keep my soul in this dark light,
> Whose black beams lighted me to lose my self?
> When I have lost my arms, my fame, my mind,
> Friends, brother, hopes, fortunes, and even my fury?
> O happy were the man could live alone,
> To know no man, nor be of any known!
>
> (5.4.62–74)[34]

Byron has changed in nothing more than a new self-awareness, which permits him to comprehend himself: "When I have lost . . . even my fury." The revelations of credulity and duplicity have not merely shunted Byron to a "simply trusted" hatred of man or of the world. He knows, and has the power to know, much more about himself than before. When the lawyers stipulate a public reading of Byron's sentence, he reluctantly concludes, "Read, if it must be, then, and I must talk" (line 85). He speaks, defending his honor rather than his innocence; almost to the play's end, Byron retains the heroic warrior's concern for personal and familial honor.

As he nears the block, Byron resolves the central image of his strength and the central tenet of his old ethic:

> He is at no end of his actions blest
> Whose ends will make him greatest, and not best;
> They tread no ground, but ride in air on storms
> That follow state, and hunt their empty forms;
> Who see not that the valleys of the world
> Make even right with the mountains, that they grow
> Green and lie warmer, and ever peaceful are,
> When clouds spit fire at hills and burn them bare;
> Not valleys' part, but we should imitate streams,
> That run below the valleys and do yield
> To every molehill, every bank embrace
> That checks their currents, and when torrents come,
> That swell and raise them past their natural height,
> How mad they are, and troubled! like low streams
> With torrents crown'd, are men with diadems.
>
> (5.4.144–58)

The river contending with the ocean or angrily overflowing its banks often appears in the two plays' imagery.[35] As he approaches death, Byron resolves the tension and violence of those images, as Henry did less completely when granting pardon in the first play (*Conspiracy* 5.2.69–78). Similarly, Byron's favorite equation of highest, greatest, and morally best now dissolves before the "new learning" taught by death.

What remains of a noble's sense of honor leads Byron to demand a violent death, a mimic battle-wound rather than the shame of execution. An anonymous soldier judges the hero with wisest sorrow:

> Now by thy spirit, and thy better Angel,
> If thou wert clear, the continent of France
> Would shrink beneath the burthen of thy death
> Ere it would bear it.
> .  .  .  .  .  .  .
>                                    I say well,
> And clear your justice: here is no ground shrinks;
> If he were clear it would; and I say more,
> Clear, or not clear, if he with all his foulness
> Stood here in one scale, and the king's chief minion
> Stood in another, here; put here a pardon,
> Here lay a royal gift; this, this, in merit
> Should hoise the other minion into air.
>
> (5.4.213–23)

His words answer Byron's frantic assertion ("All France shall feel an earthquake; with what murmur, / This world shrinks into chaos") and evoke the play's great final speech.

Begun in self-recognition, "This is some poor witness / That my desert might have outweigh'd my forfeit," the speech expands from the personal to the racial plane in a passage of almost Virgilian (or Horatian)[36] pathos—time's eternal cycle and man's brief life—and alludes to the statists for whom Byron would be a warning. Byron dies, commanding ever, ordering at once his execution and the flight of his soul, flung against death and up to heaven.

To many contemporaries, the historical Byron's death agony seemed indecently violent; the hero appeared to lack fortitude, or resignation, or both. The sudden emotional extremes attracted Chapman; indeed, he exaggerated the "contraries" coexisting in Byron and made them epitomize the hero's world. Put individually, Byron's life, like Bussy's, might be read as a conflict of Virtue, or Nature, with Fortune. Viewed more abstractly, however, Byron's life might exemplify the universe's puzzling, even frightening, refusal to submit to principle. Neither Byron nor his great antagonist, Henry IV, can be typed very easily. While Byron may be a malcontent traitor, he has equally been France's greatest military hero and a loyal servant through strenuous and unrewarding years. The "Most Christian" King dismayed (and worse) his English allies by "playing both ways with religion,"[37] and his use of La Fin, a man even Henry's friends despised, hardly earns assent, much less admiration, for the King's often pompous moralizing. When La Fin publicly accuses him, Byron vividly defines the principle the whole play has put in doubt. He summons all

> virtuous Powers in earth and heaven
> That have not put on hellish flesh and blood,
> From whence these monstrous issues are produc'd,
> That cannot bear, in execrable concord
> And one prodigious subject, contraries;
> Nor as the isle . . .
> Is sever'd from the world, can cut yourselves
> From the consent and sacred harmony
> Of life, yet live; of honour, yet be honour'd. . . .
>
> (5.2.136–44)

Byron's immediate point is that La Fin somehow manages to live against nature and in defiance of the "virtuous Powers." The speech also makes much more general assumptions, chiefly that virtues and contraries do not coexist: La Fin and his ilk are hellish flesh and blood, monstrosities and prodigies unimaginably compounded.

As the frequent images of flooding water suggest, coherence—physical and mental, emotional and theoretical—has been the play's continuous concern. Typically, external forces have given Byron his coherence, his self-definition, and his apparent consistency. Chapman created a situational man, one who depends upon circumstances for selfhood. As various external forces appear and struggle for Byron's loyalty, he divides himself, and each new "individual" reacts to a separate external demand. Peace is too complicated for Byron because it requires successive decisions, any one of which may compromise or question some other. While admitting his "intemperate speech," Byron plaintively claims, "reason ever did my deeds attend" (5.2.215–16), and his military actions do have a consistency, a logical rationale, that peacetime's more subtle pressures forbid. D'Auvergne wonderfully describes the court's instability. When the king's attitude changes, he says, the courtiers will all be

> Chang'd into water, that will instantly
> Give look for look, as if it watch'd to greet us;
> Or else for one they'll give us twenty faces,
> Like to the little specks on sides of glasses.
>
> (4.1.72–75)

Policy and the king give a courtier many faces, but Byron lacks even that frail control over his own shifting responses. Nonetheless, he tries to manufacture a face to suit each single look he receives.

Eventually, of course, Byron fails to shift fast enough to meet a very mobile reality. In prison, he rages "in walks and words; but in his looks / He comments all and prints a world of books" (5.1.134–35). The man who proclaimed a world and a self founded upon singleness and virtue's power to defeat contraries finally personifies all that world's divergent, centrifugal variety. He can discover no principle, of psychology or politics or philosophy, that organizes (and hence explains) the world and his experiences in it. Instead, it is a "firmness breeding all inconstancy": this sure and firm set world has no consistency but inconsistency; its only union is disjunction. Principles of judgment, like principles of perception, become radically debatable in *Byron's Tragedy*, and the hero dies a monument to his world's incoherence. If the hero seems uncentered and fragmented, the force opposed to him offers no clearer principle. Henry's attitudes and ideals have also been so deeply questioned that Byron's jibe appears just: "Like th' ancient gods / Are modern kings . . . since they pass'd ["wretched men"] in power, surpass'd in right" (5.3.59–60, 63). Too often, the king's apparent beliefs prove bastards to his heart's truth. Playing one force against another, juxtaposing one explanation with another, Chapman created a tragedy that challenges tragedy's principles and even its existence.

In both plays, Chapman employs art and ideas about art to develop his thematic interests and his conception of Byron's character. Of course, the two purposes cannot be neatly separated. Yet the "masque of virtues" substantiates some of Byron's claims by removing them from the interplay of motive, the struggle of charge and countercharge. While the masque does not exculpate Byron, it establishes as objectively as possible the moral and political flaws he attacks. The "history of Catiline" penetrates Byron's own psychology and provides a moral index of the hero's egotism and his ability to distort perception. Later, his remarks on tapestry monarchs and true subjects reveal how he continues to ignore or redefine art's proffered truth and insight. Sitting for his portrait or grandiloquently imagining a mountain reshaped in his own image, Byron perilously subjects nature to the sway of a transient and corrupted artistry. The *Conspiracy*'s final reconciliation temporarily rectified Byron's "imaginous fancy." "Antic vizards" fell away. His concluding frenzy, however, shows him once again splintered and refracted like the images Renaissance optical experimenters delighted in creating: "twenty faces, / Like to the little specks on sides of glasses."[38] As I suggested, Byron's character and Henry's court make perception and judgment unstable and shifting. Art's eternal veracity threatens to change "into water, that will instantly / Give look for look . . . Or else for one . . . give . . . twenty." This threat—an art that magnifies human self-conceit—becomes real in *Chabot*, and that reality destroys Chapman's artistic enterprise.

# 4

# "Free and Fast": The Perspectives of
# *Chabot, Admiral of France*

*Chabot, Admiral of France*, probably Chapman's last play,[1] unifies its dramatic action and its intellectual concerns in ways the earlier tragedies often did not. While the play's authorship and philosophical framework have been much debated, the critics who have examined the play itself discover unexpected riches. K. M. Burton, for instance, finds "no superimposed dramatic pattern; the pattern arises naturally out of the dramatist's conception of the manner in which evil penetrates the political structure"; and Takashi Sasayama claims that "every incident in *Chabot* is dramatically significant in clarifying the theme and making for the progress of the plot."[2]

Although *Chabot* may be superior to the earlier tragedies in some ways, there are many family resemblances. Once again, the central characters are a great noble and his monarch; once again, the hero violates prevailing social and political mores; once again, the hero defends himself against enemies who regard him as just another example of familiar aristocratic egotism and extravagance; once again, feuding politicians attempt to use or destroy the hero for their own advantage; once again, the conflict forces the monarch either to pardon or condemn the hero; once again, the hero disputes the king's authority to pardon. These striking similarities help to locate the play firmly in the canon, but some remarkable changes have occurred.[3] Francis I, for example, receives far more attention than Henry III (in *Bussy D'Ambois*) or even Henry IV (in the *Byron* plays). The issue over which monarch and hero struggle is now both one of personality (as it was in the earlier plays) and also one of principle. Although Chabot is better than his fellows, he lacks the glittering difference from other men that made Bussy and Byron so gloriously and dangerously self-confident. Chapman shifts his attention away from the hero's personal qualities and emphasizes the values—now purely social and political values—for which the hero stands. Thus, when Chabot defends himself with dignified eloquence, he often justifies not only his own nature but his principles as well.

As Admiral of France, Chabot holds the highest legal office below the King, and Chapman uses questions of justice to focus his other dramatic interests. Although various courtiers, chief among them Montmorency, hope to depose Chabot and replace him in the King's favor, the original conflict between king and noble turns on a legal "bill" that Chabot considers so unjust that he tears it up. To Francis, this intransigence seems whimsical or worse, and he quickly stakes his personal prestige on forcing Chabot to approve the suit. Once the King shifts from his proper role as ultimate judge to irresistible (because political) advocate, Chabot's very sense, not only of his own integrity but also of the King's ideal justice, forces him further into opposition and, of course, into greater danger. This opening situation recalls Thomas Kyd's *The Spanish Tragedy*, where another high legal official finds himself trapped by his double allegiance to the law and to the just state embodied in the monarch. Yet Chapman's play has a crucial difference from Kyd's, for there is, at least initially, no question of Francis's guilty complicity or criminal indifference. Rather, the King and Admiral are so close that Chabot willingly accepts Montmorency as a friend because the King wills it: the reconciliation needs "none / To encourage or confirm it but my own / Love and allegiance to your sacred counsel" (1.1.128–30). Again and again, Chabot returns to a fundamental point. His love for Francis and for France require him to love justice. Approving an illegal act "betrays" / The honour and the chief life of the King, / Which is his justice" (2.2.70–72). Thus, like Chapman's other tragedies, *Chabot* does concern a principle that the world denies or ignores or denigrates. Now, however, that principle has been woven into the personal relations between the two central characters. The varying health or illness of that relation makes the play's intellectual core part of its dramatic conflict.

Chapman places the two men in a world which, like Hieronimo's in *The Spanish Tragedy*, appears to be a "mass of public wrongs." Corruption in high places everywhere takes advantage of its power, and consequently any great man who acts honorably is hated and envied. Corruption has spread so far that few courtiers, even Francis himself, can seriously believe Chabot's goodness, or the goodness of any man who holds high station. As Bussy said, "authority here / Goes with corruption; something like some States, / That back worst men" (*Bussy* 4.1.38–40). "Worst men," men like the Chancellor or the Advocate or even the pliable Montmorency, fill the court and control the King's justice. Their ambition and their envy create an ugly, demeaning world, fundamentally hostile to any good, individual or institutional.

When Francis finally decides to coerce Chabot's agreement to the legal suit, he ominously distinguishes between intrinsic merit and the social benefits that the crown bestows:

> the persons that
> Your passionate heat calls into question
> Are great and many, and may wrong in you
> Your rights of kind, and dignities of fortune.
>
> (2.3.19–22)

Although the Admiral casually dismisses concern for courtly status, other characters frequently mention what an Elizabethan would call Chabot's great "port." Chabot himself acknowledges his high place when he concludes that both he and Montmorency "may be enrich'd, and raise our fortunes . . . past the height of others" (1.2.47, 49). Indeed, Chabot's display seems the only valid charge brought against him at his trial:

> . . . how this great and mighty fortune has exalted him to pride is apparent . . . in his contempt and scorn of the subject, his vast expenses in buildings, his private bounties, above royal, to soldiers and scholars . . . the number of domestic attendants, an army of grasshoppers and gay butterflies . . . his caroches shining with gold . . . he is of late so transcendently proud that men must be his mules and carry him up and down . . . till their chines crack with the weight of his insupportable pride. . . . (3.2.147–62)

Clearly, Chabot does not disdain the customary perquisites of his office. His difficulties arise not so much because he is better than other men (although he is), but because he looks like one of them. Unable to believe that Chabot is special, or as special as he claims to be, his detractors and his king assume he is essentially no different from others in their experience. Chabot's father-in-law summarizes this attitude, basically guilt by association: "Being now aton'd [with Montmorency], you must be one in all, / One in corruption . . ." (1.2.42–43).

Chabot recognizes the existence of the kind of "great man" the King mistakenly thinks him to be. His allusion to men raised above their fellows is only part of this recognition; he also knows mankind's prevailing hatred and envy. Chabot uses the very corruption of most men to defend his own confidence and uprightness:

How mad were I to rave thus in my wounds,
Unless my known health, felt in these forc'd issues,
Were sound and fit; and that I did not know
By most true proofs that to become sincere
With all men's hates doth far exceed their loves,
To be, as they are, mixtures of corruption;
And that those envies that I see pursue me
Of all true actions are the natural consequents
Which being my object and my resolute choice,
Not for my good but yours, I will have justice.

(2.3.49–58)

Chabot repeatedly answers Francis's arguments with variations of his favorite boast: "I serve . . . you . . . but for yourself, / *And* that good in your rule that justice does you" (2.3.8–10; my italics); "I seek . . . justice only, / The fount and flood both of your strength and kingdom's" (2.3.15–16).[4] The fundamental conflict is clear: Francis's mental "set" treats, or threatens to treat, Chabot as just another great noble; Chabot resolutely asserts his own vital participation in royal justice and hence in the state's existence. The struggle appears subtly in such words as *will, passion,* and *soul.* When Chabot concludes, "I will have justice," Francis immediately toys with the word *will.* He cannot see Chabot's attitude as anything but passionate obstinacy, compounded with insolent self-possession: "Is your will so strong / Now against mine, your power being so weak, / Before my favour gave them both their forces?" (2.3.59–61). When the King seeks to "spur" Chabot's "dulness" with an account of how he has received "greater dignities than any," Francis hopes that the threat of removing royal protection (and, potentially, Chabot's honors) will revive the Admiral's duty to the source of power and status. For all his pains, Francis is finally greeted with Chabot's assertion: "You merit not of me for benefits, / More than myself of you for services" (2.3.94–95).

Metaphoric development of the words *soul* and *passion, blood* and *resolve,* further delineates the two men's attitudes while emphasizing their mutual misapprehension:

<blockquote>

*King.*     Was ever heard so fine a confidence?
             Must it not prove presumption? And can that
             'Scape bracks and errors in your search of law?
             I prithee weigh yet with more soul the danger,
             And some less passion.

*Chabot.*                        Witness, heaven, I cannot,
             Were I dissolv'd, and nothing else but soul.

*King.*     [*aside.*] Beshrew my blood, but his resolves amaze me.—

(2.3.116–22)

</blockquote>

Francis uses *soul* to mean the rational faculty, untainted by what he considers the appetitive corruption of Chabot's *passion* (here, misguided confidence). The King's plea is simple. A rational man must recognize that "dignities of fortune" are insecure, may well have been won with some wrongdoing, and may only be retained through acknowledging the source of those rewards. To "weigh with more soul the danger" means to recognize that one is no different from other great men, equally subject to chance and (perhaps the same thing) equally dependent upon royal favor. Chabot uses *soul* in a strictly moral sense, as the highest ethical as well as rational faculty. He asserts that he is free from passionate corruption: if he were dissolved and nothing else but soul, he would still act as he does now.[5] Francis threatens a very different kind of dissolution, the destruction of a corrupt "great man" by Change. He cannot understand Chabot's different and higher use of the word.[6] The response, "Beshrew my blood, but his resolves amaze me," continues the play of important metaphysical concepts. Francis wittily condemns his own *blood* (the source of passion, envy, and corruption) and thus, perhaps in mock humility, associates himself with the psychological condition of the "great man" he still thinks Chabot to be. When he uses the word *resolves*, it has a double meaning: "determination" and "dissolution into soul."[7] Eventually, Francis will concede that his anger originated in "those distempers that inform" his "blood and spirits" (5.3.95–96). *The Teares of Peace* summarizes Chabot's position: Learning directs, Chapman writes, "Reason in such an Art, as that it can / Turne blood to soule, and make both, one calme man" (lines 558–59; *Poems*, p. 185).

The King expounds his own sense of reason. For him, reason means knowing the world of corruption and intrigue, chance and transience, which forms the matrix of the entire play. Reason shows the King that "he that can use actions with the vulgar, / Must needs embrace the same effects." Throughout his speech, however, runs the unresolved dissonance between his perception of "a man so rare / In one thing" and his practical experience of wealthy Chabot, "in the broad highway, / The common dust up in your eyes beating" (2.3.127–30). This double view of Chabot originally appeared in Francis's distinction between "rights of kind" (Chabot's natural integrity) and his "dignities of fortune" (secular honors dependent upon the king). The metaphoric play with *reason* and *soul* and the suggestion of Biblical echoes in the "broad highway"[8] make these exchanges central to any interpretation that finds Chabot presumptuous and ignorant of postlapsarian man and society.[9] A major obstacle to this interpretation is that Chabot *does* recognize both the world's evil and its power to destroy him:

> I were mad
> Directly, sir, if I were yet to know
> Not the sure danger, but the certain ruin
> Of men shot into law from kings' bent brow,
> There being no dream from the most muddy brain
> Upon the foulest fancy, that can forge
> More horror in the shadows of mere fame,
> Than can some lawyer in a man expos'd
> To his interpretation by the king.

> (2.3.142–50)

Chabot's firm defence of his own merits seems the final insolence and furthest reach of ingratitude. Francis, enraged, dismisses him: "Perish thy love and faith, and thee for ever!" The King immediately begins the legal proceedings he had threatened. As he does so, he draws a parallel between his angry fear of Chabot and the passions of "a distracted king . . . in just fear of his assaulted life" (2.3.211–12). Seen through the King's distorting passion, Chabot's integrity threatens the state.

Francis's chief motive is his anger at Chabot's "insolence" (4.1.219). Superficial similarities between Chabot and "great men" lead Francis to think that "bracks and errors" must exist in Chabot's "search of law." Moreover, the King envies Chabot, this "man of confidence," and envies his public stature: "To want my pity, who breaks forth like day, / Takes up all people's eyes and admiration?" (4.1.195, 20–21). Francis wants to humiliate Chabot, not condemn him. When (to the King's surprise) Chabot is actually found guilty, Francis's goal shifts from showing Chabot the insecurity of worldly status to gaining a virtuous triumph:

> I joy
> This boldness is condemn'd, that I may pardon,
> And therein get some ground in his opinion,
> By so much bounty as saves his life;
> And methinks that, weigh'd more, should sway the balance
> 'Twixt me and him, held by his own free justice.

> (4.1.166–71)

Clearly, while Francis respects Chabot, he also competes with him.[10]

The King's egocentric desire to have Chabot admit the royal bounty, and his readiness to trifle with the law in order to force the point home, explain the Admiral's otherwise foolish belief that the King but tests him. Going to the trial, Chabot can still say that Francis "by exposing / Me to this trial, means to render me / More happy to his subjects and himself" (3.1.12–14; note the allusion to public antagonism). The French historian Pasquier, Chapman's source, seems to agree that Francis simply wished to humble Chabot as a punishment for insolence. Speaking to the great men among his readers, Pasquier advises them to avoid, at all costs, a public trial if they should fall into disfavor: it is both humiliating and dangerous.[11] Still, to say that Francis wants to humiliate Chabot does not fully explain the King's attitude toward the problem of the great, good man. The play's world also postulates an accepted experience to which Chabot, Francis, the Chancellor, the Queen, and the courtiers all appeal: men in high place always have something to hide, must always fear public exposure, and hence should always depend upon royal favor to protect them from such exposure. The ambiguity and delicacy of Francis's role arise from the fact that he is the first person to understand that Chabot might represent a purity almost unimaginable in court.

Only such a mixture of beliefs about Chabot, together with inchoate and conflicting desires either to confirm his value by trial or to punish his insolence, can explain Francis's genuine surprise at the verdict and his swift attempt to salvage an ascendancy over Chabot through pardoning him. Equally, the King's amazement demonstrates his trust in French justice. When Francis says, "But he [Chabot] to do this [censure others for his own faults], more deceives my judgment / Than all the rest whose nature I have sounded" (4.1.150–51), he leaves no doubt that he once trusted Chabot's justice almost entirely, and that now, equally, he has no doubt of his own judges' decision. Attempting to pardon Chabot, Francis receives an even greater shock: "you cannot pardon me, sir . . . It is a word carries too much relation / To an offence, of which I am not guilty . . . I need no pardon" (4.1.235–37, 240). The gesture, of course, recalls Bussy's similar refusal, and Chabot's continued "prodiges" outrage the King:

> Have not our laws
> Pass'd on his actions; have not equal judges
> Certified his arraignment and him guilty
> Of capital treason; and yet do I hear
> Chabot accuse all these, and quit himself?
>
> (4.1.257–61)

The scene goes on to provide both anagnorisis and peripeteia: Chabot's refusal of pardon causes Francis to suspect that he has misjudged both Chabot's integrity and that of his courts: "I do incline / To think I am abus'd, my laws betray'd / And wrested to the purpose of my judges" (4.1.285–87). Summoned to the presence, the royal judges quickly admit that Chabot was convicted only "For threats by my Lord Chancellor on the bench / Affirming that your Majesty would have it / Made capital treason" (4.1.329–31). "This inversion / Of all . . . loyalties and true deserts" staggers the King, and the discovery of the "poisonous outrage" supports Chabot's contention that he *is* French justice. At least, without him, there is no open justice in France. True to the quicksilver nature that had earlier made him jump to pardon Chabot, the King now draws a rather pat "lesson":

> that whatsoever
> Charge or commission judges have from us,
> They ever make their aim ingenuous justice,
> Not partial for reward or swelling favour;
> To which if your king steer you, spare to obey.
>
> (4.1.442–46)

Even this flawed recognition comes too late. The trial has broken Chabot's heart—"the greatest souls are thus oft wounded" (5.1.8)— and the Admiral is dying.

Irving Ribner has called Chabot's tragedy his "education, for he must learn that such an ideal ["of perfect, unwavering justice"] is impossible in an imperfect world."[12] The true education of the play is more personal, a discovery of the nature of human relations and not man's relation to the divine, to principle, or to the Fall. At his trial, Chabot appeals "to the King's knowledge of me / How far I am in soul from such a rebel" (3.2.134–35). Cleared at last, he claims "I never had a fear of the King's justice" (4.1.383); when he continues, "And yet I know not what creeps o'er my heart, / And leaves an ice beneath it," the sensation of mortality does not come from a lost faith in justice.[13] Rather, Chabot has felt the wound to his honor, his loyalty, his proud faith in his importance to Francis and through Francis to royal justice. As Chabot's father-in-law tells the King, "though he [Chabot] be right in fame and your opinion, / He thinks you were unkind" (5.1.79–80). The strong connotations of *unkind* ("unnatural") make the larger point: Francis disrupts the natural, human relations between king and noble. Although the King quickly recovers his faith (his doubt, after all, was passionate and transitory), his loyal servant cannot so easily recoup.

When the dying Chabot relates his "crime," he describes the King's action very gently:

> But his justice then,
> That would not spare whom his own love made great,
> But gave me up to the most cruel test
> Of judges, for some boldness in defence

Of my own merits and my honest faith to him,
Was rare, past example.

(5.3.78–83)

The speech does not reveal a tragic or pessimistic, much less a new, sense that there is no justice in the world. Chabot does not mention that he stood up for justice. Instead, he echoes Francis: the subject was too bold before his king. Although Chabot claims that thoughts of the king are "balm enough to cure / A thousand wounds" (5.3.73–74), Francis offers an appropriate remedy much too late:

Give me thy heart, my dear, my honest Chabot;
And yet in vain I challenge that; 'tis here
Already in my own, and shall be cherish'd
With care of my best life; [no] violence
Shall ravish it from my possession;
Not those distempers that infirm my blood
And spirits shall betray it to a fear.

(5.3.90–96)

Francis now understands the union between the Admiral's sense of justice and his fidelity to the monarch: "He speaks the funeral of my crown that prophesies" Chabot's death (5.3.109). Since Chabot does die, we must in some sense agree that the kingdom dies with him. Chabot's final prayer assures us that his death has a private and personal significance far more than an ideological or religious one: "May all you trust have no less faith than Chabot!" (5.3.201). The play portrays the corruption of human justice, but Chabot's death cannot be admitted as evidence. His death shows that corruption reaches even the honorable bonds between king and servant, a discovery more painful to Chapman's hero than any Christian recognition of the fallen world's pervasiveness and the need for salvation through mercy.

For the Chancellor and the others who plot to replace the Admiral with the more pliant Montmorency, Francis's passionate "distempers" provide a nominally legal way to crush Chabot. Through the chinks in law and royal order caused by Francis's passion creep vermin bearing a politic doctrine of ambition and hypocrisy. When Montmorency hesitates to break his sworn friendship for Chabot, the Secretary assures him that "conscience" is "a name to fright, and terrify young statists":

the league that you have vow'd of friendship
In a true understanding not confines you,
But makes you boundless; turn not edge at such
A liberty, but look to your own fortune;

. . . . . . . . . . . .
Friendship is but a visor, beneath which
A wise man laughs to see whole families
Ruin'd, upon whose miserable pile
He mounts to glory. Sir, you must resolve
To use any advantage.

(1.1.221, 228–31, 234–38)

The world such men as the Secretary and Chancellor and Treasurer have made and the world in which their shifts and policies allow them to succeed is the world where "even virtues are made crimes," the world that "will not patiently / Endure the due rise of a virtuous man" (1.1.29, 9–10).

Chabot and Francis both concede the existence of this world: Chabot uses "what everyone knows" about the world to argue the truth of his own self-confidence. Francis uses the same common sense perception to convince himself that Chabot cannot in fact be so good as he claims, since no one else has ever been. This matrix of judgments and of convictions about life fails to dominate the play so long as its most pernicious expression belongs to the Chancellor and his ilk. Francis will perhaps be less ready to doubt honest men and to intervene in the operation of justice once he has learned the full measure of Chabot's faith. Unfortunately, this is not true. When the Queen and Montmorency hesitate to tell Francis of Chabot's illness, the King immediately assumes that they continue to envy the Admiral (5.1.46–50, 53–58). Francis's mistake shows not only that he cannot believe that Chabot might have converted others, but also the pervasive influence of an ambitious and envious world, hating virtue and consisting of politicians' supple "cheverel minds" (1.1.193).

The poison of this world spreads throughout the play's close. Francis continues his vacillating course. Having at last established Chabot's innocence, the King abruptly charges the Chancellor with corruption and orders a second trial. Originally, the King's passionate regard for his station and disregard for his personal importance to justice permitted the rival politicians their opportunity to attack Chabot. Now, however, his hatred of the Chancellor leads to overt interference in the course of justice—the very interference the Chancellor threatened at Chabot's trial. The King claims he has learned a lesson and warns his judges to treat the Chancellor fairly: "Urge what can *in justice* be against him"; "All that *due course of law* against him can / Charge"; "nothing urg'd *but justly*" (4.1.397, 414–15, 440; my italics). Alongside these remarks run others much more prejudicial and, in the strictest interpretation, self-serving. Francis calls the Chancellor's motives "impious rage," his deeds, a "riot on our laws and corrupt actions" and a "poisonous outrage," and the man himself, "this wretch," "this viper," "this polluted Chancellor." These vivid phrases, however true, are neither temperate nor unbiased. With Francis's own example before them, the judges can scarcely obey their King's "lesson." Speaking of the Chancellor's "malice show'd / Upon the Admiral," one judge says:

> please your lordships to remember, that
> Was *specially commended* by the King,
> As being most blemish to his royal person
> And the free justice of his state.
>
> (5.2.4–5, 7–10; my italics)

Even now, the King, a man of "troubled blood," cannot avoid meddling in French justice. The King admits he is an accessory before the fact:

> thus am I by his [the Chancellor's] malicious arts
> A party render'd, and most tyrannous spur
> To all the open course of his base envies,
> A forcer of my judges, and a thirst
> Of my nobility's blood, and all by one
> I trusted to make clear my love of justice.
>
> (4.1.342–47)

Although it was a fault to trust the Chancellor, Francis occasionally seems to transfer the responsibility for Chabot's trial to the Chancellor alone: the Chancellor's "fury" pursued Chabot, his "malice" made "royal freedom and empire . . . servants" (4.1.436, 407–8). In fact, only the King's "fury" permitted the trial in the first place. Two phrases have ominous overtones. The King's charge to the judges ends, "Employ your justice on this Chancellor" (4.1.412), suggesting that justice may be "employed," made a tool, just as it had in Chabot's trial. Another phrase reveals Francis's defensive and self-justifying motives. To his judges he says, "be you all that sate on him [Chabot] compurgators / Of me against this false judge [the Chancellor]" (4.1.437–38). By "compurgators," Francis may mean "fellow purgers," but that meaning would, it seems, be peculiar to Chapman. In legal jargon, a "compurgator" is "a witness to character who swore along with the person accused, in order to the acquittal of the latter"; more generally, the word means "one who testifies to or vindicates another's innocence, veracity, or accuracy; one who vouches for, or clears from any charge."[14] Chapman apparently sought the ambiguity of the King's asking his judges to testify to his own righteousness.

The Treasurer, playing his own game and intent upon protecting his own career, remarks that the Advocate's willingness to prosecute the man he had proclaimed a model judge "must imply a strange volubility in . . . tongue or conscience" (5.2.58–59). That worthy's answer makes clear the immoral source of "truth," or of some truth, in French society: while in office, "although . . . internally and privately . . . guilty of bribery of justice," a man "in public . . . is an innocent and upright judge"; "Once removed from his place by . . . the King," however, "we are . . . to forget what he hath been, and without partiality . . . lay him open to the world, a counterfeit and corrupt judge" (5.2.69–79). This explanation recalls Francis's threat to Chabot: powerful men require powerful friends. The Chancellor's office, gained through royal favor, protects him from the law; once that favor is withdrawn, the office slips away as well. The moral basis of right and wrong, true testimony and false, rests ultimately on the King's pleasure or displeasure, expressed here through status in the state.

The Advocate, or Proctor-General,[15] continues to corrupt French justice. His "noise of words" at Chabot's trial inflated any possible crime the Admiral could have committed. When called for an explanation, he tells Francis he merely followed a superior's orders:

> It was my allegiance, sir; I did enforce
> But by the directions of your Chancellor;
> It was my office to advance your cause
> Gainst all the world, which when I leave to execute,
> Flay me, and turn me out a most raw advocate.
>
> (4.1.390–94)

It is difficult to know what is most contemptible about this speech: its hypocrisy, its transfer of guilt, or the ugly pun on *raw*, with its suggestion that a less seasoned advocate might have considered justice rather than simply obeying instructions. When the Chancellor's turn comes, the Advocate abandons him without sentiment and promises Francis

> I
> Will play my law prize; never fear it, sir.
> He shall be guilty of what you please. I am studied
> In him, sir: I will squeeze his villanies,
> And urge his acts . . . home. . . .
>
> (4.1.399–403)

Some of the ironies here and in the Chancellor's speeches probably derive from the common Elizabethan and Jacobean literary hatred of lawyers. Nonetheless, we realize that the *form* of Chabot's trial and of the Chancellor's is the same. Only the names of the guilty have been changed. Thus, when the Advocate boasts that he will "play" his "law prize," his judicial function—as T. M. Parrott notes—becomes a public contest for some prize or wager. Trials do not reveal guilt or innocence, only the participants' satisfactory manipulation of a system. The Chancellor, too, was "a man studied" in his judicial victim (4.1.307); the second trial unnecessarily confirms that the Advocate's tongue serves not justice but the King's will.

As the lawyers' *playing* with legal form and the callous pun on *raw* imply, art has become corrupt in *Chabot*'s world. The earlier tragedies showed how art might serve as a pattern of experience sometimes united with, sometimes opposed to, the pattern of history. Art represented and valorized Hero's and Leander's love; art allowed the poet to condemn unceremonious love and magnify true love's spirit into eternal pattern. Later, the "history of Catiline," Byron's picture, and his illogical playing with artistic theory all served as a moral index, a significant glimpse of the false artistry, false image, and false pattern that constitute Byron's self-conception. Henry IV himself appears less admirable when the masque in *Byron's Tragedy* formulates his court's unsavory qualities in an extraexperiential art work. These uses of art have almost disappeared from *Chabot*. Instead, political manipulators and Francis in his least honorable moments subvert art for their own purposes.

Given Chapman's high conception of poetry, the ugliest example of art's direct misuse appears in the Proctor-General's attack during Chabot's trial. Praising Chancellor Poyet, he says:

> . . . and yet I may worthily too insist and prove that no grace hath been so large and voluminous as this, that he [Francis] hath appointed such upright judges at this time, and the chief of this Triumvirie, our Chancellor, by name Poyet, which deriveth from the Greek his etymology, from *Poyein*, which is, to make, to create, to invent matter that was never extant in nature; from whence also is the name and dignity of *Poeta*—which I will not insist upon in this place, although I am confident his lordship wanteth no faculty in making of verses. (3.2.5–14)

Even as it obeys Cicero's advice that the advocate praise the court, this speech ridicules itself through redundance, pomposity, and the crowning undignified tag about the Chancellor's poetic skills. Internal ridicule hardly redresses the balance, because the Proctor-General has sheared away the true "name and dignity of *Poeta*." While Chapman may glance at Horace's *Ars Poetica* ("to invent matter that was never extant in nature"), the Proctor-General's simple definition of poetry flatly contradicts the playwright's belief that fiction owes its truth to a higher nature. Poetic fury enters a transcendent, truer world, incomparably superior to this one. Manipulation, not inspiration, reigns here. For Poyet, the Proctor-General, the men of politics generally, even Francis and often Chabot, the court world is the only world. To survive and to succeed here requires incessant remaking and incessant change—of words, of "visors," and of the principles they conceal.

Art no longer detects falsity and reveals truth; it has become the very source of corruption. The Proctor-General's false etymology is a form of pun and permits his terrible misappropriation of the maker's status. While Chapman could pun as crudely as any contemporary and also sometimes used the pun for very serious meanings ("worthless," for example, in *Bussy*, 5.3.157), *Chabot*'s puns all seem firmly linked with perverse pattern and corrupt persuasion. Well before Dryden's jibe ("the lowest and most grovelling kind of wit"), puns were much debated because they were so open to false suggestion and illicit validation of immoral deeds and goals. Henry Peacham's *Garden of Eloquence* counsels: "This figure ought to be sparingly used, and especially in grave and weightie causes. . . . Also heede ought to be taken of whome it is used, and against whom it is applied."[16] The Chancellor confirms Peacham's caution when he encourages Montmorency with an evilly persuasive pun:

> our soul motion is affirm'd
> To be, like heavenly natures', circular;
> And circles being call'd ambitious lines,
> We must, like them, become ambitious ever,
> And endless in our circumventions. . . .
>
> (1.1.188–92)

The Chancellor plays upon the Latin root of "ambitious"—*ambio, ambire,* to go around, to surround—and then introduces the standard idea of a circle as an endless line. "Circumventions" neatly completes the verbal ambush. This small example cannot be dismissed as twisted logic or false etymology and then discarded along with the speech's earlier perversions of Aristotle's "animal politicum" and Plato's conception of the soul. Instead, this verbal reshaping contributes to art's endemic perversion within the play. Attacks on words and linguistic norms mirror attacks on principles and morals; indeed, the one promotes the other. So, too, pervasive corruption of art and poetry reflects a more general moral corruption.

Chabot's trial is the all-embracing example of perverse art. To detect that perversion, we must remember the analogy between poetry and patterned, meaningful experience that served Chapman so well in *Hero and Leander*. Chabot's accusers impose false patterns upon experience and evidence. Legal, rhetorical, and logical artifice all conceal the truth and offer a meretricious interpretation of life: "All your great law and learning are but words" (2.2.81). Here art does not penetrate life's various confusions to poetry's goal, "not truth, but things like truth" (Epistle Dedicatory, *The Revenge of Bussy D'Ambois*). Flexible conscience and malleable principle force the commitment to paronomasia, to false invocations of the "name and dignity of *Poeta*," and to spurious pattern.

At either end of the play stand the only examples of art used positively. One is Chabot's own allegory describing his experiences:

> The engine is not seen that wounds . . . [me]
> Past all the remedy of art or time,
> The flatteries of court, of fame, or honours:
> Thus in the summer a tall flourishing tree,
> Transplanted by a strong hand, with all her leaves
> And blooming pride upon her, makes a show
> Of Spring, tempting the eye with wanton blossom;
> But not the sun, with all her amorous smiles,
> The dews of morning, or the tears of night,
> Can root her fibres in the earth again,
> Or make her bosom kind to growth and bearing;
> But the tree withers; and those very beams
> That once were natural warmth to her soft verdure,
> Dry up her sap, and shoot a fever through
> The bark and rind, till she becomes a burthen
> To that which gave her life; so Chabot, Chabot—
>
> (5.3.49–64)

Although Chabot fails to apply his dark conceit, the meaning is clear: the trial has "transplanted" him. After his trial, although restored to the king's favor (the tree's return to earth, water, and sun), Chabot has lost his confident personal relation with Francis and his proud, self-referring belief in his judicial importance. The changes are invisible; the circumstances appear to be the same; the consequences are opposite. Once tried, or transplanted, man and tree become "a burthen / To that which gave . . . life." More interesting than this explication, however, is the process it represents: Chabot's "allegory" actually verges on being an emblem. Like many another character—Bussy, for example, and Tamyra, and Byron—Chabot chooses this static, slightly mysterious art form as a means of personal expression and self-interpretation. Chapman often employs extended comparisons, epic similes and the like, but when this habit appears in describing a character, it edges the character toward emblem, or hieroglyph, or some other static art work like Hero's scarf (*Hero and Leander* 4.37–121). The emblematic character thus seeks to understand experience through art's mediation, and those who seek to interpret the character and his meanings must proceed as if interpreting an art work.

This situation appears strikingly in the play's other positive use of art. Offering his "true censure" of Chabot's "general worth, / Virtue and judgment," Allegre regards his master as an example of anamorphic art. To understand Chabot, to discern what Allegre calls his "main form," requires an act of artistic interpretation:

> As of a picture wrought to optic reason,
> That to all passers-by seems, as they move,
> Now woman, now a monster, now a devil,
> And till you stand and in a right line view it,
> You cannot well judge what the main form is:
> So men, that view him [Chabot] but in vulgar passes,
> Casting but lateral or partial glances
> At what he is, suppose him weak, unjust,
> Bloody and monstrous; but stand free and fast
> And judge him by no more than what you know
> Ingenuously and by the right laid line
> Of truth, he truly will all styles deserve
> Of wise, just, good; a man both soul and nerve.
>
> (1.1.68–80)

As Peter Ure explains, Allegre alludes to the small Elizabethan paper constructions, or graphic art works, that seem to represent all sorts of fantastic or meaningless shapes unless viewed precisely aright.[17] Chapman's typical equation of more profound understanding with the correct physical perception of art underlies the whole analogy. To interpret the man is to interpret an art work. Comprehending both the "picture wrought to optic reason" and Chabot's true nature requires that we stand "free and fast." His static freedom requires the same of us.

Allegre continues the dichotomy between movement (moral instability, false understanding) and rest (fixed principle, just comprehension) when he criticizes Montmorency for being "wrought on with the counsels and opinions / Of other men" (1.1.84–85). He diverges from the Admiral, who is "not flexible, nor won / To move one scruple"; shaped from without, the Constable "explores not so sincerely [as Chabot] / The course he runs" (1.1.86–87, 89–90). Without straining Chapman's metaphor, one may justly see Chabot as the play's fixed center. He acts only once, when he tears the bill. The conspirators move constantly, on and off stage, whispering with one another, securing and resecuring alliances, displaying everywhere the cheverel minds the Chancellor praises. When Francis finally ceases to cast "but lateral or partial glances" and rises above the "vulgar passes," he understands Chabot and perceives the whole pattern that confuses or escapes the eye in motion.

The metaphor of motion and stasis, like the related effort to make characters into art works, links neatly with *Chabot*'s extensive use of puns as vehicles for corruption and expressions of immorality. To understand Chabot one must follow the rules of art. Only thus will the pattern—which is also the truth—emerge from a welter of contradictory perceptions. Yet word-play deliberately violates linguistic patterns and expectations when it finds multiple meanings in the same sound. Words become as polysignificant as the picture wrought to optic reason: in plural signification, they lose any stable meaning. The play's turbulent characters find perverse visual and verbal patterns— the monster, the devil, the "raw" and "seasoned" advocate, the "ambitious" line—but they can never discover "wise, just, good" and true meanings because they never stand free and fast. In sight and speech, these characters do not "know / Ingenuously," they cannot judge "by the right laid lines of truth." Instead, they aimlessly make or discover aberrant patterns and corrupt meanings; they "invent matter that was never extant in nature." Transcendent and eternal truths validate human art. Without that validation, art becomes corrupt, pliable rather than "right laid," limited rather than ingenuous.

Just such an invalid art appears throughout *Chabot*. This discovery points toward the play's central and disturbing vision of human existence: *Chabot* contains few intimations of transcendence, few hints of principles and few significant actions based on any standards other than expediency and change. Aside from Chabot, the initially good characters, Allegre and the Father-in-law, for instance, achieve little, and the characters who are eventually converted, such as Montmorency and the Queen, also have little effect upon events.

Rejecting Francis's threat to withdraw his royal protection, the Admiral makes an oddly attenuated reference to God:

> if the innocence and right that rais'd me
> And means for mine, can find no friend hereafter

Of Him that ever lives, and ever seconds
All kings' just bounties with defence and refuge
In just men's races, let my fabric ruin,
My stock want sap, my branches by the root
Be torn to death, and swept with whirlwinds out.

(2.3.29–35)

Curiously, this whole exchange between Francis and Chabot lacks any other direct reference to God or to the possibility that Chabot consciously represents principles whose ethical value depends, for him, upon a system of belief beyond this world.[18] Again, one remembers Chabot's constant portrayal of the problem as one of personal loyalty, relationship between men, and the sequence of events as a loss of faith, test, renewal of love, forgiveness, and, finally, death through the heartbreak caused by the doubt of a loved and trusted superior.

Chabot's death, to any audience accustomed to the metaphysical pyrotechnics that usually surround the death of Chapman's heroes, seems remarkably dim: no gala air, no glad embrace of a reward well earned through suffering, no confident step into a new and better world, no hint of satisfaction, much less deification. Immediately after Chabot's death, the characters sound particularly grey and resigned. They seem almost oblivious to any significance for the court-world that might be gained from the Admiral's life and death:

*Wife.*　　　His heart is broken.
*Father.*　　　　　　　　And kneeling, sir,
　As his ambition were in death to show
　The truth of his obedience.
*Montmorency.* I fear'd this issue.
*Treasurer.* He's past hope.
*King.* He has a victory in's death; this world
　Deserv'd him not. How soon he was translated
　To glorious eternity! 'Tis too late
　To fright the air with words; my tears embalm him!
*Wife.* What can become of me?
[*King*].　　　I'll be your husband, madam, and with care
　Supply your children's father; to your father
　I'll be a son. . . .

(5.3.202–13)

Chabot's victory is rather ambiguous. Although he has succeeded in saving the condemned Chancellor's life (but not his liberty or property [5.3.218–23]), the Admiral has hardly improved Francis's administration of justice. The "victory in's death" is translation to "glorious eternity," that is, escape from a world that "Deserv'd him not" and, we might add, understood him little. "Glorious eternity" no doubt means "heaven," but also, given Chabot's own emphasis on his posthumous reputation and Francis's promise that Chabot "shall boast as many monuments / As there be hearts in France" (5.3.206–8, 224–25), it seems to mean the "eternity" conferred by fame, the repute he has gained through his defence of justice. We listen in vain for any mention of Hercules (as in *Bussy D'Ambois*) or of God (as in *Byron's Tragedy*). Not only in the hero's death, but after it as well, *Chabot* is very distant indeed from Chapman's earlier political tragedies.

The lesser characters who surround Chabot do not set off the hero's differences from others so much as they convince us that Chabot's action and sacrifice are not only vain (perhaps the necessary fate of tragic heroes) but with little resonance for his society. So long as Chabot survives, just so long will his nature have even a small influence over his world. Several features of the play produce this impression of volitionless moral neutrality among the characters surrounding Chabot. The action involving the Queen and Chabot's wife degrades the conflict between their husbands: Chabot's wife is nearly featureless, alternately ranting and weeping, each to little effect; the Queen's jealousy and later change of mind inadequately reflect the King's finely articulated ambivalence toward Chabot. Montmorency, a secondary character unusually well developed for Chapman's drama, occasionally challenges our interest in Chabot himself. His dilemma—admiration and ambition—appears compellingly in several brief speeches. Nonetheless, these characters and their actions, which might have expanded the social significance of Chabot's nature and action, remain ancillary to the central relation of King and Admiral.

Once the conflict between Chabot and Francis has begun, they move further and further away from the court world. Of the basic reasons for Francis's hesitation and final discovery—his admiration for Chabot, the Admiral's behavior, the Queen's intervention, and Montmorency's change of attitude—the last two are truly minor. Compared to the complex relation between Chabot and Francis, the actions of other court-figures are pale indeed. Chabot's break with Francis and their ultimate reconciliation rests upon their personal relation, the relation between master and noble, between the principle of justice-in-the-state and private passion. Around and beyond this central pair swirls the perpetual motion of court politics, mob violence and mob justice, torture, and, eventually, the continued meddling of a king who has learned little from experience. In a sense, once his allegiance to justice has been demonstrated, Chabot must be huddled off the stage, for his utter irrelevance to the dramatic world, his isolation from it, and his inability to operate in it have become patent.

Jean Jacquot remarked that Chabot is

> plus proche de la commune humanité que les autres héros chapmaniens, qui ont tendance a s'abstraire de leur entourage pour se réfugier dans un monde idéal.[19]

As we have seen, the ideal world into which Chabot might flee remains very hazy. Jacquot's comment also turns our attention to the characters who remain after Chabot's death. The Advocate, ever willing to argue both sides, remains; the Treasurer and the Secretary, saved by cheverel minds, remain; Montmorency, shown to be a slender hope for future stern magistracy, remains. Around all the characters of this rather hermetic play lies the vast sea of the applausive multitude, as ready as the Advocate to cheer Chabot's fall (4.1.130–34) or the Chancellor's disgrace (5.2.2–3, 145–46) or Chabot's reinstatement, or (one supposes) to mourn his death and "enshrine" his memory.

The court is evidently strewn with easy traitors like Chabot's unfaithful servants (3.1.4–5) and physical cripples like the faithful Allegre. Opposed to this immorality and suffering, we find, aside from Montmorency, only the Queen, who is simple and ineffectual, Chabot's father-in-law, who cannot function at court or anywhere else except in isolation from society, and Francis, whose inability to control himself and to achieve justice has been amply demonstrated. Finally, we see the crumpled and prostrate body of Chabot himself. Just as true tragicomedy's feints and diversions may ultimately conclude with a sense of frailty, of easy loss and narrowly gained order, so *Chabot* ends with none of the optimism associated with the spectacle of a tragic hero who, though fallen, has exercised the human spirit in strange and wonderful ways and who promises unknown strengths in every man.

# Conclusion: "Coherents for the Time"

> The human understanding is of its own nature prone to suppose the existence of more order and regularity in the world than it finds.
>
> —Bacon, *Novum Organum*

Dedicating *Seaven Bookes of the Iliades* to the Earl of Essex, Chapman lectured his noble patron about poetry's eternal conjunction with the soul. No "sensuall delight," he claims, can "compare with the Felicitie of the Minde,"

> And ought not this to be so, where the incomprehensible figure of God is diffusde in sacred and everlasting Beames, where wee have in earth societie with Eternitie? Al this walkes upon the bosome of Death in the worthiest writing—and shall a man vayle to a painted Begger on horseback and goe sawcilie by such a godlike resplendence with a wall eye and an horned countenance? (*Homer*, 1:504)

The argument comes easily: it repeats Chapman's claims for poetry's eternal truth, its earthly access to heaven, its triumph over change and decay. Chapman then turns the customary Elizabethan compliment: Achilles survives in Homer (and Chapman); Essex is a modern "most true *Achilles*"; as patron, he too wins poetic immortality. Essex's reaction is unknown, but he evidently encouraged the Homeric rage; later the same year Chapman dedicates *Achilles Shield* to the earl and resumes the lecture, this time "To the Understander." Some (unnamed) critics have been so walleyed as to see "affected labour" in the first dedication. The author's counterblast:

> . . . for the darkenes there is nothing good or bad, hard or softe, darke or perspicuous but in respect, and in respect of men's light, sleight or envious perusalles (to whose loose capacities any worke worthily composde is knit with a riddle) and that the stile is materiall flowing and not ranke, it may perhaps seeme darke to ranke riders or readers that have no more soules than burbolts . . . but the truth is, my desire and strange disposition in all

thinges I write is to set downe uncommon and most profitable coherents for the time, yet further removed from abhorde affectation than from the most popular and cold digestion. (*Homer*, 1:548)[1]

Polemical as the claim may be, it is consistent and, here, framed more personally than usual.

Yet the crucial phrase—"uncommon and most profitable coherents for the time"—has some unrecognized ambiguities. These ambiguities must have been almost invisible in 1598, but as we trace Chapman's later career, they become more and more palpable. Chapman means, of course, that he alone among poets—perhaps since Homer, certainly among his contemporaries—instills truth, eternity, learning, and beauty into his poems. Other poets and most readers have the blunted souls of birdbolts. They villainize the soul and set "the scum of the body" between "Custome and Imputation" (*Homer*, 1:503). True poetry draws coherent,[2] if surprising ("uncommon") and educative ("profitable"), meanings from heaven. These the poet offers his age and thereby promises eternity. "For the time" has, however, the unhappy alternative meaning of "brief," for *a* time. Some of the passage's metaphors—"ranke riders," for example, or the rhyme in "men's light, sleight or envious perusalles"—aptly catch the world's motion, the transcience of perception and its variety. Coherence itself may sway in such a flux, and poetry assumes a momentary significance that events will soon sweep away.

❧   ❧   ❧

To understand Shakespeare's discontinuities of subject, treatment, and characterization, Philip Edwards suggests that we regard him as an artistic experimenter, testing his art and questioning its power to formulate experience.[3] However different the motive and the result, Chapman's plays reveal a coordinate purpose. Although anxious to expatiate on art and its truth and its human importance, Chapman is quite unself-conscious about artistic forms—conventions, genres, topoi—in themselves. Not for him the Shakespearean theatrical metaphor and receding dramatic perspectives. For Chapman, frustration demands invention. Intractable experience, imponderable contraries striving with one another, examples that do *not* prove axioms—these crises lead to experiment. Unlike Shakespeare, who often seems to view his subject matter as a way of exploiting his dramaturgy (rather than vice versa), Chapman willingly commits no heresy against his confident artistic beliefs. At some point, however, the *data* revolt against the *facta:* there is an insurrection of event against the thing made of event, experience against art or literature. Lacking Shakespeare's composure, Chapman marshals successive forms, conventions, and genres as potential orderings.

A fluid succession of formulas represents, then, another aspect of Chapman's attention to a mutable world. This motive qualifies Millar MacLure's otherwise accurate observation: "For Chapman the genres are instrumental, to be spoken through, dislocated, rather than rested in."[4] Proposed and discarded pattern in *Bussy* and the ambiguous cluster of interpretations running through the *Byron* plays make it difficult to fix the dramas' meanings, and that difficulty is fruitful. Yet these vertiginous successions and ambiguous codes make genre (and so forth) seem a little less "instrumental" as we lose faith, or Chapman does, in his ability to shape a securely conceived meaning. The plays demonstrate not the literary forms' utility, but their failure. Chapman tests his artistic models, great and little; he holds up first one, then another, as experimental frame (that is, explanatory system, giver of meaning) for the passing dramatic action. However odd it may be for a dramatist who often seems shut up in the same closet as Greville or Daniel, Chapman's comprehensive vision finally defeats the artistic order he seeks to impose. Chapman must experiment, not because he wants to employ literary form only so long as it is useful (MacLure's implication), but because he very much hopes the genres *will* work and will order the dramatic universe into moral and artistic significance.

Order's conflict with the plays' extravagant variety may yield new techniques, as the pressures of time and memory do when they struggle against *de casibus* and *débat* structures in *Byron's Conspiracy*. And often, Chapman's difficulties force him to write brilliant poetry in order to extricate the hero, as in *Bussy D'Ambois*. Indeed, the poet must extricate himself from his own disillusion: art attempts to conquer art's failure. Eventually, Chapman creates a world without transcendence, where the supervenient (Chabot's broken heart) mocks order and where the survivors lack even a Machiavel's graspable, immoral shape. The earlier characters, admirable and attractive as well as outrageous, give way to simple moral gymnasts, oblivious to their pain, submissive to chance and change, ignorantly resigned to their own dull world.

Chapman's divided theory and practice force him to experiment: when the theory fails to perform, he changes not the theory but its application. Theory and practice, design and accomplishment, were in fact diverging, and this division creates the tragedies' own fissured universes. *Bussy D'Ambois* especially, we may recall, reveals an extraordinary separation of "worlds"; this condition influences structure, action, language, and characterization. The two worlds resist easy labels, but one includes politics, court life, and "policy," while the other, rather cloudier one validates (as he supposes) Bussy's confidence and eventually appears as the transcendent, quasi-Epicurean "world of fire" where the hero's now immortal part resides for ever. In the *Byron* plays, Chapman studies political life and political types more closely and examines the political world's moral and psychological consequences. While the paradox doesn't have *Bussy's* almost garish simplicity, the two *Byron* plays again divide Byron's claims from his obvious moral frailty. Chapman's attitude has gained rigor: he pursues Byron's claims "ruthlessly" (Peter Ure's term), although he had treated Bussy's sympathetically and lent them Henry's royal credence.

Yet, for all the dramatist's ruthlessness, *Byron's Tragedy* has a concluding tour de force even more adventurous than Bussy's stellification. Conceding all his hero's failings—in represented self-awareness, moral sensitivity, loyalty—Chapman forges a triumphant Byron, impervious to the critical standards that discredited him throughout the preceding nine acts. This conclusion rests wholly upon Byron's challenge to death. Acknowledging his weakness and humanity, Byron opposes, and ultimately conquers, humanity's greatest enemy. The arena becomes transcendental, the stakes eternal. This finale revives the issue of the plays' divided worlds, for Byron is no longer, or not merely, the politicians' egotistical dupe: he champions humankind's deepest and most tragically insecure hopes. Thus, using different dramatic methods and creating very different theatrical effects, Chapman returns to the divided world that dominated *Bussy D'Ambois*. Success, of course, depends upon Chapman's making each world credible and managing the transitions so as to leave the actions, discoveries, and judgments of each as unchallenged as possible.

*Chabot* attempts to reconcile these two worlds.[5] Although the political world kills the hero, his faith in an uncontaminated, transcendent world of moral belief and personal integrity eventually converts the master politician, King Francis. The "other," nonpolitical, world of *Chabot* is harder to define than in the earlier tragedies, chiefly because Chabot is its sole active member, and he says very little about his beliefs. Or, rather, he says a great deal about a very few beliefs. Indeed, reconciling the two worlds does partly require narrowing and concentrating one of them very thoroughly. Nor are comparisons with the earlier tragedies simple. Monarchs and their great nobles do not have fixed places on virtue's scale. Henry IV, for instance, clearly has more personal integrity and greater moral awareness than Byron, just as Chabot exceeds his king. Still, we may remember that the *Byron* plays challenge Henry's morality; Henry's force diminishes when compared with Byron's final triumph. Moreover, the political worlds of *Bussy D'Ambois* and the *Byron* plays are much less moral than their best inhabitants.

More qualifications than these shadow *Chabot*'s power to resolve the complicated divisions within Chapman's art. The play that might crown a decade's experiment and difficulty depends for its own resolution upon two hackneyed and incredible devices: the conversion and the death by heartbreak. These devices will work, of course, but only if the audience accepts that the characters' choices and actions have vital practical as well as conceptual meaning. Francis must not change his mind, or Chabot die, simply because Chapman's design requires it. *Bussy D'Ambois* and the two *Byron* plays powerfully represent one alternative world, politics; the other alternative depends upon the actors' abilities and the effectiveness of Chapman's best dramatic poetry. *Chabot* also presents a sharply observed political world, but the hero's poetry and the role's opportunities for vivid acting are more subdued and perhaps less effective than in the earlier plays. So qualified, *Chabot* makes an earthly choice between the divided mundane and transcendent worlds in Chapman's tragedies: one world variously corrupt and weakly good, the other asserting man's greatness, his aspiration, and his potential for self-fulfillment.

❦   ❦   ❦

The political world that comes to dominate Chapman's tragedies was, I have argued, drawn from the life. No concentrated study of contemporary or classical history could provide the sinister detail and large perception Chapman so clearly commands. Nor would his artistic theory have begun to fail so palpably were he not aware that his La Fins and Savoys, Montmorencies and Montsurries, lived closer to home than historical texts from the other side of the channel. Certainly, Chapman had the opportunity to observe native courtiers and nobles at close range, and, we have seen, he had numerous, if not especially rewarding, court connections. Chapman's relations with his patrons have some startling similarities to crucial dramatic relations in his plays. These similarities deserve critical consideration because they illuminate Chapman's artistic difficulties and the evolution of his tragic drama.

As modern historians and literary scholars have amply testified, Prince Henry's death in 1612 cut short many important artistic and political developments, public and private, but Chapman—whose "Heroicall Patrone" the prince had been—may justifiably be said to have suffered as much as, perhaps more than, any other member of

Henry's artistic retinue. His urgent personal loss often breaks through the formal, and sometimes translated, mourning of his commemorative poem, "An Epicede or Funerall Song: On the most disastrous Death, of . . . Henry Prince of Wales." Describing "The parting of the Princes Servants," for example, he asks us to

> see
> How left to this, the mournfull Familie,
> Muffled in black clouds, full of teares are driven
> With stormes about the relickes of this Heaven;
> Retiring from the world, like Corses, herst,
> Home to their graves, a hundred waies disperst.
>
> (lines 148–53; *Poems*, p. 257)

In the margin of the same page, he writes: "Those that came to the Princes service seem'd (compared with the places they liv'd in before) to rise from death to the fields of life."

Many years earlier, Essex's abortive political ambitions had denied Chapman a real-life Achilles to match his Homeric portrait. In 1598, he addressed Essex as,

> Most true *Achilles* (whom by sacred prophecie *Homere* did but prefigure in his admirable object) and in whose unmatched vertues shyne the dignities of the soule, and the whole excellence of royall humanitie. . . .[6]

And with that real Achilles also departed an apparently generous Maecenas.[7] Dedicating his earliest published Homeric translation, Chapman claimed Essex's "honord countenance yet and vouchsafte reacknowledgement of one so unworthy as my selfe (being the great objects of al my labors in their first dedication) shal draw on the rest" ("To the Most Honored Earle," *Homer*, 1:506). The "rest" of the translations awaited Prince Henry's encouragement some years later, only to be interrupted once more.

In 1611, about a year before Prince Henry's death in November 1612, Chapman made his first approach to Robert Carr, Viscount Rochester and James's reigning favorite. During the print run of his translation of Homer's *Iliad*, Chapman added a sonnet "To the Most Honord, and Judiciall honorer of retired vertue, Vicount Rochester, &c."

> You that in so great eminence, live retir'd
> (Rare Lord) approve your greatnesse cannot call
> Your judgement from the inward state requir'd
> To blaze the outward; which doth never fall

In men by chance raisd, but by merit still.
He seekes not state, that curbs it being found.
Who seekes it not, never comes by it ill;
Nor ill can use it. Spring them from this ground,
And let thy fruits be favours done to Good,
As thy Good is adorn'd with royall favours;
So shall pale Envie famish with her food;
And thou spread further by thy vaine depravours.
True Greatnesse cares not to be seene but thus;
And thus, above our selves, you honour us.

It is a remarkable effort and, as Phyllis Bartlett says (*Poems*, p. 484), considerably more personal than most others of the appended sonnets. Chapman strikes a note that will continue for the remainder of his dedications: Carr "lives retired," that is, reserved or withdrawn into himself (so *OED*); he honors "retired virtue" and lacks the blaze of outward state one might expect from a meritless man raised by chance or by external forces only. He has an "inward state" superior to the court-honor and respect offered to any one in high place. Instead, Carr is a worthy man raised by merit, who curbs the pomp and display many might suppose appropriate to his "state." Chapman doesn't forget the purpose of his sonnet—reward ("thy fruits be favours done to Good")—but urges it as a natural consequence of King James's recognition of Carr's own goodness. By redistributing the royal favor, Carr starves Envy: the more he is falsely depraved, the more his true merit will be manifested.

Chapman's second and unquestionably most controversial address to Carr celebrates the marriage (26 December 1613) of Carr, now Earl of Somerset, to Frances Howard, whose previous marriage to the third Earl of Essex had been nullified on the grounds of Essex's impotence. King James had arranged that first marriage and had then, five years later, labored hard to dissolve it, offending the consciences of the Archbishop of Canterbury and several other members of an investigative commission the king eventually had to pack in order to gain the desired result. Most observers were incredulous that Frances Howard could be declared—even by a vote of 7 to 5—*virgo intacta*, and most regarded the episode as an offensive display of the favorite's domination over James.

Chapman's epithalamion, *Andromeda Liberata, or The Nuptials of Perseus and Andromeda* (1614) and its dedication display no such doubts. The entry for his poem in the *Stationers' Register* demonstrates, however, that others were less certain of the public reaction to marriage and celebratory verses. That entry further demonstrates the

link among politics, patronage, and poetry. Uniquely among all the
works entered in that register up to 1640, Chapman's poem was
licensed for printing by no fewer than four members of the Privy
Council—"the Duke of Lennox, the earle of Suffolke, the earle of
Marr, Sir Julius Caesar." Licensing was, of course, ordinarily the
prerogative of various clerics, although courtiers, aristocrats, and
officers of state might occasionally certify a work having to do with
their special interests (e.g., the Earl Marshal) or special responsibilities (e.g., raising an army or describing a foreign military campaign).[8] Of the four councillors who licensed Chapman's poem,
however, only one, Lennox, licensed even a single other work, and
that "exception" confirms the rule since it concerns Lennox's position
as Alnager General. That these four men should favor a poem support-
ing the marriage is largely explicable: Suffolk was the bride's father,
Marr, a very old friend and confidant of James, and Julius Caesar, one
of the most enthusiastic members of the commission that nullified her
first marriage. Lennox's presence is less easily explained, but Sir John
Holles testified that Lennox had privately urged the marriage "in
[Frances's] behalf"; presumably Lennox saw the Howards and their
allies as the dominant court-faction, as indeed they now were.[9] One
can only speculate on why such authoritative names appear in the
*Register.* If their appearance is a positive, aggressive act, it might
represent a move in the propaganda war to vindicate the favorite's
position, his marriage, and, by extension, the power and sway of his
allies; these men would have had no trouble getting any text published
in 1614! Alternatively, some party to the transaction, most likely
Lawrence Lisle, the publisher, might have wanted reassurance that
the poem represented the ruling party line.[10]

Chapman's pugnacious dedication and the poem's inflammatory
adulation do not bear out Walter Greg's explanation that since the
poem "naturally gave offense to the Essex faction . . . Chapman
evidently sought to put it under the protection of powerful members
of the Privy Council."[11] As the epigraph from Petrarch promises,
*Nihil veritate nec virtute remotius quam vulgaris opinio,* the dedication
and to a lesser degree the poem itself develop the envy-theme introduced at the end of the *Iliads* sonnet. Chapman's dedication begins by
translating the epigraph; it is a majority-of-one argument, a conventional claim that the more popular an idea, the less likely it is to be
true:

> As nothing under heaven is more remov'd
> From Truth & virtue, then Opinions prov'd

> By vulgar Voices: So is nought more true
> Nor soundly virtuous then things held by few. . . .
>
> (lines 1–4; Poems, p. 305)

This *in medias res* opening assumes the reader ("The Right Worthily
Honored Robert," "the Ladie Frances," or anyone else) already
knows what the "vulgar Voices" are saying, knows, that is, how
thoroughly unpopular the marriage and its antecedents are. Chapman
concludes the dedication with the same advice he gave in the *Iliads*
sonnet: Carr is to "thirst" for "inward *Goodnesse*" "Till *Scandall* pine,
and *'Bane-fed* envie burst" (lines 154, 158–59); his wife is to

> make our factious brood
> Whose forked tongs, wold fain your honor sting
> Convert their venomd points into their spring:
> Whose owne harts guilty, of faults faind in yours
> Wold fain be posting off: but arme your powers
> With such a siege of vertues, that no vice
> Of all your Foes, *Advantage* may entice
> To sally forth, and charge you with offence,
> But sterve within, for very conscience
> Of that Integritie, they see exprest
> In your cleere life. . . .
>
> (lines 161-71; Poems, p. 308)

The poem itself retells the myth of Perseus and Andromeda, with
Andromeda's "barren rock" allegorized as the very same vulgar opinion castigated in the dedication. Given the official claim that Essex's
impotence justified the divorce, readers quickly supposed that rather
than rescuing Frances from the slings and arrows of public obloquy,
making (or remaking) an "honest woman" of her, Carr had in fact
rescued his wife from a loveless, sexless marriage. The interpretation
may be vulgar, but it is also obvious and congenial to popular distaste
for recent events. Chapman was forced into an unpersuasive but
dogmatically defensive "Justification," in which he claimed that the
obvious interpretation of his poem couldn't be right because it made
no sense to describe a man, the Earl of Essex, as a "barren rock"!

Little more than a year after the poem, Carr and his wife were under
investigation for the murder of Sir Thomas Overbury, once Carr's
closest advisor and apparently an outspoken opponent of his marriage.
That investigation, and the trials and convictions that followed it,
destroyed Carr's influence. James sent the old favorite to the Tower
(May 1616) and chose a new one, George Villiers, later Duke of
Buckingham.

Although Carr eventually obtained his freedom, he gained little more beyond Chapman's dogged loyalty. That loyalty continued, after Carr's release from the Tower, in the dedications to *Pro Vere Autumni Lacrymae* (1622) and *The Crowne of all Homers Workes* (1624–25?), and, if Solve's speculations are correct, in *Chabot*'s political propagandizing.[12]

The dedications to *Pro Vere* and the last Homeric translations strongly suggest that Chapman saw Carr's condition as his own. Patron and poet suffer detraction, barbarism, misunderstanding—all of Chapman's lifelong complaints, now for the first time publicly shared by his patron, though for different reasons. His preface to *Pro Vere* alludes to the crisis over *Andromeda Liberata*'s personal application to Carr and his wife, and Chapman worries that this poem's purpose will be distorted. The poem is Vere's *"Plant of Fame"*

> Which cannot furnish with an *Anagram*
> Of just *Offence*, and Desire to wrest
> All the *free* Letters here; by such a *Test*
> To any *Blame*: for equall *Heaven* avert,
> It should return *Reproach*, to prayse *Desert*;
> How haplesse, and perverse, soever bee
> The *Envies*, and *Infortunes* following Mee:
> Whose true, and simple-onely-ayme at *Merit*,
> Makes your acceptive, and still-bettering *Spirit*
> My *Wane* view, as at *Full* still; and sustaine
> A *Life*, that other subtler *Lords* disdaine:
> Being *Suttlers* more, to *Braggart-written* Men,
> (Though still deceiv'd) then any truest *Pen*.
>
> (lines 10–22; *Poems*, p. 339)

Although Carr may remain a full moon for Chapman, both men have waned in their respective spheres of poetry and politics. "Subtler lords" have abandoned both, and Chapman implicitly fears that the dedication to Carr will open this new poem to anagramatic interpretation, wresting praise into reproach. Chapman presumably still blamed malign anagramatic interpretation for *Andromeda Liberata*'s fate, however inevitable that interpretation appears to modern, as it did to contemporary, readers.

Carr and his wife were finally released from the Tower in January of 1622; *Pro Vere* was written and printed in the summer of 1622 (*Poems*, p. 465). The poem concerns the English strategic position vis-à-vis the forces arrayed against James's son-in-law, the Elector Palatine, and concentrates on Horace Vere's entrapment in Manheim (from which he eventually retreated with honor in September 1622). The desperate military situation is not so very different from Carr's, first imprisoned and now exiled to Chiswick:

> *All* lest *Good,* That but onely aymes at *Great,*
> I know (best *Earle*) may boldly make retreat
> To your *Retreat,* from this Worlds open *Ill.*
> (lines 1–3; *Poems,* p. 339)

Nor, of course, is it so different from Chapman's own situation, both metaphorically as the embattled poet and, it seems, quite practically as a poverty-stricken man himself exiled from London during the period 1614–19.[13]

When others' scorn or indifference harrowed him, Chapman sought refuge in poetry and hermetic consolation. Dedicating *The Crowne of all Homers Workes,* he now offers Carr that consolation, or a chastened version of it:

> Since then your Lordship settles in your shade
> A life retir'd, and no Retreate is made
> But to some strength (for else tis no Retreate,
> But rudely running from your Battaile's heate),
> I give this [the translation] as your strength:
>     your strength, my Lord,
> In Counsailes and Examples, that afford
> More Guard than whole Hosts of corporeal power,
> And more deliverance teach the fatall Howre.
>     Turne not your medcine then to your disease,
> By your too set and sleight repulse of these,
> The Adjuncts of your matchless Odysses. . . .
> (lines 42–52; *Homer,* 2:508, font reversed)

The martial metaphor vividly exaggerates both the patron's situation and the poet's, but Chapman leaves no doubt that he sees Carr's situation in military terms when he devotes lines 84–116 to an extended simile comparing Carr's retreat-in-strength to Sir John Norris's exploits on the continent. In fact, court-war is worse than open-war:

> So fight out, sweet Earle, your Retreate in Peace;
> No ope-warr equalls that where private Prease
> Of never-numberd odds of Enimie,
> Arm'd all by Envie, in blinde Ambush lie,
> To rush out like an open threatning skie,
> Broke al in Meteors round about your eares.
>
> (lines 105–10)

Contemplative withdrawal—political exile or poetic meditation—offers no easy answers and demands fierce energies, as Chapman had always claimed. Yet in Homer (and by extension, perhaps in Chapman), Carr has a source of moral assurance and strength:

> Retire to him [Homer, the *Hymns*] then for advice, and skill
> To know things call'd worst Best; and Best most ill;
> Which knowne; truths best chuse; and retire to still.
>
> (lines 81–83)[14]

Failed politician and waning poet now retreat, or Chapman would have it so, to the same source of strength.

The unhappy seesaw of Chapman's attempts to secure patronage amply justifies his sense that he has been banished from the fields of life. A series of disasters quite divorced from his poetry and even from his own abrasive personality recurrently denied him sponsorship just as true and public success appeared certain. Unlike the earlier patrons, however, Carr and his special circumstances gave Chapman the opportunity to unite poetry's subject and political life, to link the genuine poet's isolation with an equivalent political exile. While Chapman did seek other noble patronage—he dedicated his Hesiod translation (1618) to Bacon shortly before that worthy's disgrace (the sequence seems inescapable) and *Caesar and Pompey* to Lionel Cranfield, Earl of Middlesex, after his—he soon came back to Carr.[15] And part of the motive lies in simple identification of poet with patron; Chapman believed, or wanted to believe, that they shared equal if different disappointments and similar compensations.

Chapman tirelessly repeated his claim that poetry, both his original drama and his translations, offered specific political instruction. Carr's career and Chapman's own worsening circumstances led him to phrase the connections more intimately and less abstractly than usual, but in a dedicatory sonnet prefacing the *Iliads*, he quite bluntly tells Lord Chancellor Ellesmere:

> That Poesie is not so remov'd a thing
>     From grave administry of publike weales,
> As these times take it; heare this Poet sing,
>     Most judging Lord: and see how he reveales
> The mysteries of Rule. . . .
>
> (lines 1–5; *Poems*, p. 396)

If Chapman believed this principle, as he plainly did, then we may justly suspect that the link also works in reverse: political realities influence poetry, as I have argued before. The final question to ask of this triangular relation (poet-patron-poetry) is whether the poet's experiences of patronage also influence his poetry.

A review of Chapman's major original works suggests that they do reflect the patron-poet relation. While remaining intensely abstract, intensely concerned with political, artistic, and moral theory, Chapman more and more decisively anchors tragic conflicts in personal relations. In *Hero and Leander* and *Bussy D'Ambois*, these relations were heterosexual and amorous, although the abortive Monsieur-Bussy alliance hints at future developments. Subsequent plays, including *The Revenge of Bussy* and *Caesar and Pompey*, lean increasingly upon a masculine pair: Byron and La Fin; Byron and Henry; Clermont and Guise; Cato and Pompey; Chabot and Francis.[16] These pairs, especially in the French plays, look back to a politically and philosophically simpler era opposed to contemporary corruption and Machiavellian manipulation. Clearly, one effect of *policy*—or modern nationhood—is to destroy human trust and to negate actions founded upon personal rather than social or power relationships. Chapman's dedications to his noble patrons, we may remember, often sound similarly elegiac, finding old virtues newly clothed or welcoming unexpected returns of primitive excellence.

These dramatic relations and their consequences may be explained in terms of Chapman's ideas, but I find something more natively his own in them. Dedicated to hermetic exclusivity, Chapman depended upon a small band of comrades (Matthew Roydon and Thomas Harriot, for example; compare Jonson's much larger circle) and an equally small group of aristocratic patrons. Few of these friends and patrons ever attained and none long held great authority. None could satisfy Chapman's ambivalent desire for detached greatness and public reward. The poet's personal or professional disappointments thus parallel his tragic heroes' experiences: the more circumstances—disgrace or death—rebuffed him, the more tightly he held onto those friendships and memories. So, too, his tragic heroes blindly cling to friends and supposed friends, to standards of trust and mutual interest, long after those friends and standards have failed or have been defeated. It can hardly be more than a pleasing coincidence and a tribute to a garish treason, but Lord Chancellor Ellesmere, inviting Chapman's patron Robert Carr to begin his defence on the charge of having murdered Sir Thomas Overbury, chooses a recent historical example, more recently dramatized:

> before you speak for yourself by way of advice, I will say unto you, in giving you two examples: Your wife, that yesterday confessed the fact

[crime]; and there is great hope of the king's mercy, if you now mar not that which she made. On the contrary, Byron, who when the king of France used all means he possibly could, to bring him to the acknowledgment of his offense, which if he had done, there was no question to be made of the king's grace. And I think there never was, nor is, a more gracious and merciful king than our master. But Byron still persisting in the denial of his fact, you know his end.[17]

Again, if only by happenstance, poet, patron, and hero are joined.

Chapman espouses a transcendental theory that offers not merely explanation but absolute value; simultaneously, he experiences and dramatizes close human relations that have no external references for their values and meanings. This overt puzzle may merely be a quirk of Chapman's personality and art. No artist deserves the consistency many critics so dearly love to find. Nonetheless, I think we may explain these divergent tendencies. Chapman's attention to great men and their personal relations increased even as he found his theory failing to master his subject matter. At the same time, Chapman himself was growing older, poorer, and less popular. His search for sponsorship also grew increasingly desperate: Essex was executed; the new scholar-prince, Henry, died just as the poet completed the *Iliad* translation and anticipated future support; Carr was accused, condemned, jailed, and never restored to favor. The surviving evidence is greater than we have for any other contemporary dramatist, and it shows that Chapman became more anxiously and more closely attached to each successive patron. The climax came, of course, with the irresponsible *Andromeda Liberata,* the blankly foolish defence of that poem, and, finally, Chapman's stubborn refusal to abandon Carr. Thus, the glorious certainty of Bussy's transcendental stature echoes Chapman's early confidence that Essex is, or can be made, a Homeric hero.[18] As the dramatic realities diverge further and further from their theoretical goals, Chapman's hopes of worldly success and patronage also recede. Eventually, the dramatic heroes can rely, or so they falsely believe, on only one other person. So, too, the poet.

These interpretations risk associating the dramatist too closely with his imaginary creations, or vice versa. Yet Chapman was a man in the world; among the period's plays his tragedies almost alone single-mindedly employ contemporary or near contemporary political history; he needed, and grievously did not find, the encouragement of a court that looked more and more like the corrupt, indifferent courts he portrayed on stage. Chapman's artistic theory was also a theory of the world; there lay its excitement and his claim to attention. The theory, I have argued, begins to fail artistically, and so too Chapman's own professional life begins to weaken and fail. Chapman, more nakedly than any other contemporary playwright, put current politics on stage, and his theory failed both its artistic test and its disciple's experiences in Jacobean London.

❦   ❦   ❦

Although those experiences were not very encouraging, the poet's role perpetually fascinated Chapman. Defining the poet's nature and claiming that place for himself are motifs throughout his critical writings, and they often appear within the poetry itself. He longed especially for the *first* poets' privileged stature: hence his devotion to Homer, his long-continued interest in Musaeus, and even the late, odd, dart into translating Hesiod. Michael Drayton's prefatory poem to the Hesiod translation mentions his friend's choice very specifically: Chapman delivers "them so well, the first and best, / That to the world in Numbers ever sung."[19] As these choices imply, and the curious double conclusion to *Hero and Leander* confirms, Chapman distinguished himself from late-born poets, no matter how excellent. Rather, he sought—and his theories tended to confer—a quasi-mystical status. While he might not charm beasts or raise Theban walls, he could, he did, seek Musaeus's place.

Chapman's search for that place influences his work in many ways, but it has some especially curious consequences for his overt use of art works. When we consider Hero's scarf, for example, or the tapestry of Catiline's conspiracy that so tempts Byron, we immediately recognize their significant relation to their contexts. Yet, how did they come to be? What power controls or determines their relation to experience? Where do they get their validity? These may appear naive questions, the more naive because the immediate answer is so simple: the art works draw meaning, indeed existence, from the creating poet. Yet, that creating poet elaborately distinguishes himself from the poet who laments Leander's death and self-consciously drowns it with floods of ink. The poet who conceived Hero and Leander's metamorphosis exists in a very different place from the dramatist who writes "things like truth" and laboriously distills historians into iambic pentameter. Chapman's most exalted place is with Musaeus, quite outside the poetry or drama he writes. He stands in some mythic relation to poetry's source and subject; he can no more be questioned than the art works that *occur* in that poetry. Musaeus and the art works represent the relation among morality and meaning and poetry. As themselves, they embody that relation and are simply significant of it.

Chapman aspired to Homer's place, or Musaeus's, but he also knew poetry's rigors and disappointments. While his "free soule" and "strange muse" sought "instructive light" from the "whole Sphere of fire," he more often sensed a "smotherd fervour" and lamented his own "stiffled verse." Chapman's willingness to express his creative anguish, often in very subjective language, accounts for his poetry's modern reputation; it links him, for example, with Donne, who is otherwise a very different poet. He had many explanations for his ill-rewarded efforts: his own human limitation, the world's ignorance, the chance that denied him recognition. Yet, this self-reflective quality made him see Homer as a living source, almost literally an unsurpassable "patron": "For though I now consume in poesie, / Yet *Homer* being my roote I can not die."[20] Moreover, this infinitely serious absorption in life's difficulties and limits explains (as the critics cannot) how he could understand Tamyra's passion—"All bars made engines to his insolent fury"—and Byron's aspiration and Chabot's calm. His career as a tragic writer shows him increasingly unable to control the life he created through the theory he believed. His art could not give the promised coherence to the worldly particularity, expedience, and decay he would not ignore.

With *Hero and Leander,* Chapman managed an almost perfect balance between his competing views of the poet and the tensions within his own theory and practice. *Bussy D'Ambois* nearly achieves a dramatic equilibrium of the same sort, but the rifts become very plain in the *Byron* plays, and *Chabot* concedes defeat. The poetic theory is not responsible for Chapman's diffculties, only the poet, who felt bound to interpret the world he saw. William Oldys—on unknown authority—records a telling anedcote:

> Indeed his Head was a Poetical Treasury Magazene or Chronicle of whatsoever was Memorable among the Poets of his Time which made him latterly much resorted to by the young Gentry of good Parts and Education. . . . [He] preserved in his own Conduct the true dignity of Poetry wch he compard to the Flower of the Sun that disdains to open its Leaves to the Eye of a Smoking Taper.[21]

The tale may be antiquarian wishful thinking, but it epitomizes Chapman's self-estimate: poetry and man—and the failings of both—were one.

# Appendix

Here I offer a survey of Chapman's pronouncements on a variety of literary, dramatic, and critical topics germane to my argument about the tragedies.

❦   ❦   ❦

Bad readers or spectators far outnumber good ones. While many of Chapman's comedies and tragedies succeeded admirably, others did not, and he often complained about the reception his poems and plays received. This mixed success, as well as his frequent trouble with authorities who objected to the political and satiric content of such pieces as *Eastward Ho!* and the *Byron* plays, might explain his attacks on the "savage multitude" (the monster that attacks Andromeda in his epithalamion for Robert and Frances Carr) as plain sour grapes. Yet these attacks are much more than a foiled satirist's ungracious dismissal. Indeed, the ill nature of most audiences justifies an important poetic strategy: the artist must darken or obscure an art the majority cannot understand and often hates.

The adjectives Chapman chooses to describe poetry's enemies (his enemies, too) get us closer to the underlying principle. Those who hate or dismiss poetry are "savage" (not civil, or civilized), "prophane" (not sacred, not hierophantically adept), and "manlesse" (not human). The audience may contaminate poetry and the "sappe of hidden Truth" within "the utter barke" (*Poems*, p. 327). The simple multitude, "reading but to curtoll a tedious houre" (*Poems*, p. 19), are perhaps less dangerous than the deluded "imaginaries in knowledge," the poets or "statists" or critics who claim learning (*Poems*, p. 245). Their chief threat lies not so much in their so-called creative accomplishments—lack of truth will deny them eternity—as in the danger they pose for true poets and true (eternal) poetry.

All these matters, except perhaps the poetaster category, are fairly traditional. Poetry's intentional obscurity, the dark required to protect the light, had long been at least an implied premise for nonliteral readings of many texts.[1] Thus, some of Chapman's obscurity is for poetry's sake: personality and tradition join to make difficulty congenial. Some writers have argued, however, that Chapman's defense of difficult poetry also represents a quality intrinsic to his theories of poetry and creativity: his evident personal struggle to create is not ineptitude but a necessary adjunct of his subject matter and his sense of its high importance.[2] Self-identified as the "interlocutor," Chapman describes his creative anguish in *The Teares of Peace:* "Peace" wonders why this "wretched man" has sought her out and why he thinks "to finde, light in obscuritie, / Eternitie, in this deepe vale of death." Chapman confesses his poems' defects, but characteristically claims they are better than other poems:

> I grant their strangenesse, and their too ill grace
> And too much wretchednesse, to beare the face
> Or any likenesse of my soule in them:
> Whose Instruments, I rue with many a Streame
> Of secret Teares for their extream defects,
> In uttering her true forms: but their respects
> Need not be less'ned, for their being strange,
> Or not so vulgar, as the rest that range
> With headlong Raptures, through the multitude:
> Of whom they get grace, for their being rude.
>
> (*Poems*, p. 179)

In a curious fashion, Chapman comes back to an ultimately Horatian view of stylistic decorum: he could write no other way because "absolute Poems" require "high, and harty invention exprest in most significant, and unaffected phrase" (*Poems*, p. 49). Plainness responds to and produces barbarism. To create and understand truthful poetry requires effort, and the poet may produce tortured verse. At the same time, however, obscurity may also produce pleasure because it requires effort and promises discovery. Chapman opens his justification of *Andromeda Liberata* by writing that "*Learning*, hath delighted from her Cradle, to hide her self"; we delight in finding the hidden heart. Elsewhere, he explains that he varies his poetry "from popular custome, even for the pure sakes of ornament and utilitie" (*Poems*, p. 49). In this formula, ornament cannot be separated from utility: obscurity is both necessary and beautiful. Ornament, utility, and obscurity all derive from "Reason," which is "ground, structure and ornament, / To all inventions, grave and permanent" (*Poems*, p. 381).

❦   ❦   ❦

Chapman's idea of a good audience relies on his theory of poetry's origin and effect. Indeed, the poet's creative act and his audience's response are closely related. Chapman borrows the Platonic doctrines he found in *Alcibiades II* (possibly spurious), *Phaedrus*, and *Ion*, as well as Ficino's exposition and translation of those doctrines and dialogues. Both *Alcibiades II* and Ficino's *In Platonis Ionem, vel de furore poetico* appear, for example, in Chapman's dedication of the *Odysseys:*

> . . . He that knocks at the Gates of the *Muses*; *sine Musarum furore*, is neither to be admitted entrie, nor a touch at their Thresholds. . . . There being in *Poesie* a twofold rapture, (or alienation of soule . . .) one *Insania* . . . by which the infected is thrust beneath all the degrees of humanitie: & *ex homine, Brutum quodammodo redditur* . . . the other is, *Divinus furor*; by which the sound and divinely healthfull, *supra hominis naturam erigitur, & in Deum transit.*[3]

The Latin definitions of the two forms of *rapture* come straight from Marsilio Ficino. Chapman himself translates the *divinus furor* when he calls *Andromeda Liberata* "this poore Rage / Of forespoke *Poesie*" that can "Discover all the good and bad of man . . . Erect him past his human Period / And heighten his transition into God" (*Poems*, pp. 305–6). Here lies poetry's greatest good. It can guide the true reader to a supraterrestrial realm of perfection and eternity. Poetry assists our spiritual and moral perfection.

The reader's learning and knowledge gain poetry's benefits. Chapman carefully distinguishes his concept of "Learning" from acquaintance with books or success in practical affairs, however complex.[4] Early in his career, he claims as a fit audience "these searching spirits, whom learning hath made noble, and nobilitie sacred" (*Poems*, p. 49). So, too, in 1614, he writes:

> . . . nought more true
> Nor soundly virtuous then things held by few:
> Whom *Knowledge* (entred by the sacred line,
> And governd evermore by grace divine,)
> Keepes in the narrow path to spacious heaven,
> And therefore, should no knowing spirit be driven
> From fact, nor purpose. . . .
>
> (*Poems*, p. 305)

"Sacred line" means all true poetry: through such poetry the reader enters (receives, achieves) knowledge and is evermore governed by divine grace. The phrase might mean scripture alone, but Chapman tended to view scripture, Homer, and other true poetry almost as one.[5]

Phyllis Bartlett suggested that Chapman's reader should ideally experience a chastened version of the poet's own inspiration; this view relies on the poet's favorite light-imagery and descriptions of his perfect readers as "those that before-hand, have a radiant, and light-bearing intellect."[6] Poet, poem, and reader are related more complexly, I think. Poetic skill requires "invocation, fasting, watching" and demands "drops of . . . [poets'] soules like an heavenly familiar" (*Poems*, p. 19), or to continue the magical figure, "charms made of unlerned characters are not consecrate by the Muses which are divine artists" (*Poems*, p. 49). Chapman feels his poetry deserves the reader's effort; in fact, the better the poetry—the more truthful—the more effort the reader must supply. No doubt Chapman's creative experience included entrancement, an almost fiery spiritual invasion, but poetry survives because it manifests and incorporates eternal truth. The true reader's experience involves a similar incorporation. A slight wrenching might describe that experience in terms of Plato's concept of "participation," rather than the more mystical Neoplatonic union among human and angelic or divine intelligences that Bartlett implies. Other statements substantiate this observation. For example, wishing that his "stiffled verse" might more perfectly express his soul's meaning, Chapman tells his friend Thomas Harriot,

> under all those formes you should discerne
> My love to you, in my desire to learne.
> Skill and the love of skill do ever kisse:
> No band of love so strong as knowledge is. . . .
>
> (*Poems*, p. 382)

To the Earl of Essex, Chapman writes, "The soules of al the recorded worthies that ever liv'de become eternally embodyed even upon earth" through poets who "are their earthlie Elisummes." Those "worthilie-termed" poets' writings allow us to enjoy "this true manner of communication and combination of soules" because in our souls, in poetry, "wee have in earth societie with Eternitie." Finally, with a revealing simile, he writes, "For, as Number, Sound and Ryme can challenge no inclusion of the soule without divine invention, judgement and disposition, no more can the soule expect Eternitie on earth without such eternall writing."[7] The words Chapman chooses—*kiss, communication and combination, society, inclusion*—suggest that the reader experiences a meeting or perception aided by learning, rather than inspiration per se. So far as I can see, the reader or subject of poetry does not lose individuality or subjectivity, as Chapman himself seems to have done when Homer's "breath in flames, that did instruct (me thought) / And (as my soule were then at full) they wrought" (*Poems*, p. 174).

❦ ❦ ❦

Chapman defined his proper audience very carefully and analyzed the process of creating art with equal care. Precisely what did Chapman think poetry had to offer his audience? He liked the Homeric passage describing Jove's golden chain and allegorized it variously. Jove, speaking Chapman's English, says:

> . . . see let downe our golden chaine,
> And at it let all Deities their utmost strengths constraine
> To draw me to the earth from heaven: you never shall prevaile
> Though with your most contention ye dare my state assaile.
> But when my will shall be disposed to draw you all to me,
> Even with the earth it selfe and seas ye shall enforced be.
> Then will I to Olympus' top our vertuous engine bind
> And by it everie thing shall hang by my command inclind.
> So much I am supreme to Gods, to men supreme as much.
>
> (*Iliads* 8.16–24; *Homer*, 1 : 167)[8]

That golden chain might image poetry itself, for Chapman believed poetry drew heaven down to earth and made earthly things divine. Poetry's power to make eternal appears throughout Renaissance defenses, usually as part of dedications seeking support from the duly eternalized patron, but the commonplace should not lose its striking force for being common. By calling poets "earthlie Elisummes," Chapman gives his version of the idea a slight twist: poet, poetry, and poetic subject all achieve immortality through art's mediation. Immortality, in turn, depends upon truth. Chapman argues the point more syllogistically than usual in dedicating *Seaven Bookes of the Illiades:*

> If the crowne of humanitie be the soule, and the soule an intellectual beam of God, the essence of her substance being intellection and intellection or understanding the strength and eminence of her faculties, the differencing of men in excellencie must be directed onelie by their proportions of true knowledge. Homericall writing, then, being the native deduction, image and true heire of true knowledge, must needes in desert inherite his father's dignitie.
>
> (*Homer*, 1 : 505)

Other discussions make clear that while poetry's eternity depends upon its truthfulness, that truth might originate with the inspired poet, with his subject, or (the most common formula) with their interaction. Chapman lists various subjects that endorse poetry's immortality: "dimme and obscure prints of divinity, and the sacred history"; "grounds of naturall, or rules of morall Philosophie, for the recommending of some vertue, or curing some vice in generall"; "memorable Examples for the use of policie and state" (*Poems*, p. 327).

Poetry also has an active duty:

> . . . where high *Poesies* native habite shines,
> From whose reflections flow eternall lines:
> *Philosophy* retirde to darkest caves
> She can discover. . . .
>
> (*Poems*, p. 384)

Poetry has intrinsic qualities that enforce an active search for knowledge. Complaining about other translators, Chapman stipulates that Homer's meaning can only be found through an equally powerful poetic investigation:

> They fail'd to search his deepe and treasurous hart.
> The cause was since they wanted the fit key
> Of Nature, in their down-right strength of Art,
> With Poesie to open Poesie—
>
> (*Homer*, 1:10)

*Poeta nascitur*, and translators too. Chapman of course considers the soul, like truth and proper learning, to be immortal. This equation leads to some odd phrases: poetry as "this great inflamer of all powers / That move in humane soules" is fairly common, but "the right vertuous touch / Of a well-written soule to vertue moves" returns us once more to the curious mutuality of the poet's soul, the reader's soul, and poetry (*Homer*, 1:4). The well-written soul's "Promethean facultie / Can create men and make even death to live" (*Homer*, 1:6).[9] Explaining the phrase "Promethean Poets" ("The Shadow of Night," line 131), Chapman notes:

> He cals them Promethean Poets in this high conceit, by a figurative comparison betwixt them, that as Pro. with fire fetcht from heaven, made men: so Poets with the fire of their soules are sayd to create those Harpies, and Centaures, and thereof he calls their soules Geniale. (*Poems*, p. 22)

"Fire fetcht from heaven" inflames the reader's soul just as it does the poet's. It represents eternal truth and confers immortality on poet and poetry.

❦ ❦ ❦

Given Chapman's demands upon his audience and his high estimate
of poetry's truth, his defense of lying and his commitment to the stage
come as a surprise. Yet he indignantly claims there is no

> . . . such reality of wisdome's truth in all humane excellence as in Poets'
> fictions—that most vulgar and foolish receipt of Poeticall licence being of
> all knowing men to be exploded (accepting it as if Poets had a tale-telling
> priviledge above others), no Artist being so strictly and inextricably con-
> fined to all the lawes of learning, wisedome and truth as a Poet. (*Homer*,
> 1 : 14)

The striking use of *reality* reminds us that Chapman understands
poetry's truth as a universal and transcendental quality often missed in
day-to-day existence and the sorry productions of most human artistry. The fire Promethean poets fetch from heaven burns more
brightly, more truly, than any mundane conflagration, however real or
naturally explicable. The famous defense of poetic invention prefaced
to *The Revenge of Bussy D'Ambois* shows Chapman's distinctions
between a factual truth and a truth more true though less "autentical":

> For the autentical truth of either person or action, who (worth the respect-
> ing) will expect it in a poem, whose subject is not truth, but things like
> truth? Poor envious souls they are that cavil at truth's want in these natural
> fictions; material instruction, elegant and sententious excitation to virtue,
> and deflection from her contrary, being the soul, limbs, and limits of an
> autentical tragedy. (*Tragedies*, p. 77)

Here Chapman tries to mediate between an appeal to verisimilitude
("natural fictions") and Jonson's "truth of argument."[10] The balanced
use of "autentical" suggests that facticity (e.g., Clermont D'Ambois
did not exist) has no claim upon "true" tragedy (the kind of punning
that appears in "autentical tragedy").

"Things like truth" cannot be just an allusion to Aristotelian proba-
bility; rather, the phrase needs to be assimilated to Chapman's pervasive distinction between eternal truths, or eternal learning, or
"soul," and the successful but deceptive varieties of truth, even including "mere" fact, which swarm the world. Truth, like Peace, like
the poet, does reside among men although it may be ignored, despised, or poverty-stricken. Truth can be rescued and preserved, even
apotheosized, by the poet. Very simply, poetic licence cannot be
permitted because it gives mundane "reality" too much truth. Whatever material comes to hand, a myth or French or Roman history,

deserves no respect per se but finds value only so far as the poet's "doctrinall" or "sententious" or "virtuous" purposes shape it.[11]

Chapman's ideas about poetry and its power have too much energy to be dismissed as abstract vaporings or even as self-serving excuses. The "reality of wisdome's truth" may, perhaps, demand a stage as its best forum. He very specifically applauds theatrical performance—or "scenical representation"—because it gives "personal and exact life" to "all-moving truth."[12] In 1595, apparently before he had written any plays, Chapman devoted a sonnet to the theater's fascination and its benefit: the Muses "Have most inspirde, and showne theyr glories there" and the "Theaters of *Athens* and of *Rome*" did not "live by soothing moods, and serving tymes."[13] Dedicating *The Widow's Tears,* he dismisses the charge of theatrical frivolity: "Free judgement weighs nothing by the Name, or Forme . . . but will accept acceptable matter, as well in Plaies; as in many lesse materialls, masking in more serious Titles" (*Comedies,* p. 479; font reversed).

In his fine commendatory poem to *Sejanus,* Chapman analyzes the play's quality. First, as might be expected, he compliments Jonson's didactic achievement:

> Thy *Poeme,* therefore, hath this due respect,
>   That it lets passe nothing, without observing,
> Worthy Instruction; or that might correct
>   Rude manners, and renowme the well deserving. . . .
>
> (*Poems,* p. 360)

Chapman equates *poem* and *play.* A few other dramatists used the words as synonyms, but Chapman's high regard for poetry makes the usage especially significant.[14] The next lines continue with an extremely revealing hierarchy of responses:

> Performing such a lively Evidence
>   In thy Narrations, that thy Hearers still
> Thou turnst to thy Spectators; and the sense
>   That thy Spectators have of good or ill,
> Thou inject'st joyntly to thy Readers soules.

"Narrations" could mean "fables, which are a false narration resembling true," but Chapman has a narrower definition in mind: he later attacked "certaine insolent objections made against the length of my speeches, and narrations" in *The Memorable Masque.*[15] For Chapman, *narrations* is likely to mean any expository speech, the function the *narratio* fulfills in an oration, or the messenger/report speeches that naturally appear in the classically-based *Sejanus.* In either case, these narrations have the power to make listeners see. Chapman puns on "lively Evidence" and "Spectators": the actors and text manifest (*e-videre*) the subject to the hearers' and readers' imaginative sight.[16] Jonson's dramatic speeches compel his audiences to visualize what is described. Great dramatic poetry is not merely spoken verse. By praising the narrations, Chapman acknowledges the power of dramatic speech to transform its audience because it is speech that strikes more than the ear alone.

Defending *Caesar and Pompey*'s "division of acts and scenes," Chapman recalls the principle hinted in "lively Evidence." Division offers "the more perspicuity and height of celebration"; dramatic form clarifies a play's subject and dignifies it just as the "high" tragic style does. "Scenical representation," Chapman continues,

> is so far from giving just cause of any least diminution, that the personal and exact life it gives to any history, or other such delineation of human actions, adds to them lustre, spirit, and apprehension. (*Tragedies*, p. 341)[17]

As the earlier conjunction of didacticism and "lively Evidence" suggested, Chapman believes that performance offers a particular to join with the general validity that dramatic poetry discovers in its subject matter. When the audience sees the "personal and exact life" provided by specific human actors, they more readily and more pleasurably understand the play's "delineation of human actions." To press Chapman's thought further than he went, one might even return to his defense of "things like truth" and observe that (logically) no "history" can be enacted by any other than its first actors (e.g., Caesar, Pompey, Cato). Dramatic imitation becomes, *ipso facto*, like its original truth rather than that truth itself, played once and for all.

Drama possesses exact and vivid life. We apprehend human action through the actors' personal enactment. Chapman emphasizes the life on stage, the moment-to-moment conflict, acts, and speeches. These views and Chapman's chosen tragic subjects (French and Roman history) may explain why allegorical readings of his drama, as opposed to similar interpretations of the nondramatic poetry, have not succeeded very well.[18] If we apply the distinction between allegorical and oratorical poetry to Renaissance drama, common sense as well as most contemporary practical discussions of drama's methods will throw drama toward the oratorical pole.[19] Roughly speaking, allegorical techniques will help interpret two dramatic features: broad *données* (e.g., Bussy's "Herculean" characterization)[20] and specific local episodes or passages (e.g., the echoes of Hercules at the crossroads with which *Bussy* begins or the shadowy presence of Bruno's *Lo Spaccio della bestia trionphante* elsewhere in the play).[21] More elaborate structures, analogous to a long poem's narrative organization, cannot be expected.[22]

❧    ❧    ❧

F. P. Wilson observed that "Chapman's beliefs may not be summed up in a phrase—for they were as peculiar to himself as Milton's. . . ."[23] And I have not attempted a summation. The audience, poetry's origin and effects, the qualities poetry manifests, the varied nature of drama and its particular power—these matters are not Chapman's whole theory, but they are especially appropriate to my general argument. I have focused on two areas: what poetry has to offer its audience and the way that audience responds to poetry. In these matters, Chapman did not distinguish between dramatic and nondramatic poetry. His goals and methods remain the same. Everywhere he views art as the mediating agent between the divine and secular: "the right vertuous touch / Of a well-written soule to vertue moves." Poems and audience have souls, and through that divine element they participate in the eternal and the true, or so he hoped.

# Notes

For frequently cited works, the abbreviations from the Note on Texts and References are retained throughout the following notes.

## Introduction: "The Most Curious Maker of Them All"

1. See Joel E. Spingarn, ed., *Critical Essays of the Seventeenth Century* (1907; reprint, Bloomington: Indiana University Press, 1957), 1:138. For the relationship of Chapman, Drayton, and Reynolds, see below and the presentation copy of Chapman's *The Crowne of all Homers Workes* (ca. 1624) with Chapman's holograph inscription to Reynolds (see *Homer*, 2:503). In *Mythomystes*, Reynolds calls Chapman "my old friend" (Spingarn, ed., *Critical Essays*, 1:165).

2. "An Invective Wrighten by Mr. George Chapman Against Mr. Ben: Johnson" (lines 127–31 [*Poems;* pp. 376–77]); the poem is in Ashmole MS 38. It has long been thought that Chapman collaborated with Jonson on the staged version of *Sejanus*, and Jonson courteously mentions a "second pen" in his preface to the quarto. The debate is reviewed and a strong case for Chapman argued in R. P. Corballis, "The 'Second Pen' in the Stage Version of *Sejanus*," *Modern Philology* 76 (1978–79): 273–77. Byron's Senecan intoxication (*Byron's Conspiracy* 1.2.22–52) is remarkably similar to Sejanus's soliloquy opening act 5 of Jonson's play.

3. Chapman rebuts the charge of "affected labour" in 1598 (*Homer*, 1:548).

4. Algernon Swinburne, *George Chapman* (London: Chatto and Windus, 1875), p. 103.

5. See, respectively, Franck L. Schoell, *Etudes sur l'humanisme continental en Angleterre* (Paris: Champion, 1926); Ennis Rees, *The Tragedies of George Chapman: Renaissance Ethics in Action* (Cambridge: Harvard University Press, 1954); Nancy von Pogrell, *Die philosophische-poetische Entwincklung George Chapmans* (Hamburg: Friedrichsen, de Gruyter, 1939).

6. Jonathan Dollimore, *Radical Tragedy: Religion, Ideology and Power in the Drama of Shakespeare and his Contemporaries* (Chicago: University of Chicago Press, 1984), p. 82; more generally, see Dollimore's chap. 4 on mimetic realism and the nature of reality.

7. Some elements of Chapman's theory are especially relevant to my argument: his views on the bad audience and the good; poetry's supposed truth; the nature of dramatic representation. The Appendix offers a brief survey.

8. Chambers's assertion in *The Elizabethan Stage* (Oxford: Clarendon Press, 1923), 3:250 derives from Bertram Dobell's series of inaccurate extracts and commentaries in *The Athenaeum* 74, pt. 1 (23 and 30 March, 6 and 13 April 1901). For agreement, see: *Poems*, p. 480; Elkin Calhoun Wilson, *Prince Henry and English Literature* (Ithaca: Cornell University Press, 1946), pp. 74 and 145 n.45; J. W. Williamson, *The Myth of the Conqueror: Prince Henry Stuart* (New York: AMS, 1978), pp. 40 and 86. A sewer, like the cupbearers, carvers, and ushers, attended the royal

personage at meals, but the position was not strictly menial and holders were frequently gentry: the future Earl of Ancram was groom and later page of the bedchamber to James; George Villiers, fourth son of a knight and eventually Duke of Buckingham, began his career at court as a cupbearer to the king; Thomas Carew was once sewer to James.

9. See *Letter-Book*, pp. 293 and 453, where I, too, mistakenly ascribe the petition to Chapman.

10. See, respectively, P[ublic] R[ecord] O[ffice] (London) SP14/15, ff. 137–38 and PRO SP14/72/111.

11. Roy Strong, *Henry, Prince of Wales and England's Lost Renaissance* (London: Thames and Hudson, 1986), p. 180, citing PRO LC 2/4/6.

12. See Pam Wright, "A Change of Direction: The Ramifications of a Female Household, 1558–1603," in *The English Court: from the Wars of the Roses to the Civil War*, ed. David Starkey (London and New York: Longman, 1987), pp. 154–56. Among other dramatists, Samuel Daniel was groom (at fifty pounds per year) and then gentleman extraordinary of Queen Anne's Privy Chamber, a post considerably superior to that Chapman apparently held.

13. See, e.g., *Poems* pp. 199–200, 385–89; *Letter-Book*, pp. 293–94 (item 88), 396 (item 139), 443, 457.

14. For the description of Drayton as "the Prince's poet" and the claim that Jones designed the title pages of the complete Homer and Drayton's *Polyolbion*, see Strong, *Henry, Prince of Wales*, pp. 61 and 130–31, respectively.

15. See, respectively, Ann Fanshawe, *The Memoirs of Ann Lady Fanshawe*, ed. E. J. Fanshawe (London: John Lane, 1907), p. 9, and George Chapman, *The Iliads of Homer*, ed. Richard Hooper, 2d ed. (London: J. R. Smith, 1865), 1:li. Sir Henry Fanshawe was remembrancer of the exchequer (1601–16) and a close friend of John Chamberlain. His seat, Ware Park, was near Chapman's home town of Hitchin, Herts., with which he maintained a life-long association and where his elder brother Thomas was a substantial figure; see C. J. Sisson and Robert Butman, "George Chapman, 1612–22: Some New Facts," *Modern Language Review* 46 (1951): 185–90 and R. L. Hine, *Hitchin Worthies: Four Centuries of English Life* (1932; reprint, Hitchin: Eric Moore, 1974), passim, esp. p. 57.

16. See J. R. Dasent, ed., *Acts of the Privy Council* 32 (London: HMSO, 1907), pp. 190 and 213. Walsingham had earlier semidiplomatic experience with France: see "the [eight] payments to him for journeys to and from France carrying letters to or from Henry Cobham, ambassador to France" in 1580–81 and 1582–83, recorded in David Cook, "Dramatic Records in the Declared Accounts of the Treasurer of the Chamber 1558–1642," *Malone Society Collections*, 6 (1962 for 1961), p. 141.

17. *A True and Perfect Discourse of the Practices and Treasons of Marshall Biron* (1602), a pamphlet "translated from the French," was entered in the *Stationers' Register* on 5 August, a bare two weeks after Biron's execution on 31 July (21 July, English style).

18. If this interpretation is correct, Chapman was lying when he defended the two plays to Sir George Buck, claiming "I see not myne owne Plaies" and therefore should not be held responsible for politically offensive performances (see *Letter-Book*, pp. 246, 435–37).

19. See John Chamberlain, *The Letters of John Chamberlain*, ed. N. E. McClure (Philadelphia, Pa.: American Philosophical Society, 1939), 1:273; William Cecil was also an intimate of Prince Henry (see Strong, *Henry, Prince of Wales*, esp. pp. 44–45). Lady Walsingham was one of the court ladies who escorted Queen Anne south from Scotland in 1603. She helped costume (and probably danced in) a masque for the

queen at Hampton Court (December 1603) and certainly performed in Jonson's *Masque of Blackness* (1605) and *Masque of Beauty* (1608); see John Nichols, *The Progresses, Processions, and Magnificent Festivities of James I* (London: Nichols, 1828), 1:167, 3:1061, 1:489, 2:174, respectively. The Walsinghams were jointly chief keepers of the Queen's Wardrobe, so it is not impossible that some obsolescent court finery might have found its way to the Blackfriars stage, just as Queen Elizabeth's apparel had been used for Queen Anne's masque at Hampton Court in December 1603.

20. See Millar MacLure, *George Chapman: A Critical Study* (Toronto: University of Toronto Press, 1966), p. 133.

21. Godfrey Goodman, *The Court of King James the First*, ed. J. S. Brewer (London: Bentley, 1839), 1:30.

22. See Neil Cuddy, "The Revival of the Entourage: the Bedchamber of James I, 1603–1625," in Starkey, ed., *The English Court*, pp. 173–225; quotation from pp. 179–80. For similar distinctions on the English and Scottish styles of monarchy, see Jenny Wormald, "James VI and I: Two Kings or One?" *History* 68 (1983): 204–5. R. Malcolm Smuts suggests some of the differences between Elizabeth's court and James's as they were perceived publicly in *Court Culture and the Origins of a Royalist Tradition in Early Stuart England* (Philadelphia: University of Pennsylvania Press, 1987), pt. 1, esp. pp. 26–31.

23. In the Conclusion, I suggest that Chapman explained his own career to himself in the terms he used both in the plays and to his patrons; for the moment, though, I want only to stress Chapman's historical immersion in the very *kinds* of events he dramatizes.

24. See chap. 3 for comment on this scene; the opening of *Bussy*, act 5, scene 3, is very similar, and there are related, if less full, scenes in Chapman's other tragedies.

25. For further discussion, see my "The Arts of the Dramatist," in *The Cambridge Companion to English Renaissance Drama*, ed. A. R. Braunmuller and Michael Hattaway (Cambridge: Cambridge University Press, 1990), pp. 53–90.

26. *Tragedies*, p. 598. Peter Ure, writing about "Chapman's Tragedies" in J. R. Brown and Bernard Harris, eds., *Jacobean Theatre*, Stratford-upon-Avon Studies 1, rev. rpt. (1960; London: Arnold, 1965), asserts that all of Chapman's plays from *The Revenge of Bussy* onward explore "what happens when political power and moral authority are not coincident . . ." (p. 241). I would extend the generalization: as we have seen, "moral authority" is often hard to locate.

27. Any writer about Chapman sooner or later touches the issue. An early counterargument appears in Richard Gerber's "Ubermensch und Treue: zur umstrittenen Entwincklung von George Chapmans Drama," *Anglia* 76 (1958): 510–35, esp. 510–14, although Gerber proceeds to redichotomize the tragedies along the lines his title suggests. It may be possible that Stoic ethics become increasingly predominant as the Neoplatonic metaphysic begins to fail; Chapman reacts at the ethical level to a wider and larger theoretical failure.

28. Ernst Cassirer, *Individual and Cosmos in Renaissance Philosophy* (1927), trans. Mario Domandi (New York: Harper, 1964), p. 61.

29. The first quotation comes from the dedication to *Caesar and Pompey* (*Tragedies*, p. 341); the second appears in the "Justification" of *Andromeda Liberata* (*Poems*, p. 327).

30. If what looks like the true moves us, what is really true will move us much more; *Francisci Robortelli . . . in librum Aristotelis de arte poetica explicationes . . .* (Florence, 1548), p. 93. This (mis)reading of *Poetics*, chap. 9, was popular; see Gerald Else, *Aristotle's Poetics: The Argument* (Cambridge: Harvard University Press, 1957),

pp. 320–21, and Leon Golden and O. B. Hardison, Jr., *Aristotle's Poetics: A Translation and Commentary for Students of Literature* (Englewood Cliffs, N.J.: Prentice-Hall, 1968), p. 160. Note, too, that Robortello uses *true* (in poetry) to mean "possible" or "credible" rather than accomplished fact: "Verisimilia nos movent, quia fieri potuisse credimus, ita rem accidisse. Vera nos movent, qui scimus ita accidisse . . ." (Robortello, p. 93).

31. I mean, of course, metaphysics and theologically oriented philosophy, not natural philosophy. "History" was the safest arena for speculative political philosophy as well.

32. W. J. Bouwsma, *Venice and the Defense of Republican Liberty* (Berkeley and Los Angeles: University of California Press, 1968), chap. 1. On European historiography in England, see F. J. Levy, "Hayward, Daniel and the Beginnings of the Politic History in England," *Huntington Library Quarterly* 50 (1987): 1–37.

33. See H. A. Kelly, *Divine Providence in the England of Shakespeare's Histories* (Cambridge: Harvard University Press, 1970): ". . . The practice of writing from a providential point of view, which was strongly influenced, especially in the sixteenth century, by the didactic concept of historiography . . . eventually gave way to . . . an analysis of causes on a natural level. Providential interpretations, since they involved . . . absolutely unverifiable conjectures as to the divine reasoning . . . were set aside as mere idle speculation" (p. 300). Kelly's long section on "Shakespeare's Double Tetralogy" (pp. 203–95) shows how Shakespeare freed his plays from the sources' imposed patterns and shaped a new, independent, and dramatic "moral ethos and mythos" from their materials.

For further discussion of changes in historiography, see J. W. Thompson, *A History of Historical Writing* (New York: Columbia University Press, 1942), esp. chaps. 30 and 31; F. S. Fussner, *The Historical Revolution: English Historical Writing and Thought 1580–1640* (London: Routlege, 1962); F. J. Levy, *Tudor Historical Thought* (San Marino, Calif.: Huntington Library, 1967). For suggestions on how "advanced" historiography and drama interrelated in the period, see my "*King John* and Historiography," *ELH* 55 (1988): 309–32.

34. A. P. Rossiter, ed., *Woodstock: A Moral History* (London: Chatto and Windus, 1946). The same author's *English Drama from Early Times to the Elizabethans* (London: Hutchinson, 1950) shows very clearly how the moralities' Cromwellian and Marian political involvement contributes to high Elizabethan and Jacobean political-historical tragedy (see "Interlude of Church and State," pp. 122–38). For seventeenth-century developments, see Judith Doolin Spikes, "The Jacobean History Play and the Myth of the Elect Nation," *Renaissance Drama*, n.s., 8 (1977): 117–49. Irving Ribner, *The English History Play in the Age of Shakespeare*, rev. ed. (London: Methuen, 1965), traces some important Continental historians' influence (pp. 14–19).

35. The standard treatment, Ribner's *English History Play*, restricts itself to plays using British subject matter and naturally excludes Chapman. Ribner's definition of the history play—"An adaptation of drama to the purposes of history" (rev. ed., p. 27)—coupled with his view of history itself does not produce many observations germane to my topic. He categorizes thus: "It is almost possible to divide extant history plays into two groups, the one embodying a dramatic structure stemming from the miracle play and the other one stemming from the morality" (p. 28). A later chapter concerning *Edward II*, *Woodstock*, and *Edward III* is called "Historical Tragedy and Moral History," but Ribner does not pursue the implicit terminological possibilities.

36. For the background of historical and political thought, see Felix Gilbert,

*Machiavelli and Guicciardini* (Princeton: Princeton University Press, 1965); Felix Raab, *The English Face of Machiavelli: A Changing Interpretation 1500–1700* (London: Routledge, 1964); Friedrich Meinecke, *Machiavellism: The Doctrine of Raison D'Etat and its Place in Modern History,* trans. Douglas Scott (New Haven: Yale University Press, 1957); and J. W. Allen, *Political Thought in the Sixteenth Century* (1928; reprint, London: Methuen, 1941).

37. T. B. Tomlinson represents an extreme position in *A Study of Elizabethan and Jacobean Tragedy* (Cambridge: Cambridge University Press, 1964); he includes a chapter entitled, "Decadence: The Hollowness of Chapman and Ford." Dollimore places the drama in the wider context of European scepticism; see especially *Radical Tragedy,* pt. 3, "Man Decentred."

38. That the choice was unusual is a commonplace; the closest surviving example is Marlowe's *Massacre at Paris.* Chapman's and Marlowe's plays are the central evidence, for example, in A. H. Smith's *Les Evénements politiques de France dans le théâtre du siècle d'Elisabeth* (Paris: Larose, 1906); Smith was thereafter reduced to discussing *Love's Labour's Lost, Thierry and Theodoret,* and the ghostly contents of Henslowe's diary. The danger of such subject matter became manifest when the French ambassador objected to the *Byron* plays in 1608. His report on the incident specifically mentions that playing resumed "a condition qu'ils [the actors] ne representeront plus aucune histoire moderne ni ne parleront des choses du temps a peine de la vie" (quoted from Chambers, *The Elizabethan Stage,* 3:258). This prohibition, as much as any putative "philosophical" change, must have influenced Chapman's subsequent choice of tragic subjects—the "things like truth" of *The Revenge of Bussy D'Ambois,* the Roman history of *Caesar and Pompey,* and safely "ancienne" history of *Chabot* (Francis I, after all, was a Valois, not a Bourbon). Of course, other dramatists wrote political tragedies, but they tended to select lurid domestic events from Italian city-states (e.g., Webster's two tragedies) or events concerning England's temporary or long-standing national enemies (e.g., Thomas Middleton's *A Game at Chess* or John Fletcher and Philip Massinger's *Sir John van Olden Barnevelt).*

39. For an exhaustive study of the plays' dates, see Albert H. Tricomi, "The Dates of the Plays of George Chapman," *English Literary Renaissance* 12 (1982): 242–66.

40. See E. H. Gombrich, "*Icones Symbolicae:* The Visual Image in Neo-Platonic Thought," *Journal of the Warburg and Courtauld Institutes* 11 (1948): 163–92; a much expanded version appears in Gombrich, *Symbolic Images: Studies in the Art of the Renaissance, II* (Oxford: Phaidon Press, 1972), pp. 123–91. See also D. P. Walker, *Spiritual Magic from Ficino to Campanella* (London: Warburg Institute, 1958) and the same author's *The Ancient Theology* (London: Duckworth, 1972).

41. *Tragedies,* p. 78. Parrott glosses "most divine philosopher" as Epictetus (p. 577). Preconception has here overtaken common sense: Chapman's dedicatory epistle to the *Odysseys* quotes Ficino as if he were the master himself: "*Qui Poeticas ad fores accedit, &c.* (sayes the Divine Philosopher) . . ." (*Poems,* p. 408). That philosopher is Plato: I know of no passage in Epictetus's *Discourses* that mentions the doctrine here ascribed to the "most divine philosopher." See also Schoell, *Etudes,* pp. 5–6, and Jean Jacquot, *George Chapman (1559–1634): sa vie, sa poésie, son théâtre, sa pensée* (Paris: Ed. Les Belles Lettres, 1951), p. 260.

42. See Jackson I. Cope, *The Theater and the Dream: From Metaphor to Form in Renaissance Drama* (Baltimore: Johns Hopkins University Press, 1973), pp. 32–53, and R. B. Waddington, *The Mind's Empire: Myth and Form in George Chapman's Narrative Poems* (Baltimore: Johns Hopkins University Press, 1974), chaps. 3 and 6.

43. Millar MacLure remarks, "I am not altogether convinced that there is a clear

line of development in Chapman's thought, passing comfortably from the Achillean to the Ulyssean ideal" (*George Chapman*, p. 132). This view has been thoroughly substantiated in Richard S. Ide's *Possessed with Greatness: The Heroic Tragedies of Shakespeare and Chapman* (Chapel Hill: University of North Carolina Press, 1980), pp. 160–67. Chapman's oeuvre resists simple schematization; he was a typical Renaissance syncretist whose sources encouraged eclecticism. Just as Ficino relies on Aquinas (see, e.g., M. J. B. Allen, ed. and trans., *The "Philebus" Commentary* [Berkeley and Los Angeles: University of California Press, 1975], pp. 86–89, 294–97, 374–79), so a reader of Cicero would find Cato, Hercules, and Ulysses listed as exemplary wise men (see Eugene M. Waith, *The Herculean Hero in Chapman, Marlowe, Shakespeare and Dryden* [London: Chatto and Windus, 1962], p. 30).

## Chapter 1. "Spirit to Dare and Power to Do": The Two Worlds of *Bussy D'Ambois*

1. See *Bussy*, p. 147 and John Dryden, *Of Dramatic Poesy and Other Critical Essays*, ed. George Watson (London: Dent, 1962), 1:274–79.

2. Millar MacLure, *George Chapman: A Critical Study* (Toronto: University of Toronto Press, 1966), p. 112. For summaries of criticism, see Brooke's *Bussy*, pp. liv–lvii, and MacLure, *George Chapman*, pp. 112–113.

3. While Monsieur does admire Bussy here, R. W. Dent suggests to me that the phrase "great heart" may qualify the praise. Dent cites several passages in which "great heart" stands for overweening, unjustified, and dangerous human pride. For example, Arthur Dent, *The Plaine Mans Path-Way to Heaven* (1601): God will strike "till hee haue broken our stout stomackes, and made our great hearts come downe" (p. 237); Thomas Dekker, *Old Fortunatus* (1600), 1.1.63: "down great heart, downe" (in Fredson Bowers, ed., *Dramatic Works of Thomas Dekker* [Cambridge: Cambridge University Press, 1953–61], 1:118). To these may be added Second Lord's words addressed to Barnavelt's corpse: "Farwell, great hart: full low thy strength now lyes, / he that would purge ambition this way dies" (John Fletcher and Philip Massinger, *The Tragedy of Sir John van Olden Barnavelt*, ed. T. H. Howard-Hill, Malone Society Reprints [Oxford, 1980], lines 3002–3); Parrott claims Fletcher imitated *Byron's Tragedy* in Barnavelt's final speech (*Tragedies*, p. 623).

4. Quoted from Brooke's note on 1.2.142; unlike Brooke, I would retain the first quarto's comma after "the place" to indicate apposition.

5. See Chapman, *Bussy D'Ambois*, ed. Maurice Evans (London: Benn, 1965), pp. xx–xxiv. Details of *Lo Spaccio*'s original publication appear in *The Expulsion of the Triumphant Beast*, ed. and trans. Arthur Imerti (New Brunswick, N.J.: Rutgers University Press, 1964), pp. 21 and 281 n.2. This translation is hereafter cited as *The Expulsion*.

6. For example, see Frances Yates, *Giordano Bruno and the Hermetic Tradition* (Chicago: University of Chicago Press, 1968), and Jean Seznec, *The Survival of the Pagan Gods* (1940), trans. Barbara Sessions (New York: Harper, 1961).

7. This argument for Luna-Woman-Tamyra's power over Bussy is strengthened by Monsieur: "If great men / And wise make 'scapes to please advantage / 'Tis with a woman" (3.2.145–47).

8. The scene was effective (or popular) enough to be parodied in Beaumont and Fletcher's *The Maid's Tragedy*, act 4, scene 2.

9. Jonathan Goldberg, *James I and the Politics of Literature* (Baltimore: Johns Hopkins University Press, 1983), p. 160; Goldberg sees Bussy as a "hero of absolutism" (p. 155) who figures royal absolutism rather than individualism.

# Notes to Pages 38–41 161

10. See Edwin Muir, " 'Royal Man': Notes on the Tragedies of George Chapman," rpt. in Max Bluestone and Norman Rabkin, eds. *Shakespeare's Contemporaries* (Englewood Cliffs, N.J.: Prentice-Hall, 1961), pp. 233–34. Chapman's friend, Henry Reynolds, joins the Golden Age with Eden: "What could they [the "wise Auncients"] meane by their *Golden-Age* . . . But the state of Man before his Sin? and consequently, by their Iron Age, but the worlds infelicity and miseries that succeeded his fall?" (*Mythomystes* in Spingarn, *Critical Essays*, 1: 175–76).

11. Louis I. Bredvold, "The Naturalism of Donne in Relation to Some Renaissance Traditions," *Journal of English and Germanic Philology* 22 (1923): 471–503; see esp. pp. 477–88 and 493.

12. See Samuel Daniel's superb translation in Daniel, *Complete Works in Verse and Prose*, ed. A. B. Grosart (1885; reprint, New York: Russell and Russell, 1963), 1: 260–61. John Wolfe had published a complete Italian text of *Aminta* in 1591, so it is not fanciful to think Chapman or some of his audience knew the text. On its English popularity, see G. K. Hunter, *Dramatic Identities and Cultural Tradition* (Liverpool: Liverpool University Press, 1978), pp. 136–40.

13. See, respectively, Cicero, *De Finibus*, book 3; Seneca, *Epistolae Morales* 90; and *The Expulsion*, pp. 203, 207, and 231.

14. Cf. *The Expulsion*, pp. 126 and 145.

15. See Thomas Starkey, *A Dialogue between Reginald Pole and Thomas Lupset*, ed. Kathleen M. Burton (London: Chatto and Windus, 1948), pp. 26–40.

16. Harry Levin, *The Myth of the Golden Age in the Renaissance* (Bloomington: Indiana University Press, 1969), p. 117.

17. Raymond B. Waddington, *The Mind's Empire: Myth and Form in George Chapman's Narrative Poems* (Baltimore: Johns Hopkins University Press, 1974), p. 23.

18. Gordon Braden's reading of *Tamburlaine* does not mention Chapman but implicitly describes what he might have learned about heroic characterization, if not heroic rhetoric, from that play; see Braden, *Renaissance Tragedy and the Senecan Tradition: Anger's Privilege* (New Haven: Yale University Press, 1985), pp. 182–97.

19. Bruno makes the same rather common point: see *The Expulsion*, p. 231. Tamyra's attitude toward Henry is very important. The King is a moral and sensible, if rather ineffective, monarch: see Robert P. Adams, "Critical Myths and Chapman's Original *Bussy D'Ambois*," *Renaissance Drama* 9 (1966): 156. MacLure disagrees: "The King . . . after all, has no *character* of his own" (*George Chapman*, p. 121); cf. *Tragedies*, p. 544.

20. E. M. Waith, *The Herculean Hero in Marlowe, Chapman, Shakespeare and Dryden* (London: Chatto and Windus, 1962), chap. 4, examines this aspect of *Bussy.*

21. See Erwin Panofsky, *Hercules am Scheideweg*, Studien der Bibliothek Warburg, 18 (Leipzig and Berlin: Teubner, 1930), pp. 37–128 and plates 30–65. Many late fifteenth- and sixteenth-century northern woodcuts show Hercules lying down, for example, most of those in the many editions of Sebastian Brant's popular *Stultifera Navis* (1497). Annibale Caracci's Farnese Palace fresco established what Panofsky calls the "canonical" iconography: Hercules sits between Virtue and Vice in a woodland setting that includes the rocky path through barren country to Virtue on one side, and the luxuriant, downward path to voluptuous indolence on the other. Annibale's work is too late (1595) to have influenced Chapman even through copies; Chapman must have known Brant's *The Ship of Fools*.

Panofsky considers the mixed subjects—Judgment of Paris, Dream of Scipio, Choice of Hercules—and varied stylistic traditions that underlie Hercules' positions and the landscapes of his choice; see esp. pp. 37–42, 55–64, 103–7, and 124–28.

22. See Edgar Wind, *Pagan Mysteries in the Renaissance*, rev. ed. (New York: Norton, 1968), pp. 81n. and 82.

23. See John Rupert Martin, *The Farnese Gallery* (Princeton: Princeton University Press, 1965), pp. 28–30, where he also cites Ficino's letter to Lorenzo de'Medici (*Opera Omnia*, 1576, p. 991) and the *Philebus* commentary.

24. For instance, Thomas Starkey, *Dialogue*, p. 24.

25. See G. B. Nenna, *Nennio or A Treatise of Nobility*, trans. William Jones (London, 1595), esp. sig. H3r–H4r where the Judgment of Paris is analyzed as a choice of active, contemplative, or "delightful" lives. The treatise's second book constantly emphasizes *learning* as training in, and practice of, virtue. This material may have attracted Chapman (his prefatory poem is in *Poems*, p. 353). Peter Bement believes the active-contemplative dichotomy runs throughout Chapman's work; see his *George Chapman: Action and Contemplation in His Tragedies*, Salzburg Studies in English Literature, 8 (Salzburg: Universität Salzburg, 1974), esp. chaps. 2 and 3. For Bement, Bussy begins "as a contemplative" (p. 105) and Chapman has merged "the melancholy scholar and the malcontent tool-villain" (p. 114). I disagree. Although Bement reaches a balanced conclusion that acknowledges *Bussy*'s experimental qualities, his initial approach sacrifices the play's valid refusal to take sides.

26. The preceding paragraph owes much to Hallett Smith, *Elizabethan Poetry* (1952; reprint, Ann Arbor: University of Michigan Press, 1968), chap. 1; see also my *George Peele* (Boston: G. K. Hall, 1983), chap. 3.

27. Monsieur's comment—"Turn'd to earth, alive? / Up man, the sun shines on thee" (1.1.54–55)—may suggest the corrupted soul's immersion in matter; the "sun" would then refer to the physical-spiritual principle that radiates heat and divine knowledge and power to individual human souls. Monsieur perverts these metaphors in lines 57ff.

28. Monsieur calls Bussy's withdrawl "sloth" (Accidia, a deadly sin) in line 64 and goes on to recite Plutarchian examples of military glory.

29. Compare, for example, Bussy finely costumed and accompanied by two pages (act 5, scene 2) with Monsieur's initial appearance (act 1, scene 1), a juxtaposition Brooke notes in his edition, p. xxix. The 1988 Old Vic production of the play showed that this analogy could work theatrically.

30. MacLure, *George Chapman*, p. 121.

31. In a chapter subtitled "The Saving Stereotypes of Female Heroism," Lisa Jardine defines Jacobean convention: "Virginity is the acme of female virtue. It is to femaleness what valour is to maleness." See *Still Harping on Daughters: Women and Drama in the Age of Shakespeare* (Brighton, England: Harvester, 1983), p. 176.

32. See Brooke's edition, pp. xliii f., and Robert Adams, "Critical Myths and Chapman's Original *Bussy D'Ambois*," *Renaissance Drama* 9 (1966): 154. E. M. Waith has suggested links between *Bussy D'Ambois* and chivalric romance, especially in Chapman's handling of the love affair; see *Ideas of Greatness: Heroic Drama in England* (London: Routledge, 1971), pp. 127–29.

33. See Brooke's edition, p. xliv.

34. This passage raises the vexed question of night's morality. To judge from "Hymnus in Noctem" and scattered remarks elsewhere (especially the letter to Roydon preceding *Ovids Banquet of Sence*), Chapman apparently took a hermetic or Neoplatonic line on the issue of secrecy, concealment, and darkness—actual or metaphorical. In *Herculean Hero*, pp. 98–103, Waith argues convincingly for a multivalent response to night and its associate, magic. Caught between the stock associations and Chapman's eccentric attitudes, the audience responds ambivalently, and that response, as Waith shows, suits Chapman's presentation of the love affair. For agreement, see Joel B. Altman, *The Tudor Play of Mind: Rhetorical Inquiry and the Development of Elizabethan Drama* (Berkeley and Los Angeles: University of Califor-

nia Press, 1978), p. 314. Bement, *George Chapman: Action and Contemplation*, pp. 114–24, finds that "night" in the play's last four acts is "false night," a view that makes the play structurally monstrous and undermines Chapman's skill and beliefs. For further treatment of the play's imagery and its sources, see Gunilla Florby, *The Painful Passage to Virtue: A Study of George Chapman's "The Tragedy of Bussy D'Ambois" and "The Revenge of Bussy D'Ambois,"* Lund Studies in English, 61 (Lund: Gleerup, 1982), chap. 3.

35. Later, using similar metaphors, Bussy argues that "our Griefs and Joys / Hold several sceptres in us" (4.1.25–26); he admits that "authority" (control of the passions "hous'd behind the shield of Nature") "goes with corruption" (knowledge of, and submission to, "tyrannous law, treachery, or beastly need"). For a valuable investigation of these ideas, see Stephen Booth's commentary on sonnet 146 in *Shakespeare's Sonnets: Edited with an Analytic Commentary* (New Haven: Yale University Press, 1977), pp. 501–17.

36. See Muir, " 'Royal Man,' " p. 233. Tamyra's reciprocal characterization strongly qualifies this view: see Robert B. Heilman, *Tragedy and Melodrama: Versions of Experience* (Seattle: University of Washington Press, 1968), p. 197: "The careful treatment of her conflicting emotions gives a tragic direction not fully realized in the more univocal characterization of Bussy."

37. See Louis B. Wright, "Stage Duelling in the Elizabethan Theatre" (1927), rpt. in *The Seventeenth-Century Stage*, ed. G. E. Bentley (Chicago: University of Chicago Press, 1968), pp. 159–69. The fact that Chapman was using child actors probably does not affect the argument: he was prepared to risk putting Tamyra's torture and Bussy's death on stage.

38. Adams, "Critical Myths," p. 150, makes this comparison and so describes the language.

39. Waddington, *The Mind's Empire*, p. 31, claims that Bussy now resembles the colossal and hollow statues that he castigated in his first soliloquy; this view ignores the facts that Bussy, were he to "become" a statue, would be both life-size and "marble" (5.3.145), without the overweening and empty pomposity of those earlier statues.

40. "Thunderbolt" could apparently mean a permanent stellar object which might have "stuck" (remained fixed in the heavens); see Brooke's note at 5.3.193 and A. S. Ferguson, "The Plays of George Chapman," *Modern Language Review* 13 (1918): 18.

41. See Brooke's note at 5.3.157 and compare Bussy's resonant response to Maffé's puzzlement at what makes the hero important: "no merit in the world sir" (1.1.172).

42. Compare Altman, *Tudor Play of Mind*, pp. 302–30. Altman's very different method (a study of plays as if they were arguments *in utramque partem*) yields an interpretation that supports the one offered here, although I believe he pays insufficient attention to the verse and "surface" conflict. In *Possessed with Greatness: The Heroic Tragedies of Shakespeare and Chapman* (Chapel Hill: University of North Carolina Press, 1980), Richard S. Ide believes that Bussy resigns "his titanic heroism in favor of Christian magnanimity" and that "Bussy's titanic spirit . . . has been perfected at the end by moral virtue" (pp. 95–96).

43. From the Stoics (originally Epicurus), the Neoplatonists took the idea of a cyclical conflagration of sublunar nature, which would then begin to retrace the path it had followed in previous cycles. See Thomas Whittaker, *The Neo-Platonists: A Study in the History of Hellenism*, 2d rev. ed. (Cambridge: Cambridge University Press, 1918), p. 73. Ide finds the Friar's eulogy "authoritative," but doubts that Chapman believes "that Bussy's flame will ignite a universal conflagration out of which cleansing fires the world will be born anew" (*Possessed with Greatness*, pp. 96–97).

## Chapter 2. War and Peace in *The Conspiracy of Charles, Duke of Byron*

1. Two contributions to *Essays in Dramatic Literature: The Parrott Presentation Volume,* ed. Hardin Craig (Princeton: Princeton University Press, 1935) exemplify these inappropriate critical responses. In "Political Theory in the Plays of George Chapman," Charles W. Kennedy makes overstringent distinctions: "The figure of Henry IV is opposed to that of his rebellious Marshall; justice and virtue opposing corruption and disloyalty . . . at no time is the sympathy of the reader enlisted in his [Byron's] behalf. His attitude toward Henry is that of a traitorous subject, and he is presented by Chapman as an example of disloyalty directed to ambitious striving for personal interest" (p. 80). Craig himself chides the playwright in "Ethics in the Jacobean Drama: The Case of Chapman": "He [Chapman] also betrays admiration" for Tamyra and Byron (p. 39), and "Chapman goes further than ethics permitted in sympathizing with sin" (p. 42). Peter Ure's "The Main Outline of Chapman's Byron," *Studies in Philology* 47 (1950): 568–88 examines the King's relation with Byron and corrects many misinterpretations although later critics have not always heeded the corrective; Ure's essay has been reprinted in *Elizabethan and Jacobean Drama: Critical Essays by Peter Ure,* ed. J. C. Maxwell (Liverpool: Liverpool University Press, 1974). I refer to the two plays as *Byron's Conspiracy* and *Byron's Tragedy,* or simply, *Conspiracy* and *Tragedy.*

2. For the ascent and descent pattern, related to *de casibus* organization, see G. K. Hunter, "*Henry IV* and the Elizabethan Two-Part Play," *Review of English Studies,* n.s., 5 (1954): 236–48. Ure, "Main Outline," argues for the influence of a common topos of heroic biography—the "competition" of Virtue and Fortune—mixed in this play with speculation on Machiavellian political theory. Chapman's borrowings from Plutarch, *De Alexandri Magni Fortuna Aut Virtute,* suggest that work as a source for the pattern, but Machiavelli and Ralegh, among many others, also discussed it. Hardin Craig finds a pervasive "psychological determinism" in the play; psychological interpretations as well as magical and astrological ones are discussed below. For the two plays as a "political morality," see Chapman, *The Conspiracy and Tragedy of Charles, Duke of Byron,* ed. John Margeson (Manchester: Manchester University Press, 1988), p. 25.

3. Just what history Chapman used as a source is debatable. Most critics believe Chapman drew exclusively upon a work by his cousin Edward Grimeston[e]: *A General Inventorie of the History of France* (London, 1607), a translation of works by Jean de Serres, Palma Cayet, and Pierre Matthieu. Marion Jones and Glynne Wickham, in "The Stage Furnishings of George Chapman's *The Tragedy of Charles, Duke of Byron,*" *Theatre Notebook* 16 (1962): 113–17, argue that earlier printed sources, including Palma Cayet and Matthieu, may have been used. This view does not account for Chapman's frequent verbal similarities to Grimeston unless one postulates that dramatist and historian would translate the same text into the same words. However derived, Chapman's historical information comes largely from the three French historians, and I have usually quoted Grimeston for convenience.

4. No audience could possibly notice the similarity in the theater, but Chapman echoes this line in Byron's speech describing "Noble, happy beasts, / That die, not having to their wills to live; / They use no deprecations nor complaints" (*Tragedy* 4.1.139–41).

5. William Empson, *Some Versions of Pastoral* (London: Chatto and Windus, 1950), p. 57; see his chap. 2.

6. Cf. D. J. Palmer, "Art and Nature in *As You Like It,*" *Philological Quarterly* 49 (1970): 33, where he remarks "those situations in tragedy, where the leading figures discover their own circumstances reflected in some chance meeting with a stranger, as Hamlet identifies himself with the actor's passion for Hecuba, or with Fortinbras' quixotic sense of honor, or with the grief of Laertes, and as Lear sees his own image in 'poor Tom.'"

7. Objecting to Jusserand's praise of this scene as the work "d'un psychologue et d'un maître dramaturge," Parrott evidently thinks the scene merely establishes Byron's credulous simplicity (*Tragedies*, p. 594). Parrott further claims, as he almost always does when source and drama coincide, that Grimeston did Chapman's job for him, but the editor has overlooked the play's difference from the history. Opposite the marginal comment, "The Duke of *Savoyes* policy," Grimeston writes, "The Dukes proceeding therein was very cunning and Judicious, for often times he would begin a discourse of the valour & courage of the Duke *Biron,* to sound the Kings opinion, who did not alwayes give him the glory of those goodly executions, whereof hee vanted [vaunted]. The Duke did still advertise the Duke *Biron* of any thing the King sayd of him, that might any way alter him . . ." (ed. 1607, p. 883).

8. See Wolfgang Clemen, *English Tragedy Before Shakespeare: The Development of Dramatic Speech,* trans. T. S. Dorsch (London: Methuen, 1961), pp. 46n, 49, and 54.

9. As T. F. Van Laan remarks in *The Idiom of Drama* (Ithaca: Cornell University Press, 1970), "One of the few kinds of statements a spectator is likely to accept at face value consists of the various narrated reports of the unstaged portion of the plot, the past and intervening events" (p. 129). By playing with this conventional credulity— undermining by Henry's and Savoy's argument our memory of the past—Chapman engages us in Byron's dilemma and Henry's indifference. Later in the play (5.1), Chapman makes perfectly traditional use of the reported action, as he had in *Bussy D'Ambois,* act 2, scene 1.

10. For example, Grimeston writes, "And the Warre ended, hee thought that having no more use of his valour, hee should have no more credit . . . he found that men loose themselves, being to much at their own ease" (ed. 1607, p. 960). Compare Palma Cayet, *Chronologie septenaire de l'histoire de la paix . . .* (Paris, 1605): "Il [Byron] voyait la guerre finie, & les espees remises au forreau: il jugea que sa valeur n'auroit plus de credit, & qu'il estoit inutile en temps de paix" (p. 285). Such important Jacobean plays as *Coriolanus, The White Devil,* and *The Maid's Tragedy* employ the returned or demobilized soldier as a figure at once offering a new perspective on "peace" and a soul seeking metaphysical justification.

11. In the appropriate context of the English rebuke to Byron, we learn that the Dauphin has been born (*Conspiracy* 4.1.144ff.). Birth and fecundity are yet another criticism of Byron's sterile militarism.

12. Here is Grimeston's account: "She thanked the King for his remembrance of her: but she said she could . . . not but feele an extreme torment, to see her selfe deprived of the sight and presence of the object which shee most desired. . . . From these speeches shee fell into some bitternesse of Complaints, which shee delivered with a little vehemencie, saying; That after she had succored this Prince with her Forces, Purse, and Meanes, and if she could have done it, with her own bloud, and had as much desired the happy successe of his affayres as himselfe, and the ruine of his Enemies more than himselfe, they had made no accompt of her, forcing her to thinke that the love they bare her was but for hope of commodities they might drawe from her, the which being dried up, all affection was cold. That they had sought her in the torment to forget her when the time was calme. That they preferred newe friendship before the olde, Wisdome before Justice, and Profit before Reason" (Grimeston, *General Inventorie,* p. 945). For a description of Queen Elizabeth's

deliberate humbling of Biron at their first meeting, see John Stowe, *The Annales of England* (London, 1605), p. 1411.

13. John Webster, "To the Reader," lines 37–43, in *The White Devil*, ed. J. R. Brown, 2d ed. (London: Methuen, 1966).

14. See Ure, "Main Outline," p. 572, and Dollimore, *Radical Tragedy*: the "realism" of Jacobean tragedy "problematises subjectivity rather than foregrounding man as a spiritual or psychological unity" (p. 176).

15. Compare Robert Dallington, *The View of Fraunce* (London, 1604), giving an opinion formed ca. 1598:

> See here a people, among whom it was a slander to doe well, and glorie to
> excell others in cruelty: therefore saith a Poet of theirs,
>
> . . . . . . . . . . . . . . . . . . .
> If the worst Frenchmen now are best of all rewarded,
> If the most honest men are now the least regarded
> Let's turne Traytors awhile, this time rewards offences:
> Who hath no mischief wrought, can get no recompences.
>
> (sig. F4v)

Dallington was gentleman of the Privy Chamber to Prince Henry (see Strong, *Henry, Prince of Wales,* pp. 30–31); some personal familiarity with Dallington may have added to Chapman's characteristic interest in France.

16. "Dread," Deighton's emendation for "dead" (line 22) is accepted by John B. Gabel in Chapman, *The Plays of George Chapman: The Tragedies*, gen. ed. Alan Holaday (Cambridge: D. S. Brewer, 1987). It is a plausible emendation, but unnecessary; see *OED, s.v. dead,* adj., II.14, "Of sound: without resonance, dull, muffled." Byron's association of the past with death—what he has done no longer "lives"—seems to me powerful and part of the pervasive allusions to time and memory.

Commenting on Henry's laughter, Alexander Leggatt finds that *The Conspiracy* "frequently moves in the direction of comedy"; "The King's laugh is a startling *coup de théâtre;* for the audience it brings both surprise and relief. Aware that Byron is supposed to be a tragic hero of some kind, we have found him, all too often, simply ridiculous. . . . The King's laugh clears the air: Byron *is* ridiculous; it is not only safe but proper to laugh at him." See Leggatt, "Tone and Structure in Chapman's *Byron,*" *Studies in English Literature, 1500–1900* 24 (1984): 309 and 317. I discuss *The Conspiracy*'s final, comic scene at the beginning of the next chapter.

17. Byron does obey his prince, at least in war: "I alone took Amiens . . . In spite of all the pitchy fires she cast, . . . Till she show'd yours [Henry's], and took her natural form" (*Conspiracy* 5.2.148–49, 151).

18. In speaking of the hero's "self-awareness," I mean specifically to avoid the connotations of "self-knowledge" since that term implies a view of human nature as fixed and unchanging and values that knowledge above all others; I do not hold these views, nor, for that matter, did Chapman. By self-awareness, I mean such things as a character's represented awareness of his or her circumstances, awareness of the interplay of choice and contingency, awareness of the fallibility but also the inescapability of explanations and explanatory systems; despite the prefix, self-awareness is dramatized information and emotion on behalf of the audience, not the character. Cf. Dollimore, *Radical Tragedy,* p. 179 on Renaissance self-consciousness versus modern individualistic self-knowledge.

19. The association is traditional; see, for example, Jean Seznec, *The Survival of the Pagan Gods,* trans. Barbara F. Sessions (1953; reprint, New York: Harper, 1961), pp.

140–41, where he cites, among other sources, *Somnium Scipionis*, 2:3; see also *Conspiracy* 3.2.257–58 and below. In "Chapman's Byron and Apollo's Virtue," *Explorations in Renaissance Culture* 3 (1976): 37–47, Mary E. Williams argues that "allusions to myths involving Apollo funciton . . . in clarifying the relative moral positions of the characters [i.e., Byron and Henry]" (p. 37).

20. "Mental imbalance" is the gist of Una Ellis-Fermor's view in *The Jacobean Drama*, 4th ed. (New York: Vintage, 1964), pp. 65–67.

21. See *Conspiracy* 1.1.183–94 (Henry vs. Byron); 2.2.187–94 (Byron); 3.2.170–74 (Byron); *Tragedy* 4.1.63–65 (Byron). Parrott also cites *Chabot*, 5.1.16–19, "De Guinana," lines 50–62 (*Poems*, p. 354), and "Of Friendship," lines 6–12 (*Poems*, p. 241).

22. Waith discusses the Senecan implications and interprets the scene in *Ideas of Greatness*, pp. 133–34. Contemporary French authors and artists portrayed Henry (not Byron) as Hercules. For example, see *Labyrinthe royal d'Hercule gaulois triomphant . . .* (Avignon, 1601?). Corrado Vivanti's excellent "Henry IV, the Gallic Hercules," *Journal of the Warburg and Courtauld Institutes* 30 (1967): 176–97 traces the evolution of this iconography and shows how Hermes came to be linked with Henry's pacific and learned qualities. The medal commemorating Henry's defeat of Savoy shows the king as Hercules defeating the Hydra.

23. See Edgar Wind, *Pagan Mysteries in the Renaissance*, rev. ed. (New York, N.Y.: Norton, 1968), pp. 68–69 and nn. 56–57; E. M. Waith, *The Herculean Hero in Marlowe, Chapman, Shakespeare and Dryden* (London: Chatto and Windus, 1962), pp. 44–45, 206–7, and nn. 18–23; Gordon Braden, *Renaissance Tragedy*, esp. chaps. 2 and 6 (quotation from p. 13). When a later hero, Chabot, is angered by injustice, one of his admirers claims "in the heart hath anger his wisest seat" (*Chabot*, 1.1.35), echoing Ephesians 4:25–27.

24. *Godfrey of Bulloigne, or the Recoverie of Jerusalem . . .* (London, 1600), A4r–v. Waith (see n. 23) first introduced Tasso into the discussion of Chapman's heroes; Ide, *Possessed with Greatness*, invokes Tasso to define "the normative social and psychological contexts in the *Byron* plays that weigh against the hero and at the same time weigh in favor of the hero" (p. 134).

25. Byron's words recall Horace: "Ira furor brevis est" (*Epistles* 1.2.62).

26. Ure, "Main Outline," p. 582.

27. Hardin Craig proposes "psychological determinism" as an interpretation (see n. 1 above); Ure correctly rejects the theory. In *Possessed with Greatness*, Ide regards Craig's view as a "likely but . . . partial response" (p. 151); Ide also describes Byron and La Fin in terms of "fiend" and "magician" (pp. 136ff.).

28. Writing of the *thymos* ("the ambitious, competitive part of the soul") as "a natural attribute of a warrior aristocracy," Braden generalizes: "Roman modes of self-regard become part of a powerful continuity of medieval aristocratic values. What characterizes the Renaissance is indeed the tenacity of these values even under changing social and political conditions; the real event in cultural history is the persistence of essentially chivalric standards as their content alters or even disappears" (*Renaissance Tragedy*, p. 77). Chapman and his audiences were experiencing the final convulsions of "medieval aristocratic values" in the political conflicts of late sixteenth- and early seventeenth-century England: see "English Politics and the Concept of Honour, 1485–1642" and "At a Crossroads of Political Culture: the Essex Revolt, 1601," in Mervyn James, *Society, Politics and Culture: Studies in Early Modern England* (Cambridge: Cambridge University Press, 1986), pp. 308–465; James describes the Essex fiasco as "the last honour revolt" (p. 416).

29. *Conversion* (line 48) is a logical term defining permissible substitutions of

negatives in a true positive statement in order to arrive at other true statements, and vice versa; see Thomas Wilson, *The Rule of Reason, conteinyng the Arte of Logique* (London, 1553), ff. 20v and 21v. Cf. *Byron's Tragedy*, 4.1.146.

30. Patricia Demers summarizes previous comments and reproduces an appropriate image (dedicated to Sidney with the motto "Non locus vir, sed vir locum ornat") from Geoffrey Whitney's *Choice of Emblems* (1586); see Demers, "The Conspiracy and Tragedy of Charles Duke of Byron [*sic*]: The Evaporation of Honour," *Renaissance and Reformation* 11 (1975): 90 and 95, n. 14.

31. Mark Eccles, "Sir George Buc, Master of the Revels," in *Thomas Lodge and Other Elizabethans*, ed. C. J. Sisson (Cambridge: Harvard University Press, 1933), p. 461, supposes the anonymous English counsellor who speaks these lines to be the historical Robert Cecil, Earl of Salisbury, and principal secretary to Elizabeth and James.

32. Ide finds an allusion to Ficinian spiritual magic in the scene (*Possessed with Greatness*, p. 136). The stage business itself (to which Picoté calls the audience's attention) is very unusual in dramatic tradition and remarkably similar to a moment in Æschylus's *Agamemnon*. In both plays, the central character is asked to step upon a carpet symbolic of his future (blood and death; Catiline and conspiracy); although Agamemnon is more sensitive than Byron to the implications of treading upon the carpet, the audience realizes that each man does so through hubris.

Chapman's references to Greek drama are generally secondhand, via Plutarch or Erasmus or some other intermediary, and this scene may owe nothing to the Greek play. Although editions of Æschylus appeared in 1518 and 1552, an accurate *Agamemnon* text did not appear until the Vettori-Estienne edition of 1557. Moreover, of the three Greek tragedians, Æschylus seems to have been the least well represented in English libraries: among pre-1608 printed and manuscript book catalogues I have examined, only Thomas James, *Catalogus . . . Bibliothecae . . . quam . . . Thomas Bodleius . . . nuper instituit . . .* (Oxford, 1605) lists an Æschylus (the 1557 edition, in fact). Seneca's *Agamemnon*, translated by John Studley in *Seneca His Tenne Tragedies* (London, 1581), substitutes a shirt for the prophetic carpet. Thus, the similarities between the *Agamemnon* and *Byron's Conspiracy* cannot be explained in any very simple way.

33. The simile of "offensive sounds" returns early in *Byron's Tragedy* when Henry recalls that Byron once refused foreign blandishments: "they found him still . . . a most wise Ulysses to their words, / Stopping his ears at their enchanted sounds" (1.1.77, 79–80).

## Chapter 3. Rare Virtues and Their Impair in *The Tragedy of Charles, Duke of Byron*

1. A. P. Rossiter, *English Drama from Early Times to the Elizabethans* (London: Hutchinson, 1950), p. 152. Making a very different argument from mine, R. A. Foakes observes, "In these plays [on Byron] Chapman wrote what *Bussy D'Ambois* is sometimes said to be, a tragedy of ideas"; see Foakes, "Tragedy at the Children's Theatres after 1600: A Challenge to the Adult Stage," in *Elizabethan Theatre II*, ed. David Galloway (Hamden, Conn.: Archon, 1970), p. 57 and cf. p. 59.

2. The word *legally* skirts the question of justice. To Jean Bodin, a *politique*, there were no lawful grounds for rebellion against a sovereign who had gained the throne in the proper manner; a tyrant (in Bodin's definition) could be overthrown, but not a rightful king who acted tyrannically or immorally. Thus, Bodin says, "where the kings

themselves have the soveraigntie without all doubt of question . . . it is not lawful for any one of the subjects in particular, or all of them in generall, to attempt any thing either by way of fact, or of justice against the honour, life, or dignitie of the soveraigne: albeit that he had committed all the wickedness, impietie, and crueltie that could be spoken. . . ." All quotations of Bodin are from *The Six Bookes of a Commonweale*, trans. Richard Knolles (London, 1606); the one cited here is from book 2, chap. 5; p. 222. Bodin's text appeared earlier in French (1576) and Latin (1586). See also J. W. Allen, *Political Thought in the Sixteenth Century* (1928; reprint, London: Methuen, 1941), pp. 426–31. Bodin is cited not as a specific source for any of the play's political theory, but as a contemporary political theorist who had a great influence upon European historiography, including the French sources Chapman used.

3. See Jean Bodin, *Six Books of the Commonwealth*, ed. and trans. M. J. Tooley (Oxford: Blackwell, 1955), p. xix; see also James I, *The Political Works of James I*, ed. C. H. MacIlwain (Cambridge: Harvard University Press, 1918).

4. These lines recall an important element in Kyd's *Spanish Tragedy*, a play that also dramatizes the relation between the stage world and real world, life and dramatic reality. When Revenge explains to Andrea why he has been drawm "here" (i.e., the theater, the limbo from which the two characters view the play's action), he says: "Here sit we down to see the mystery, / And serve for Chorus in this tragedy" (1.1.90–91 in Philip Edwards's Revels edition [London: Methuen, 1959]). See also Anne Righter Barton, *Shakespeare and the Idea of the Play* (Harmondsworth, England: Penguin, 1967), pp. 71ff. and Philip Edwards, *Thomas Kyd and Early Elizabethan Tragedy*, Writers and Their Work, 192 (London: Longmans, Green, 1966), pp. 31–34.

5. Inga-Stina Ewbank mentions this masque very briefly in her essay, " 'These Pretty Devices': A Study of Masques in Plays," in *A Book of Masques: In Honour of Allardyce Nicoll*, ed. T. J. B. S[pencer] and S. W. W[ells] (Cambridge: Cambridge University Press, 1967), pp. 407–48; for *Byron's Tragedy*, see p. 421. Ewbank cites Grimeston's account of the historical masque but does not go beyond the simple allegory of reconciliation.

6. Edward Grimeston, *A General Inventorie of the History of France* (London, 1607), p. 958.

7. Pierre Matthieu, *Histoire de France et des choses memorables* . . . (Paris, 1605), 2 vols., 2 : 89r (book 5, narration 1).

8. Jean Bertaut, *Oeuvres Poètiques* . . . dernière edition (Paris, 1620), pp. 558–59.

9. "Dapsile, or Liberality" seems to be a synthetic allegorical creation like Teras or Eronusis in *Hero and Leander*, where Chapman also mentions "bounty-loving Dapsilis" (4.237). Johann Scapula, *Lexicon Graeco-Latinum novum* (Basel, 1605), Chapman's aid in translating Homer, defines *dapsilis* as "largus, copiosus, abundans, uber." The word normally describes organic fecundity and spatial amplitude. By making *Liberality* a synonym, Chapman seems to appeal to the complex history of Aristotelian ethical thought (see William Harris, *Skelton's Magnyfycence and the Cardinal Virtue Tradition* [Chapel Hill: University of North Carolina Press, 1965], pp. 46–70, and Rosemond Tuve, *Allegorical Imagery: Some Mediaeval Books and Their Posterity* [Princeton: Princeton University Press, 1966], chap. 2). Liberality, in Renaissance Aristotelian thought, might be "magnificence," which—given Mme. D'Entragues's private situation—may further be "Liberty," the triumph of appetite and lower human nature over reason. Cf. Byron's complaint about the "two abhorred twins . . . stern War and Liberty" (*Tragedy* 3.1.33–34), the linking of magnanimity and magnificence (*Tragedy* 4.2.145–55), and *OED*, *s.v.* "liberty."

10. For more detailed discussion, see E. K. Chambers, *The Elizabethan Stage*

(Oxford: Clarendon, 1923), 3:257–58, and *Letter-Book*, pp. 435–37. In "The Original Version of Chapman's *Tragedy of Byron*," *Journal of English and Germanic Philology* 63 (1964): 433–40, John B. Gabel asserts that neither masque nor argument-scene was part of Chapman's original design and that Parrott's act and scene divisions (which faithfully follow the original quarto) are mistaken and misleading. What remains is a "mutilated playhouse version," saddled with "interpolated scenes" (i.e., the masque and the now excised slapping incident), which may not even be Chapman's (p. 440). There is no evidence for Gabel's thesis, although the censor has certainly mauled the text. Given that Chapman's epistle dedicatory complains of the censorship, that he probably corrected proof (see Gabel's introduction in Chapman, *The Plays of George Chapman: The Tragedies*, ed. Alan Holaday [Cambridge: D. S. Brewer, 1987], p. 270), that the 1625 issue is unrevised, and that Gabel's argument finally depends upon his interpretation of an ambiguous letter to Sir George Buck, copied in Folger MS. V.a. 321, f. 49r (see Gabel, pp. 434–36 and the facsimile and transcript in *Letter-Book*), I see no reason to doubt that Chapman wrote the masque and meant to print it where he allowed it to appear, in a publication that evidently interested him deeply. For further disagreement with Gabel's argument, see George Ray, *Chapman's "The Conspiracy and Tragedy of Charles, Duke of Byron"* (New York: Garland), 2:383–84.

For a conjectural reconstruction of the omitted scene, concentrating on Henry IV's dynastic and extramarital interests, see John Loftis, *Renaissance Drama in England & Spain: Topical Allusion and History Plays* (Princeton: Princeton University Press, 1987), p. 100.

11. Although queen and mistress were usually hostile to one another, various temporary truces were arranged; in any case, there seems to be no historical record of physical conflict. Citing the frequent contemporary parallels between Essex and Byron (mentioned in *Tragedy* 4.1.132ff. and 5.3.139ff.), Arthur H. Smith suggested that Chapman here alludes to a widely rumored, though quite possibly apocryphal, ear-boxing Elizabeth gave Essex; see *Les Evénements politiques de France dans le théâtre anglais du siècle d'Elisabeth* (Paris: Emile Larose, 1906), pp. 85–86, and *Letter-Book*, p. 417.

12. Matthieu, *Histoire de France*, 2:88v.

13. So Samuel M. Pratt contends in "Jane Shore and the Elizabethans," *Texas Studies in Language and Literature* 11 (1969–70): 1294 and n. 6.

14. Peter Ure considers the masque a symbol of harmony and part of Chapman's plan to make Henry the perfect king (see "The Main Outline," p. 583). In his edition, George Ray does "not establish the relevance of Cupid's masque, but . . . the masque serves as a thematic inset, an emblem of royal power"; see Chapman, *The Conspiracy and Tragedy of Charles, Duke of Byron*, ed. George Ray (New York: Garland, 1979), 2:385. Similarly, John Margeson finds "that the connection of the lyric celebration of virtue in the masque to the main action of the play is very tenuous"; see his edition of *The Conspiracy and Tragedy* (Manchester: Manchester University Press, 1988), p. 42. On the contrary, I find the masque relevant indeed and part of the play's criticism of Henry and his court.

15. See Grimeston, *General Inventorie*, pp. 1046–51; Cayet, *Chronologie septenaire de l'histoire de la paix*, pp. 495–96; Matthieu, *Histoire de France*, 2:265r–371v (here again, Grimeston's chief source). Chapman used historical accounts of D'Auvergne's arrest in dramatizing Clermont's capture in *The Revenge of Bussy*, act 4, scene 1.

16. See the usually fulsome Agrippa D'Aubigné, *Histoire universelle* . . . 3 vols. (Maille, 1618–20): "La Fin . . . home cauteleux par dessus tout autre, qui depuis son jeune age avoit fait litiere de toute crainte de Dieu, de sa religion de toute foi, amitie,

obligations & naturel, pour faire ses affaires aux despens de telle choses . . ." (3:468; book 5, chap. 4) and cf. 3:493 for La Fin's motives.

17. For contemporary and modern assessments of La Fin and details of his death, see Maurice Dumoulin, "Jacques de la Fin: études et documents sur la secondé moitré du XVIᵉ siècle," *Bulletin historique et philogique* (Paris, 1896 for 1895), 150–287. Well into the English seventeenth century, La Fin had a traitor's name; see Edward Waterhouse, *Fortescutus Illustratus, or a Commentary on that nervous Treatise De Laudibus Legum Angliae* (London, 1663), p. 401.

18. Robert Ornstein, *The Moral Vision of Jacobean Tragedy* (Madison: University of Wisconsin Press, 1960), p. 68.

19. See, e.g., Grimeston, *General Inventorie*, p. 961, "Princes promise all . . ." or p. 941 (for 939), ". . . for Princes are Masters of the Lawes. . . ."

20. This observation is a commonplace. See, e.g., Meinecke, *Machiavellism*, p. 50: "And there were others who made a great show of fighting it [Machiavellianism], but at the same time borrowed from it freely." In *The Advancement of Learning*, Bacon writes, "Is not the ground, which Machiavel wisely and largely discourseth concerning governments, that the way to establish and preserve them is to reduce them *ad principia* in religion and nature . . ." (3:348) and "We are much beholden to Machiavel and others, that write what men do and not what they ought to do" (3:430). Parenthetical citations refer to James Spedding and R. L. Ellis, eds., *Works of Francis Bacon*, 14 vols. (London: Longman, 1857–74). See also Napoleone Orsini, *Bacone e Machiavelli* (Genova: Ed. degli Orfini, 1936). On Bodin and Machiavelli, see Meinecke, *Machiavellism*, pp. 56–64.

21. Knolles, trans., *Six Bookes*: "is hee [the prince] not bound to obay his owne lawes? I say that this law [against theft and murder] is not his, but the law of God and nature, whereunto all princes are more straitly bound than their subjects: in such sort as that they cannot be from the same exempted, either by the Senat, or the people, but they must bee enforced to make their appearance before the tribunall seat of almightie God: For God taketh a straiter account of princes than of others . . ." (book 1, chap. 8; p. 104).

22. Ornstein, *Moral Vision*, p. 69. Ornstein errs by trusting to an implied parallelism between "if, because" and "And [if] that. . . ." In fact, Henry hypothesizes two different relations between the king and the laws. One relation he accepts: the king is above his own laws (see Bodin, 1.8). The other relation he rejects, although he concedes some evil kings may espouse it: the king is not bound by God's justice and God's laws. Henry is quite conventional (and "medieval" in Ornstein's terms) in bowing only to divine law, or to natural law, which many theoreticians considered much the same thing; Henry properly condemns the hypothetical king who does not acknowledge God's jurisdiction. See Allen, *Political Thought*, pp. 416–17.

23. Knolles, trans., *Six Bookes*: "it may be that this last point ["the impunitie of offendors"] is therein of greatest consequence or importance, and yet the least of all regarded. Which is as I have before touched, so must I also oftentimes repeat the same, for that the princes and magistrates which desire to be accounted mercifull, do oftentimes turne upon their owne heads the same punishment that the offendors deserved . . . all princes and Commonweals . . . have no more certaine cause of their ruine and decay, than the want of due execution of justice. To punish the rebellious, is also one of the meanes to prevent and meet with rebellions yet to come . . ." (book 4, chap. 7; pp. 542–43).

24. Note the values of realm and dynasty implicit in this assertion; Henry's concentration upon son and kingdom is absolute and single-minded.

25. Chapman here employs one of his favorite laudatory epithets, "learn'd," in a consciously (because conspicuously) inappropriate and ironic fashion. See Ure, "Main Outline," p. 583. Critics usually deny that Chapman has this sort of dramatic self-awareness and sense of the power of reversal after long repetition.

26. *Roundness* recalls Chapman's frequent use of *circular* to express moral perfection and personal self-sufficiency; the idea that the stars were untainted by the human sin that had corrupted all below the moon is sound Renaissance cosmology. That the astrologically inclined Byron should appeal to them is startling, but understandable in the context of La Brosse's remarks in *Conspiracy*, act 3, scene 3, if not Byron's angry challenges in that scene.

27. This explanation of Henry's hesitation reminds us of Monsieur's judgment, "Now shall we see that Nature hath no end / In her great works, responsive to their worths . . ." (*Bussy* 5.3.1ff.). It is just such a conclusion Henry wishes to avoid.

28. Parrott (*Tragedies*, p. 617) does not approve of Henry's reentrance immediately after this speech; it does not occur in Grimeston (a fact that may account for Parrott's displeasure). Against the obvious liabilities (Henry's violent attack and lavish self-praise, both pointed out by Parrott), one must balance the important fact (realized, I admit, only in retrospect) that the King's last words to Byron are "Away with him!" Momentarily, Byron senses the finality and the disgrace in those words.

29. The repetition of what I take to be a charged word, *liberty*, is important. Its use here (with *freedom* and *animal wilfullness*) supports the reading offered in connection with the masque (above, n. 9). *Savage*, according to the *OED*, had almost the sole contemporary meaning of "animalistic."

30. That is, *blood* here means "physical action" and, technically, "choler"—different meanings from those demanded in *Conspiracy*, act 2, scene 3.

31. William Shakespeare, *Coriolanus*, ed. Philip Brockbank (London: Methuen, 1976), 4.7.55.

32. See Hiram Haydn, *The Counter-Renaissance* (1950; reprint, Gloucester, Mass.: Peter Smith, 1966), p. 24. Haydn asserts, correctly I believe, that these matched pairs of "contraries" reflect a traditional, sixteenth-century Christian humanism rather than any Donne-like acknowledgment that "new Philosophy calls all in doubt."

33. An emblem tradition lies behind the image of "A slave bound face to face with Death till death," which also occurs at *Bussy* 3.2.399 and 5.1.108–11. See Andrea Alciati, *Emblemata*, in Roville's 1550 or Bonhommes's 1551 Lyons editions, and Geoffrey Whitney, *A Choice of Emblems* (Leiden, 1586), p. 99. The tyrant Mezentius, "contemptor deum," devised this punishment (*Aeneid* 8.484ff.) which the emblem book writers softened (a little) by allegorizing their pictures as "impar conjugam." See also Mario Praz, *Studies in Seventeenth Century Imagery*, Studies of the Warburg Institute 3 (London: Warburg Institute, 1939 and 1947), 1:206 and 2:6–7. For another example of emblems in Chapman's plays, see my " 'The Natural Course of Light Inverted': An *Impresa* in Chapman's *Bussy D'Ambois*," *Journal of the Warburg and Courtauld Institutes* 34 (1971): 356–60.

34. Compare Gordon Braden's comment on Marlowe's *Tamburlaine, Part 2:* "It is on the English stage that the villain hero, experimented with elsewhere, comes into his own, not merely as a cautionary example, but also as a limiting case of energies we would be proud to share. The result goes beyond the mere valorization of villainy to an exploration of how much hostility to social and moral norms can in fact be incorporated into the terms of social membership" (*Renaissance Tragedy*, p. 196). Byron is precisely unlike Braden's tentative view of Tamburlaine's death in not being reincorporated into society and its memory.

35. See above, chap. 2, n. 21, and compare the cannon images in *Conspiracy* 1.1.151ff. and 1.2.34–35.

36. Waith points out the similarity between these lines and Horace *Odes* 4.7; Ennis Rees, *The Tragedies of George Chapman*, pp. 91 and 206 n. 94 cites two more generalized passages from the *Iliads*.

37. For a concise account of diplomatic relations in the crucial period, as well as English reactions, see J. B. Black, *Elizabeth and Henry IV . . . Anglo-French Relations, 1598–1603* (Oxford: Blackwell, 1914). John Loftis considers the Franco-Hispanic political situation as Chapman represents it; see *Renaissance Drama in England & Spain*, pp. 87–104.

38. Ernest B. Gilman, *The Curious Perspective: Literary and Pictorial Wit in the Seventeenth Century* (New Haven: Yale University Press, 1978), chaps. 1, 2, and 3, surveys the scientific background and experiments. Webster liked Chapman's image well enough to imitate it in a play whose epistle dedicatory specifically praises Chapman; see Webster, *The White Devil*, ed. J. R. Brown, Revels Plays, 2d ed. (London: Methuen, 1966), 1.2.110–12.

## Chapter 4. "Free and Fast": The Perspectives of *Chabot, Admiral of France*

1. See G. E. Bentley, *The Jacobean and Caroline Stage* (Oxford: Clarendon Press, 1941–68), 5:1088–91, where he accepts T. M. Parrott's dating (1621–22) with a query. An earlier date for original composition, 1612–14, followed by revision ca. 1621, was offered by Irving Ribner, "The Meaning of Chapman's *Tragedy of Chabot*," *Modern Language Review* 55 (1960): 321–31, and reprinted substantially unchanged in his *Jacobean Tragedy: The Quest for Moral Order* (London: Methuen, 1962). Thelma Herring discusses the dating issue on pp. 168–70 of "Chapman and an Aspect of Modern Criticism," *Renaissance Drama* 8 (1965): 153–79, and Albert H. Tricomi has argued that the play was written in 1611–12 and never revised (see "The Dates of the Plays of George Chapman," *English Literary Renaissance* 12 [1982]: 242–66). On the play's authorship, see n. 3.

2. See K. M. Burton, "The Political Tragedies of Chapman and Jonson," *Essays in Criticism* 2 (1952): 412, and Takashi Sasayama, "Chabot, Admiral of France: the Last Phase of Chapman's Craftsmanship," *Shakespeare Studies* (Tokyo) 1 (1962): 27.

3. *Chabot*'s original title page attributes the play to Chapman and James Shirley. For a discussion of the authorship controversy and of the play's putative Stoicism, see my " 'A Greater Wound': Corruption and Human Frailty in Chapman's *Chabot, Admiral of France*," *Modern Language Review* 70 (1975): 241–59. Allen Bergson's "The Worldly Stoicism of George Chapman's *The Revenge of Bussy D'Ambois* and *The Tragedy of Chabot, Admiral of France*," *Philological Quarterly* 55 (1976): 43–64 makes the most subtle argument for Stoicism in the play, but largely at the expense of any recognizable Stoicism beyond a "conflict between an absolute principle and a shifting, unstable reality" (p. 53). Bergson's focus on the "irony" of Chabot's "worldly stoicism" confirms many of my conclusions without proving the case for any very strictly philosophical or ethical Stoicism.

4. Ribner and MacLure have shown the dangerous lengths to which Chabot goes in displaying his sense of his own justice and incorruptibility; see Ribner, "Meaning of *Chabot*," p. 326, and Millar MacLure, *George Chapman: A Critical Study*, p. 148. For examples see 2.3.53–57 and 106–7.

5. Strozza, the visionary philosopher of *The Gentleman Usher*, describes himself as "nought else but soule . . . Free from the passions of my fuming blood" (4.3.51–52; *Comedies*, p. 185); for Strozza and a brief epilogue on Chabot, see Jackson I. Cope, *The Theatre and the Dream*, pp. 33–52 and 75–76, respectively. Chabot's use of *dissolve* would probably remind the audience of the word's specifically religious reference, which derives from the Vulgate's "cupio dissolvi" (Philippians 1:23). Although neither the Geneva nor King James translation uses the word *dissolve* at this point, many writers did when referring to Paul's wish. See Hyder E. Rollins, ed., *Tottel's Miscellany* (Cambridge: Harvard University Press, 1928–29), 1:125: "Wherefore with Paul let all men wish, and pray / To be dissolvde of this foule fleshy masse" (D. Sand [?], "Comparison of lyfe and death," 2.20–21); the Geneva Bible (1560) has this marginal note beside II Corinthians 5:1: "After this bodie shalbe dissolved, it shalbe made incorruptible and immortal"; John Donne, *Biathanatos* (New York, N.Y.: Facsimile Text Society, 1930): "S. *Paul* had some allowable reasons, to *desire to be dissolved, and to be with Christ*" (p. 121). Cf. Milton, "Il Penseroso," lines 161–66.

6. For Francis's meaning, compare the use of *dissolve* in *Byron's Conspiracy:*

> The blood turns in my veins; I stand on change,
> And shall dissolve in changing; 'tis so full
> Of pleasure not to be contain'd in flesh.
>
> (1.2.27–29)

7. R. G. Howarth has shown that *resolve* and *dissolve* could be synonyms. In his *Diary, Drama and Poetry* (Capetown: The University, 1971), pp. 176–77, he finds that item 2054 in *England's Parnassus* (there attributed to Chapman) is really the opening of Tamburlaine's "Divine Zenocrate" speech (*Tamburlaine, Part 1*, 5.2); the copyist has substituted *dissolved* for Marlowe's *resolved*.

8. For example, Matthew 7:13—"for wide is the gate and broad is the way that leadeth to destruction, and many there be which goe in thereat" (King James translation). Compare the common Biblical antithesis between *gate* (a place of judgment) and *highway.*

9. See Ribner, "Meaning of *Chabot*," pp. 326ff.

10. The subplot between the Queen and Chabot's wife exists chiefly to demonstrate the possibility of envying Chabot not for his rectitude (although a hint of this creeps in at 2.1.23–24), but for his status and extravagance. When Chabot allegorizes his experiences (5.3.49–64), he compares his pretrial existence with a tree "with all her leaves / And blooming pride . . . tempting the eye with wanton blossom. . . ."

11. Etienne Pasquier, *Les Recherches de la France* . . . (Paris, 1621), book 6, chap. ix:

Je vous ay recité deux Histoires dont pourrez recueillir deux leçons: . . . L'autre que jamais un seigneur qui pour avoir eu bonne part en faveur du roy son Maistre, a esté employé aux grandes affaires, tombant en son indignation, ne doit permettre s'il luy est possible de tomber ès mains de la Justice, & qu'on luy face son procez, quelque innocence qu'il pense resider en luy. D'autant que se qu'il estimoit, pendant sa vogue, un peccadile, venant devant les yeus des Juges, est non seulement estimé peché mortel, ains criminel.

This text will not bear the weight Ribner gives it: see "Meaning of *Chabot*," pp. 323–24.

12. Ribner, "Meaning of *Chabot*," p. 324. For a detailed discussion of Ribner's thesis and a disagreement with it on grounds similar to those offered here, see Thelma

Herring, "Chapman and an Aspect of Modern Criticism," *Renaissance Drama* 8 (1965): 167–69.

13. Ribner, "Meaning of *Chabot*," p. 329.

14. See *OED*, *s.v.* 1 and 2. The second meaning appears, as *OED* notes, in *The Ball*, a play entered in the *Stationers' Register* along with *Chabot* on 24 October 1638 and attributed to Chapman and James Shirley. For a full discussion, see Chapman, *The Comedies of George Chapman*, ed. T. M. Parrott (New York: Dutton, 1914), pp. 869–71. In Parrott's text, *The Ball* 3.4.134–36, reads: "because you sha' not trouble friends / To be compurgators, I'll be satisfied, / If you will take your own oath."

15. The two characters are assumed to be the same: the Advocate disappears without explanation after the fourth act and the Proctor-General assumes his functions. "Advocate" seems to be Parrott's editorial creation: see Parrott, ed., *Tragedies*, pp. 647 and 649.

16. See William G. Crane's facsimile edition (Gainesville, Florida: Scholars' Facsimiles and Reprints, 1954), f. 56. For further details of paronomasia (or "paranomasia") and agnominatio, see Richard A. Lanham, *A Handlist of Rhetorical Terms* (Berkeley and Los Angeles: University of California Press, 1968), pp. 3 and 73. There are more examples, not all of them what a modern would call "puns," in Abraham Fraunce's *Arcadian Rhetoric* (1588), chapter 25. A common early word for "pun" is, of course, "quibble," which carries the meaning of evasion or equivocation I see in *Chabot*.

17. Ure, "The Main Outline," pp. 568–69, and see Ure's edition of *Richard II*, 5th ed. (London: Methuen, 1961), 2.2.18, note. See also Ernest B. Gilman, *The Curious Perspective*, chapter 3. Chapman used the analogy often; see *Eugenia*, lines 174–75 (*Poems*, p. 276); *Ovids Banquet of Sence*, stanza 3 (*Poems*, p. 54); and *All Fools* 1.1.46–48 (*Comedies*, p. 238). Parrott has a long note on the last use in his edition of *The Comedies of George Chapman*, p. 713. Ben Jonson's prefatory poem to Nicholas Breton, *Melancholike Humours* (London, 1600) uses the conceit and condemns "such as looke asquint . . . comming with a laterall viewe" (lines 7, 9). Jonson goes on to compare the act of regarding the "cunning piece wrought perspective" with poetry: "being eyed directly, I divine, / His [Breton's] proofe their praise, will meete, as in this line" (lines 13–14). See "Uncollected Poetry," *The Complete Poetry of Ben Jonson*, ed. W. B. Hunter (New York: Norton, 1963), p. 326. For many other examples, see Inga-Stina Ewbank, "Webster's Realism, or, 'A Cunning Piece Wrought Perspective,'" in *John Webster*, ed. Brian Morris (London: Benn, 1970), pp. 159–78.

18. Although Asall's commonplace at 1.1.102–7 suggests a secularly oriented moral universe for the play, scenes similar to *Chabot* 2.3 in Chapman's other tragedies usually refer much more overtly to the divine, to God, and to the transcendent. See, for example, *Byron's Conspiracy* act 3, scene 2 and *Byron's Tragedy* act 4, scene 2.

19. Jean Jacquot, *George Chapman*, p. 192. In his edition of *Chabot* (Philadelphia: University of Pennsylvania, 1906), Ezra Lehman contends, "The play, which is essentially a comedy, is converted into a tragedy. The fifth act is an excresence. The first four acts have all the elements of serious comedy; there is nothing in them to prepare for the tragic scene of the fifth act. We have a fine example of a reconciling drama up to the beginning of that act" (pp. 34–35). More aptly, Allen Bergson (see above, n. 3) observes, "After the death of . . . [Chabot] we are made to face an ironic image of the surviving court going about its cynical self-interested business" (p. 63).

## Conclusion: "Coherents for the Time"

1. Nicoll mistakenly prints this text in italic.

2. Nicoll glosses *coherent* as "consistent or logical thought" (*Homer*, 1:698); he cites only this passage from *Achilles Shield* and marks the meaning as unknown to *OED*. This single instance does not justify *logical* (or even perhaps *thought*), and I should prefer to find overtones of Latin usages—for example, *intelligible* and *self-sufficient* or *self-maintaining*. Describing Luther's position on angels and genii, Chapman uses *coherence* to mean natural harmony or the cosmic consistency of plenitude and degree: "As if a Man should take away the interjected Aire; betwixt the Earth and the Moone: That Man must likewise dissolve, all the coherence and actuall unitie of the universe; leaving *vacuum in Medio;* and necessary Bond of it all . . ." (Chapman, trans., *The Georgicks of Hesiod . . .* [London, 1618], B4r margin).

3. Philip Edwards, *Shakespeare and the Confines of Art* (London: Methuen, 1968).

4. MacLure, *George Chapman*, p. 229.

5. This suggestion was first made, although not developed, by G. R. Hibbard in "Goodness and Greatness: An essay on the Tragedies of George Chapman and Ben Jonson," *Renaissance and Modern Studies* 11 (1967): 5–54; see esp. pp. 32–33.

6. "To the most Honord . . . Earle," prefixed to *Seaven Bookes of the Iliades; Homer*, 1:504, with some corrections. For a persuasive argument that Chapman's first Homeric work is "topical translation" "doctored" to appeal to, advise, and encourage Essex in his Irish military ambitions, see John C. Briggs, "Chapman's *Seaven Bookes of the Iliades:* Mirror for Essex," *Studies in English Literature* 21 (1981): 59–73. Briggs also shows that Chapman removed many of the topical distortions when he republished his translation in the new century, almost a decade after Essex's rebellion.

7. The only textual evidence for Essex's aid occurs in the dedications of *Seaven Bookes of the Iliades* and *Achilles Shield*, although one may wish to find further support among the documents in *Letter-Book*. The dedications do not, however, support Bartlett's claim that "it is evident from the dedication [to *Achilles Shield*] that Essex had not paid any attention to the earlier volume and Chapman wanted to strike again while the iron was hot" (*Poems*, p. 479). How the iron might be hot if the first assertion is true Bartlett does not explain.

8. Information on licensing in this paragraph derives from W. W. Greg, *Licensers for the Press, &c. to 1640* (Oxford: Oxford Bibliographical Society, 1962).

9. Undated letter to Carr; see: *The Letters of John Holles 1587–1637*, ed. P. R. Seddon (Nottingham: Thoroton Society, 1975–86), 3:511.

10. Lisle also published the masque Thomas Campion wrote for the wedding and eleven editions or impressions of Thomas Overbury's "A Wife" and other literary characters from the first in 1614 through 1622. Overbury is generally believed to have opposed the Carr-Howard marriage and to have been poisoned for his opposition; some scholars have argued, perhaps anachronistically, that "A Wife" and/or "A very very Woman" represents Overbury's attack on Frances Howard. See James E. Savage, ed., *The "Conceited Newes" of Sir Thomas Overbury and his Friends* (Gainesville, Fla.: Scholars' Facsimiles and Reprints, 1968), pp. xiii–xviii.

11. Greg, *Licensers for the Press*, p. 87.

12. See Norma Dobie Solve, *Stuart Politics in Chapman's "Tragedy of Chabot,"* University of Michigan Publications in Language and Literature, 4 (Ann Arbor: University of Michigan Press, 1928). Albert Tricomi strongly attacks Solve's thesis in "The Dates," pp. 261–63.

13. The absence is speculative: see Sisson and Butman, "George Chapman, 1612–1622," pp. 189–90.

14. Jonathan Goldberg thinks Chapman is referring to himself here (poet becoming patron's patron), and Chapman seems at times to have confused himself with Homer; the lines in question do, however, refer to "your *Homer*" (line 77). See Goldberg, *James I and the Politics of Literature* (Baltimore: Johns Hopkins University Press, 1983), p. 134.

15. The choice of Bacon and the ostensible reason for translating Hesiod are both rather strained:

> Antient wisedome, being so worthily eternis'd; by the now-renew'd Instance of it in your Lordship; and this ancient Authour, one of the most Authentique, for all wisedome . . . To what Sea owe these poore Streames their Tribute, but to your Lordships Ocean? The rather, since others of the like Antiquity, in my . . . *Homer*, teach These their way, and adde comfort to their Courses; by having received right cheerfull countenance and approbation from your Lordships most grave and honourd predecessor. (Chapman, trans., *The Georgicks of Hesiod*, A2r)

Although Chapman subsequently alludes to *De Sapientia Veterum* (B2r, margin), note that his judgment has not improved: Bacon's "predecessor" was Thomas Egerton, who presided as high steward at Robert Carr's trial, and Bacon himself was chief prosecutor in Carr's trial for murder. For further discussion of Chapman and Carr, see my "Robert Carr, Earl of Somerset, as Collector and Patron" in *The Mental World of the Jacobean Court*, ed. Linda Levy Peck (Cambridge: Cambridge University Press, 1991).

16. It would be consonant with my argument here to ask if these dramatic relations have a source (or an object) in the Jacobean court. Several critics have claimed that James's relations with his favorites were obliquely represented on stage; see: Glynne Wickham, "*The Two Noble Kinsmen*, or *A Midsummer Night's Dream, Part II?*" *Elizabethan Theatre VII*, ed. G. R. Hibbard (Hamden, Conn.: Archon, 1980), pp. 167–96; Richard Harris, "Gender confusion and sexual politics in *The Two Noble Kinsmen*," in *Drama, Sex and Politics*, ed. James Redmond, Themes in Drama 7 (Cambridge: Cambridge University Press, 1985), pp. 69–76; Peter Holland, "Style at the Swan," *Essays in Criticism* 36 (1986): 193–209. Wickham (p. 183) explicitly links Theseus-Pirithous with James-Robert Carr. I would further suggest that Beaumont and Fletcher often displace the king-favorite relation into a relation between an older and a younger aristocrat, Melantius and Amintor, for example, in *The Maid's Tragedy*.

17. T. B. Howell, ed. and comp., *Cobbett's Complete Collection of State Trials* (London: Longman et al., 1809–26), 2 : 992.

18. The parallel between the dramatic heroes and Chapman's experience of patronage can of course be made self-defeatingly rigid: Essex died two and one-half years before the likeliest date of *Bussy's* first performance. I would claim that the curve of Chapman's expectation continued to rise until 1612; after Essex's death, Chapman found a place in Prince Henry's household and could anticipate years of faithful support. When the Prince died, Chapman's future must have seemed the darker for having recently been so bright.

19. Chapman, trans., *The Georgicks of Hesiod*, A4r; italics in original.

20. The quotations in this paragraph come from "To . . . M. Harriots" (*Poems*, pp. 381–84).

21. Oldys made these notes in his second copy of Gerald Langbaine's *An Account of the English Dramatick Poets* (London, 1691), p. 58, some time after 1727; the volume is now British Library shelfmark C. 28.g.1. Oldys's last line alludes to the closing of Chapman's dedication to *The Crowne of all Homers Workes* (*Poems*, p. 416).

# Appendix

1. See, for example, Daniel's dedicatory epistle to *Delia* (in Arthur Colby Sprague, ed., *Poems and A Defence of Ryme* [1930; reprint, Chicago: University of Chicago Press, 1965], p. 9). In his *Apology*, Sidney urges his reader "To beleeve, with me, that there are many misteries contained in Poetrie, which of purpose were written darkely, least by prophane wits it should bee abused" (in G. Gregory Smith, ed., *Elizabethan Critical Essays* [London: Oxford University Press, 1904], 1:204). Margaret Bottrall, "George Chapman's Defence of Difficulty in Poetry," *Criterion* 16 (1936–37): 638–54, collects many Continental Renaissance observations in Chapman's vein; Michael Murrin has done the same in *The Veil of Allegory: Some Notes Toward a Theory of Allegorical Rhetoric in the English Renaissance* (Chicago: University of Chicago Press, 1969), chap. 1.

2. In addition to Bottrall, see C. K. Cannon, "Chapman on the Unity of Style and Meaning," *Journal of English and Germanic Philology* 68 (1969): 245–64.

3. "To . . . Robert, Earle of Somerset" (*Poems*, p. 408), lines 69–84; the Latin quotes Ficino verbatim, while later in the same passage *Alcibiades II*, 147c, appears in Greek (see Schoell, *Etudes*, p. 2).

4. See Millar MacLure, *George Chapman: A Critical Study*, esp. pp. 7–9 and 73–76. For a discussion by Chapman, see *Teares of Peace*, lines 409–561 (*Poems*, pp. 182–85).

5. See the epistle dedicatory to *Ovids Banquet of Sence*, lines 40–42, where Chapman writes that he does not affect "glory for mine owne sleight labors, but desirous others should be more worthely glorious, nor professing *sacred* Poesie in any degree" (*Poems*, p. 50; my italics). For related views, see *Poems*, pp. 327 and 384.

6. For Bartlett's remarks, see *Poems*, pp. 6–7; for Chapman's, the epistle dedicatory to *Ovids Banquet of Sence*, line 49 (*Poems*, p. 50). Clark Hulse discusses Chapman as an inspired poet and especially the relation of inspiration to form in *Metamorphic Verse: The Elizabethan Minor Epic* (Princeton: Princeton University Press, 1981), pp. 124–26 and 138–40.

7. "To . . . the Earle of Essexe" (before *Seaven Bookes of The Iliades*), lines 24–28, 34–35, 39–40, 43–46 (*Homer*, 1:503–4).

8. In *Caesar and Pompey*, 4.1.127–36, Cato defines Jove's golden chain as "our pure souls." Bartlett, in *Poems*, p. 424, cites two further instances.

9. See John Webster's remark, below, n. 16.

10. For Jonson, see "To the Readers" in *Sejanus*, ed. Jonas Barish (New Haven: Yale University Press, 1965), p. 27, and J. A. Bryant, Jr., "The Significance of Ben Jonson's First Requirement for Tragedy: 'Truth of Argument,'" *Studies in Philology* 49 (1952): 195–213.

11. See the "Justification" of *Andromeda Liberata*, lines 27–35 (*Poems*, p. 327).

12. The first two phrases are from Chapman's dedicatory epistle to *Caesar and Pompey* (*Tragedies*, p. 341) and the last, from *Andromeda Liberata*, line 48 (*Poems*, p. 311).

13. Sonnet 10 in "A Coronet for His Mistresse Philosophie," lines 2–3 (*Poems*, p. 86); Bartlett mistakenly repunctuates the entire sonnet.

14. Chapman recognized that the public might consider the usage unusual; in his commendatory poem for John Fletcher's *The Faithful Shepherdess*, he writes, "A Poeme and a play too! why tis like / A scholler that's a Poet . . . one cannot both fates beare" (lines 3–4, 6; *Poems*, p. 363). Nashe's preface to Greene's *Menaphon* also joins poet and scholar: "I deeme him farre unworthy the name of a scholar . . . that is not a Poet, either in whole or in part" (in Ronald B. McKerrow, ed., *The Works of Thomas*

*Nashe*, corr. ed., F. P. Wilson [Oxford: Blackwell, 1958], 3:321). Chapman called the *Byron* plays "poor dismembered poems" (*Tragedies*, p. 152).

15. The first definition comes from Hoby's translation of Matthieu Coignet, *Politique Discourses on trueth and lying* (1586); reprint in Smith, ed., *Elizabethan Critical Essays*, 1:341; the second passage is from *Comedies*, p. 569.

16. In a preface that praises the "full and height'ned style of Master Chapman," John Webster claims that in *The White Devil* he has chosen not to "as it were lifen death, in the passionate and weighty *Nuntius*" (see Brown, ed., *The White Devil*, pp. 3–4). *Lively* is a significant word in late sixteenth- and seventeenth-century discussion of drama, poetry, and acting; see, for example, R. A. Foakes's survey in "The Profession of Playwright," in *Early Shakespeare*, ed. J. R. Brown and Bernard Harris, Stratford-upon-Avon Studies, 3 (London: Edward Arnold, 1961), pp. 28–29. Lisideius, the French apologist in Dryden's "Essay of Dramatic Poesy," specifically attributes liveliness to narrative speeches. See especially the paragraph beginning, "The words of a good writer, which describe it lively, will make a deeper impression of belief in us than all the actor can persuade us to . . . " (in John Dryden, *Of Dramatic Poesy and Other Critical Essays*, ed. George Watson [London: Dent, 1962], 1:51).

17. *History* here seems to have the modern restricted meaning rather than the more generous Elizabethan meaning (any story or narrative regardless of form or factual basis).

18. The most comprehensive attempt is Waddington's *The Mind's Empire;* the second chapter offers a revised version of an earlier essay originally entitled, "Prometheus and Hercules: The Dialectic of *Bussy D'Ambois.*" I particularly disagree with allegorical readings of the drama that promote continuous mythic meanings for the play, or which, through those myths, trace specific doctrinal propositions.

19. Waddington (see n. 18) depends upon the discussion, including the allegory/oratory distinctions, in Murrin, *The Veil of Allegory.* Yet Murrin approaches drama very cautiously, in part because of his theory and in part because the genre resists such interpretations: see especially pp. 8–9, 14, and 16.

20. See Waith, *The Herculean Hero*, chaps. 1, 2, and 4.

21. For the first example, see chap. 1; for the second, *Bussy D'Ambois*, ed. Maurice Evans (London: Benn, 1965), pp. xx–xxiv.

22. While Chapman promised to write a "Poeme of the mysteries / Reveal'd in Homer" (*Homer*, 1:10), he never did. Henry Reynolds, the recipient of one of Chapman's few surviving autograph dedications, testifies that Chapman found no natural mysteries (i.e., the Neoplatonic arcana Reynolds himself sought) in Greek literature: "One, and the best, of our Greeks translators hath ingenuously confest to mee, that for more then matter of Morality hee hath discovered little in his Authors meanings. Yet my good old friend . . . must pardon mee . . ." (from *Mythomystes* in Spingarn, ed., *Critical Essays*, 1:165).

23. See Frank Percy Wilson, *Elizabethan and Jacobean* (Oxford: Clarendon Press, 1945), pp. 14–15.

# Bibliography

Standard reference works (for example, the *Oxford English Dictionary,* the *Dictionary of National Biography*) are not entered here, nor are modern standard editions of classical texts. Chapman's translations are entered under his name. Publishers and printers are not listed for works printed before 1700.

Adams, Robert P. "Critical Myths and Chapman's Original *Bussy D'Ambois." Renaissance Drama* 9 (1966): 141–61.

Alciati, Andrea. *Emblemata.* Lyons, 1550.

Allen, J. W. *Political Thought in the Sixteenth Century.* London: Methuen, 1941.

Altman, Joel B. *The Tudor Play of Mind: Rhetorical Inquiry and the Development of Elizabethan Drama.* Berkeley and Los Angeles: University of California Press, 1978.

Aubigné, Agrippa d'. *Histoire universelle.* 3 vols. Maille, 1618–20.

Bacon, Francis. *Works of Francis Bacon.* Edited by James Spedding and R. L. Ellis. 14 vols. London: Longman, 1857–74.

Barton, Anne Righter. *Shakespeare and the Idea of the Play.* Harmondsworth, England: Penguin, 1967.

Bement, Peter. *George Chapman: Action and Contemplation in His Tragedies.* Salzburg Studies in English Literature, 8. Salzburg: Universität Salzburg, 1974.

Bentley, Gerald Eades. *The Jacobean and Caroline Stage.* 7 vols. Oxford: Clarendon Press, 1941–68.

Bergson, Allen. "The Worldly Stoicism of George Chapman's *The Revenge of Bussy D'Ambois* and *The Tragedy of Chabot, Admiral of France." Philological Quarterly* 55 (1976): 43–64.

Bertaut, Jean. *Oeuvres Poètiques.* . . . Dernière edition. Paris, 1620.

Black, J. B. *Elizabeth and Henry IV being a short study of Anglo-French Relations, 1598–1603.* Oxford: Blackwell, 1914.

Bodin, Jean. *The Six Bookes of a Commonweale.* 1576 (French), 1586 (Latin), Translated by Richard Knolles. London, 1606.

———. *Six Books of the Commonwealth.* Edited and translated by M. J. Tooley. Oxford: Blackwell, 1955.

Booth, Stephen. *Shakespeare's Sonnets: Edited with an Analytic Commentary.* New Haven: Yale University Press, 1977.

Bottrall, Margaret. "George Chapman's Defence of Difficulty in Poetry." *Criterion* 16 (1936–37): 638–54.

Bouwsma, W. J. *Venice and the Defense of Republican Liberty.* Berkeley and Los Angeles: University of California Press, 1968.

Braden, Gordon. *Renaissance Tragedy and the Senecan Tradition: Anger's Privilege.* New Haven: Yale University Press, 1985.

Braunmuller, A. R. "The Arts of the Dramatist." In *The Cambridge Companion to English Renaissance Drama, 1570–1640*, edited by A. R. Braunmuller and Michael Hattaway, 53–90. Cambridge: Cambridge University Press, 1990.

————. *George Peele*. Boston: G. K. Hall, 1983.

————. " 'A Greater Wound': Corruption and Human Frailty in Chapman's *Chabot, Admiral of France." Modern Language Review* 70 (1975): 241–59.

————. "*King John* and Historiography." *ELH* 55 (1988): 309–32.

————. " 'The Natural Course of Light Inverted': An *Impresa* in Chapman's *Bussy D'Ambois." Journal of the Warburg and Courtauld Institutes* 34 (1971): 356–60.

————. "Robert Carr, Earl of Somerset, as Collector and Patron." In *The Mental World of the Jacobean Court*, edited by Linda Levy Peck. Cambridge: Cambridge University Press, 1991.

Bredvold, Louis I. "The Naturalism of Donne in Relation to Some Renaissance Traditions." *Journal of English and Germanic Philology* 22 (1923): 471–503.

Briggs, John C. "Chapman's *Seaven Bookes of the Iliades:* Mirror for Essex." *Studies in English Literature, 1500–1900* 21 (1981): 59–73.

Bruno, Giordano. *The Expulsion of the Triumphant Beast*. Edited and translated by Arthur Imerti. New Brunswick, N.J.: Rutgers University Press, 1964.

Bryant, J. A., Jr. "The Significance of Ben Jonson's First Requirement for Tragedy: 'Truth of Argument.' " *Studies in Philology* 49 (1952): 195–213.

Burton, K. M. "The Political Tragedies of Chapman and Jonson." *Essays in Criticism* 2 (1952): 397–412.

Cannon, C. K. "Chapman on the Unity of Style and Meaning." *Journal of English and Germanic Philology* 68 (1969): 245–64.

Cassirer, Ernst. *Individual and Cosmos in Renaissance Philosophy*. 1927. Translated by Mario Domandi. New York, N.Y.: Harper, 1964.

Cayet, Pierre Victor Palma. *Chronologie septenaire de l'histoire de la paix*. Paris, 1605.

Chamberlain, John. *The Letters of John Chamberlain*. Edited by N. E. McClure. 2 vols. Philadelphia: American Philosophical Society, 1939.

Chambers, Edmund K. *The Elizabethan Stage*. 4 vols. Oxford: Clarendon Press, 1923.

Chapman, George. *Bussy D'Ambois*. Edited by Nicholas Brooke. London: Methuen, 1964.

————. *Bussy D'Ambois*. Edited by Maurice Evans. London: Benn, 1965.

————. *Chabot Admiral of France*. Edited by Ezra Lehman. Philadelphia: University of Pennsylvania, 1906.

————. *Chapman's Homer*. Edited by Allardyce Nicoll. 2 vols. Bollingen Series, 41. New York, N.Y.: Pantheon, 1956.

————. *The Comedies of George Chapman*. Edited by T. M. Parrott. London: Routledge, 1914.

————. *The Conspiracy and Tragedy of Charles, Duke of Byron*. Edited by George Ray. 2 vols. New York, N.Y.: Garland, 1979.

————. *The Conspiracy and Tragedy of Charles, Duke of Byron*. Edited by John Margeson. Manchester: Manchester University Press, 1988.

————, trans. *The Georgics of Hesiod*. London, 1618.

————, trans. *The Iliads of Homer*. Edited by Richard Hooper. 2d ed. 2 vols. London: J. R. Smith, 1865.

———. *The Plays of George Chapman: The Comedies*. Alan Holaday, general editor. Urbana: University of Illinois Press, 1970.

———. *The Plays of George Chapman: The Tragedies*. Alan Holaday, general editor. Cambridge: D. S. Brewer, 1987.

———. *The Poems of George Chapman*. Edited by Phyllis B. Bartlett. New York, N.Y.: Modern Language Association, 1941.

———. *The Tragedies of George Chapman*. Edited by T. M. Parrott. London: Routledge, 1910.

Chapman, George et al. *A Seventeenth-Century Letter-Book: A Facsimile of Folger MS. V. a. 321*. With transcription, annotation, and commentary by A. R. Braunmuller. Newark: University of Delaware Press, 1983.

Clemen, Wolfgang. *English Tragedy Before Shakespeare: The Development of Dramatic Speech*. 1955. Translated by T. S. Dorsch. London: Methuen, 1961.

Cook, David. "Dramatic Records in the Declared Accounts of the Treasurer of The Chamber 1558–1642." *Malone Society Collections* 6 (1962 for 1961).

Cope, Jackson I. *The Theater and the Dream: From Metaphor to Form in Renaissance Drama*. Baltimore: Johns Hopkins University Press, 1973.

Corballis, R. P. "The 'Second Pen' in the Stage Version of *Sejanus*." *Modern Philology* 76 (1978–79): 273–77.

Craig, Hardin, ed. *Essays in Dramatic Literature: The Parrott Presentation Volume*. Princeton: Princeton University Press, 1935.

Cuddy, Neil. "The Revival of the Entourage: the Bedchamber of James I, 1603–1625." In *The English Court: from the Wars of the Roses to the Civil War*, edited by David Starkey, 173–225. London and New York: Longman, 1987.

Dallington, Robert. *The View of Fraunce*. London, 1604.

Daniel, Samuel. *Complete Works in Verse and Prose*. Edited by A. B. Grosart. 5 vols. 1885–96. Reprint. New York: Russell and Russell, 1963.

———. *Poems and A Defence of Ryme*. Edited by Arthur Colby Sprague. Reprint. Chicago: University of Chicago Press, 1965.

Dasent, J. R., ed. *Acts of the Privy Council* 32. London: HMSO, 1907.

Dekker, Thomas. *Dramatic Works of Thomas Dekker*. Edited by Fredson Bowers. 4 vols. Cambridge: Cambridge University Press, 1953–61.

Demers, Patricia. "The Conspiracy and Tragedy of Charles Duke of Byron [*sic*]: The Evaporation of Honour." *Renaissance and Reformation* 11 (1975): 85–96.

Dent, Arthur. *The Plaine Mans Path-Way to Heaven*. London, 1601.

Dobell, Bertram. "Newly Discovered Documents of the Elizabethan and Jacobean Periods." *The Athenaeum* 74, pt. 1 (23 and 30 March, 6 and 14 April, 1901).

Dollimore, Jonathan. *Radical Tragedy: Religion, Ideology and Power in the Drama of Shakespeare and his Contemporaries*. Chicago: University of Chicago Press, 1984.

Donne, John. *Biathanatos*. New York, N.Y.: Facsimile Text Society, 1930.

Dryden, John. *Of Dramatic Poesy and Other Critical Essays*. Edited by George Watson. 2 vols. London: Dent, 1962.

Dumoulin, Maurice. "Jacques de la Fin: études et documents sur la seconde moitié du XVIᵉ siècle." *Bulletin historique et philogique*. Paris, 1896 for 1895, pp. 150–287.

Eccles, Mark. "Sir George Buc, Master of the Revels." In *Thomas Lodge and Other Elizabethans*, edited by C. J. Sisson, 409–506. Cambridge: Harvard University Press, 1933.

Edwards, Philip. *Shakespeare and the Confines of Art*. London: Methuen, 1968.

————. *Thomas Kyd and Early Elizabethan Tragedy*. Writers and Their Work, 192. London: Longmans, Green, 1966.

Ellis-Fermor, Una. *The Jacobean Drama*. 4th ed. New York: Vintage, 1964.

Else, Gerald. *Aristotle's Poetics: The Argument*. Cambridge: Harvard University Press, 1957.

Empson, William. *Some Versions of Pastoral*. London: Chatto and Windus, 1950.

Ewbank, Inga-Stina. " 'These Pretty Devices': A Study of Masques in Plays." In *A Book of Masques: In Honour of Allardyce Nicoll*, edited by T. J. B. S[pencer] and S. W. W[ells], 407–48. Cambridge: Cambridge University Press, 1967.

————. "Webster's Realism, or, 'A Cunning Piece Wrought Perspective.' " In *John Webster*, edited by Brian Morris, 159–78. London: Benn, 1970.

Fanshawe, Ann. *The Memoirs of Ann Lady Fanshawe*. Edited by E. J. Fanshawe. London: John Lane, 1907.

Ferguson, A. S. "The Plays of George Chapman." *Modern Language Review* 13 (1918): 1–24.

Ficino, Marsilio. *Opera Omnia*. Basel, 1576.

————. *The "Philebus" Commentary*. Edited and translated by Michael J. B. Allen. Berkeley and Los Angeles: University of California Press, 1975.

Fletcher, John, and Philip Massinger. *The Tragedy of Sir John van Olden Barnavelt*. Edited by T. H. Howard-Hill. Malone Society Reprints. Oxford, 1980.

Florby, Gunilla. *The Painful Passage to Virtue: A Study of George Chapman's "The Tragedy of Bussy D'Ambois" and "The Revenge of Bussy D'Ambois."* Lund Studies in English 61. Lund: Gleerup, 1982.

Foakes, R. A. "The Profession of Playwright." In *Early Shakespeare*, edited by J. R. Brown and Bernard Harris, 11–33. Stratford-upon-Avon Studies 3. London: Arnold, 1961.

————. "Tragedy at the Children's Theatres after 1600: A Challenge to the Adult Stage." In *Elizabethan Theatre II*, edited by David Galloway, 37–59. Hamden, Conn.: Archon, 1970.

Fraunce, Abraham. *Arcadian Rhetoric*. London, 1588.

Fussner, F. S. *The Historical Revolution: English Historical Writing and Thought 1580– 1640*. London: Routlege, 1962.

Gabel, John B. "The Original Version of Chapman's *Tragedy of Byron*." *Journal of English and Germanic Philology* 63 (1964): 433–40.

Gerber, Richard. "Ubermensch and Treue: zur umstrittenen Entwincklung von George Chapmans Drama." *Anglia* 76 (1958): 510–35.

Gilbert, Felix. *Machiavelli and Guicciardini*. Princeton: Princeton University Press, 1965.

Gilman, Ernest B. *The Curious Perspective: Literary and Pictorial Wit in the Seventeenth Century*. New Haven: Yale University Press, 1978.

Goldberg, Jonathan. *James I and the Politics of Literature*. Baltimore: Johns Hopkins University Press, 1983.

Golden, Leon, and O. B. Hardison, Jr. *Aristotle's Poetics: A Translation and Commentary for Students of Literature*. Englewood Cliffs, N.J.: Prentice-Hall, 1968.

Gombrich, E. H. "*Icones Symbolicae*: The Visual Image in Neo-Platonic Thought." *Journal of the Warburg and Courtauld Institutes* 11 (1948): 163–92.

――――. *Symbolic Images: Studies in the Art of the Renaissance, II*. Oxford: Phaidon Press, 1972.

Goodman, Godfrey. *The Court of King James the First*. Edited by J. S. Brewer. 2 vols. London: Bentley, 1839.

Greg, Walter W. *Licensers for the Press, &c. to 1640*. Oxford: Oxford Bibliographical Society, 1962.

Grimeston, Edward. *A General Inventorie of the History of France*. London, 1607.

Harris, Richard. "Gender confusion and sexual politics in *The Two Noble Kinsmen*." In *Drama, Sex and Politics*, edited by James Redmond, 69–76. Themes in Drama 7. Cambridge: Cambridge University Press, 1985.

Harris, William. *Skelton's Magnyfycence and the Cardinal Virtue Tradition*. Chapel Hill: University of North Carolina Press, 1965.

Haydn, Hiram. *The Counter-Renaissance*. 1950. Reprint. Gloucester, Mass.: Peter Smith, 1966.

Heilman, Robert B. *Tragedy and Melodrama: Versions of Experience*. Seattle: University of Washington Press, 1968.

Herring, Thelma. "Chapman and An Aspect of Modern Criticism." *Renaissance Drama* 8 (1965): 153–79.

Hibbard, George R. "Goodness and Greatness: An essay on the Tragedies of George Chapman and Ben Jonson." *Renaissance and Modern Studies* 11 (1967): 5–54.

Hine, R. L. *Hitchin Worthies: Four Centuries of English Life*. Rev. ed. Hitchin, England: Eric Moore, 1974.

Holland, Peter. "Style at the Swan." *Essays in Criticism* 36 (1986): 193–209.

Holles, John. *The Letters of John Holles 1587–1637*. Edited by P. R. Seddon. 3 vols. Nottingham: Thoroton Society, 1975–86.

Howarth, R. G. *Diary, Drama and Poetry*. Capetown: The University, 1971.

Howell, T. B., ed. and comp. *Cobbett's Complete Collection of State Trials*. 33 vols. London: Longman et al., 1809–26.

Hulse, Clark. *Metamorphic Verse: The Elizabethan Minor Epic*. Princeton: Princeton University Press, 1981.

Hunter, G. K. *Dramatic Identities and Cultural Tradition*. Liverpool: Liverpool University Press, 1978.

――――. "*Henry IV* and the Elizabethan Two-Part Play." *Review of English Studies*, n.s., 5 (1954): 236–48.

Ide, Richard S. *Possessed with Greatness: The Heroic Tragedies of Shakespeare and Chapman*. Chapel Hill: University of North Carolina Press, 1980.

Jacquot, Jean. *George Chapman (1559–1634): sa vie, sa poésie, son théâtre, sa pensée*. Paris: Edition Les Belles Lettres, 1951.

James I. *The Political Works of James I*. Edited and introduced by C. H. MacIlwain. Cambridge: Harvard University Press, 1918.

James, Mervyn. *Society, Politics and Culture: Studies in Early Modern England*. Cambridge: Cambridge University Press, 1986.

James, Thomas. *Catalogus . . . Bibliothecae . . . quam . . . Thomas Bodleius . . . nuper instituit . . .* Oxford, 1605.

Jardine, Lisa. *Still Harping on Daughters: Women and Drama in the Age of Shakespeare*. Brighton, England: Harvester, 1983.

Jones, Marion, and Glynne Wickham. "The Stage Furnishings of George Chapman's *The Tragedy of Charles, Duke of Byron.*" *Theatre Notebook* 16 (1962): 113–17.

Jonson, Benjamin. *The Complete Poetry of Ben Jonson.* Edited by W. B. Hunter. New York: Norton, 1963.

———. *Sejanus.* Edited by Jonas Barish. New Haven: Yale University Press, 1965.

Kelly, Henry Ansgar. *Divine Providence in the England of Shakespeare's Histories.* Cambridge: Harvard University Press, 1970.

Kyd, Thomas. *The Spanish Tragedy.* Edited by Philip Edwards. London: Methuen, 1959.

Lanham, Richard A. *A Handlist of Rhetorical Terms.* Berkeley and Los Angeles: University of California Press, 1968.

*Labyrinthe royal d'Hercule gaulois triomphant* . . . Avignon, 1601(?).

Leggatt, Alexander. "Tone and Structure in Chapman's *Byron.*" *Studies in English Literature 1500–1900* 24 (1984): 307–26.

Levin, Harry. *The Myth of the Golden Age in the Renaissance.* Bloomington: Indiana University Press, 1969.

Levy, F. J. "Hayward, Daniel and the Beginnings of Politic History in England." *Huntington Library Quarterly* 50 (1987): 1–37.

———. *Tudor Historical Thought.* San Marino, Calif.: Huntington Library, 1967.

Loftis, John. *Renaissance Drama in England & Spain: Topical Allusion and History Plays.* Princeton: Princeton University Press, 1987.

MacLure, Millar. *George Chapman: A Critical Study.* Toronto: University of Toronto Press, 1966.

Marlowe, Christopher. *The Poems.* Edited by Millar MacLure. London: Methuen, 1968.

Martin, John Rupert. *The Farnese Gallery.* Princeton: Princeton University Press, 1965.

Matthieu, Pierre. *Histoire de France et des choses memorables.* . . . 2 vols. Paris, 1605.

Meinecke, Friedrich. *Machiavellism: The Doctrine of Raison D'Etat and its Place in Modern History.* 1924. Translated by Douglas Scott. New Haven: Yale University Press, 1957.

Muir, Edwin. " 'Royal Man': Notes on the Tragedies of George Chapman." In *Shakespeare's Contemporaries,* edited by Max Bluestone and Norman Rabkin, 230–37. Englewood Cliffs, N.J.: Prentice-Hall, 1961.

Murrin, Michael. *The Veil of Allegory: Some Notes Toward a Theory of Allegorical Rhetoric in the English Renaissance.* Chicago: University of Chicago Press, 1969.

Nashe, Thomas. *The Works of Thomas Nashe.* Edited by Ronald B. McKerrow. Corrected edition, F. P. Wilson. 5 vols. Oxford: Blackwell, 1958.

Nenna, Giovanni Battista. *Nennio or A Treatise of Nobility.* Translated by William Jones. London, 1595.

Nichols, John. *The Progresses, Processions, and Magnificent Festivities of King James I.* 4 vols. London: Nichols, 1828.

Ornstein, Robert. *The Moral Vision of Jacobean Tragedy.* Madison: University of Wisconsin Press, 1960.

Orsini, Napoleone. *Bacone e Machiavelli.* Genova: Ed. degli Orfini, 1936.

Palmer, D. J. "Art and Nature in *As You Like It.*" *Philological Quarterly* 49 (1970): 30–40.

Panofsky, Erwin. *Hercules am Scheideweg*. Studien der Bibliothek Warburg 18. Leipzig and Berlin: Teubner, 1930.

Pasquier, Etienne. *Les Recherches de la France* . . . Paris, 1621.

Peacham, Henry. *Garden of Eloquence*. London, 1593.

Pogrell, Nancy von. *Die philosophische-poetische Entwincklung George Chapmans*. Hamburg: Friedrichsen, de Gruyter, 1939.

Pratt, Samuel M. "Jane Shore and the Elizabethans." *Texas Studies in Language and Literature* 11 (1969–70): 1293–1306.

Praz, Mario. *Studies in Seventeenth Century Imagery*. Studies of the Warburg Institute 3. 2 vols. London: Warburg Institute, 1939 and 1947.

Raab, Felix. *The English Face of Machiavelli: A Changing Interpretation 1500–1700*. London: Routledge, 1964.

Rees, Ennis. *The Tragedies of George Chapman: Renaissance Ethics in Action*. Cambridge: Harvard University Press, 1954.

Ribner, Irving. *The English History Play in the Age of Shakespeare*. Rev. ed. London: Methuen, 1965.

———. *Jacobean Tragedy: The Quest for Moral Order*. London: Methuen, 1962.

———. "The Meaning of Chapman's *Tragedy of Chabot*." *Modern Language Review* 55 (1960): 321–31.

Robortello, Francisco. *Francisci Robortelli . . . in librum Aristotelis de arte poetica explicationes* . . . Florence, 1548.

Rossiter, A. P. *English Drama from Early Times to the Elizabethans*. London: Hutchinson, 1950.

———, ed. *Woodstock: A Moral History*. London: Chatto and Windus, 1946.

Sasayama, Takashi. "Chabot, Admiral of France: the Last Phase of Chapman's Craftsmanship." *Shakespeare Studies* (Tokyo) 1 (1962): 15–32.

Savage, James E., ed. *The "Conceited Newes" of Sir Thomas Overbury and his Friends*. Gainesville, Fla.: Scholars' Facsimiles and Reprints, 1968.

Scapula, Johann. *Lexicon Graeco-Latinum novum*. Basel, 1605.

Schoell, Franck L. *Etudes sur l'humanisme continental en Angleterre*. Paris: Champion, 1926.

Seneca, L. A. *Seneca His Tenne Tragedies*. Translated by John Studley et al. London, 1581.

Seznec, Jean. *The Survival of the Pagan Gods*. 1940. Translated by Barbara Sessions. New York: Harper, 1961.

Shakespeare, William. *Coriolanus*. Edited by Philip Brockbank. London: Methuen, 1976.

———. *Richard II*. 5th ed. Edited by Peter Ure. London: Methuen, 1961.

Sisson, C. J., and Robert Butman. "George Chapman, 1612–22: Some New Facts." *Modern Language Review* 46 (1951): 185–90.

Smith, Hallett. *Elizabethan Poetry*. 1952. Reprint. Ann Arbor: University of Michigan Press,.1968.

Smith, G. Gregory, ed. *Elizabethan Critical Essays*. 2 vols. London: Oxford University Press, 1904.

Smith, Arthur H. *Les Evénements politiques de France dans le théâtre du siècle d'Elisabeth*. Paris: Larose, 1906.

Smuts, R. Malcolm. *Court Culture and the Origins of a Royalist Tradition in Early Stuart England*. Philadelphia: University of Pennsylvania Press, 1987.

Solve, Norma Dobie. *Stuart Politics in Chapman's "Tragedy of Chabot."* University of Michigan Publications in Language and Literature 4. Ann Arbor: University of Michigan Press, 1928.

Spikes, Judith Doolin. "The Jacobean History Play and the Myth of the Elect Nation." *Renaissance Drama*, n.s., 8 (1977): 117–49.

Spingarn, Joel E., ed. *Critical Essays of the Seventeenth Century*. 3 vols. 1907. Reprint. Bloomington: Indiana University Press, 1957.

Starkey, Thomas. *A Dialogue between Reginald Pole and Thomas Lupset*. Edited by Kathleen M. Burton. London: Chatto and Windus, 1948.

Stowe, John. *The Annales of England*. London, 1605.

Strong, Roy. *Henry, Prince of Wales and England's Lost Renaissance*. London: Thames and Hudson, 1986.

Swinburne, Algernon. *George Chapman*. London: Chatto and Windus, 1875.

Tasso, Torquato, *Godfrey of Bulloigne, or the Recoverie of Jerusalem*. Translated by Edward Fairfax. London, 1600.

Thompson, J. W. *A History of Historical Writing*. 2 vols. New York: Columbia University Press, 1942.

Tomlinson: T. B. *A Study of Elizabethan and Jacobean Tragedy*. Cambridge: Cambridge University Press, 1964.

Tottel, Richard. *Tottel's Miscellany*. Edited by Hyder E. Rollins. 2 vols. Cambridge: Harvard University Press, 1928–29.

Tricomi, Albert H. "The Dates of the Plays of George Chapman." *English Literary Renaissance* 12 (1982): 242–66.

*A True and Perfect Discourse of the Practices and Treasons of Marshall Biron*. London, 1602.

Tuve, Rosemond. *Allegorical Imagery: Some Mediaeval Books and Their Posterity*. Princeton: Princeton University Press, 1966.

Ure, Peter. "Chapman's Tragedies." In *Jacobean Theatre*, edited by J. R. Brown and Bernard Harris, 227–47. Stratford-upon-Avon Studies 1. Rev. reprint. London: Arnold, 1965.

———. *Elizabethan and Jacobean Drama: Critical Essays by Peter Ure*. Edited by J. C. Maxwell. Liverpool: Liverpool University Press, 1974.

———. "The Main Outline of Chapman's Byron." *Studies in Philology* 47 (1950): 568–88.

Van Laan, T. F. *The Idiom of Drama*. Ithaca: Cornell University Press, 1970.

Vivanti, Corrado. "Henry IV, the Gallic Hercules." *Journal of the Warburg and Courtauld Institutes* 30 (1967): 176–97.

Waddington, Raymond B. *The Mind's Empire: Myth and Form in George Chapman's Narrative Poems*. Baltimore: Johns Hopkins University Press, 1974.

Waith, Eugene M. *The Herculean Hero in Chapman, Marlowe, Shakespeare and Dryden*. London: Chatto and Windus, 1962.

———. *Ideas of Greatness: Heroic Drama in England*. London: Routledge, 1971.

Walker, D. P. *The Ancient Theology*. London: Duckworth, 1972.

———. *Spiritual Magic from Ficino to Campanella*. London: Warburg Institute, 1958.

Waterhouse, Edward. *Fortescutus Illustratus, or a Commentary on that nervous Treatise De Laudibus Legum Angliae.* London, 1663.

Webster, John. *The White Devil.* 2d ed. Edited by J. R. Brown. London: Methuen, 1966.

Whitney, Geoffrey. *A Choice of Emblems.* Leiden, 1586.

Whittaker, Thomas. *The Neo-Platonists: A Study in the History of Hellenism.* 2d rev. ed. Cambridge: Cambridge University Press, 1918.

Wickham, Glynne. "*The Two Noble Kinsman, or A Midsummer Night's Dream, Part II?*" In *Elizabethan Theatre VII,* edited by G. R. Hibbard, 167–96. Hamden, Conn.: Archon, 1980.

Williams, Mary E. "Chapman's Bryon and Apollo's Virtue." *Explorations in Renaissance Culture* 3 (1976): 37–47.

Williamson, J. W. *The Myth of the Conqueror: Prince Henry Stuart.* New York: AMS, 1978.

Wilson, Frank Percy. *Elizabethan and Jacobean.* Oxford: Clarendon Press, 1945.

Wilson, Elkin Calhoun. *Prince Henry and English Literature.* Ithaca: Cornell University Press, 1946.

Wilson, Thomas. *The Rule of Reason, conteinyng the Arte of Logique.* London, 1553.

Wind, Edgar. *Pagan Mysteries in the Renaissance.* Rev. ed. New York: Norton, 1968.

Wormald, Jenny. "James VI and I: Two Kings or One?" *History* 68 (1983): 187–209.

Wright, Louis B. "Stage Duelling in the Elizabethan Theatre." 1927. In *The Seventeenth-Century Stage,* edited by Gerald Eades Bentley, 156–69. Chicago: University of Chicago Press, 1968.

Wright, Pam. "A Change of Direction: The Ramifications of a Female Household, 1558–1603." In *The English Court: from the Wars of the Roses to the Civil War,* edited by David Starkey, 147–72. London and New York: Longman, 1987.

Yates, Frances. *Giordano Bruno and the Hermetic Tradition.* Chicago: University of Chicago Press, 1968.

# Index

George Chapman's writings, including translations, appear here as separate subentries under his name. Aristocrats appear under their family names with a cross-reference from the respective titles by which they are most commonly known. Only the main text and appendix are indexed.